Middle Dorset Variability and Regional Cultural Traditions

A case study from Newfoundland and Saint-Pierre and Miquelon

Sylvie LeBlanc

BAR International Series 2158
2010

Published in 2016 by
BAR Publishing, Oxford

BAR International Series 2158

Middle Dorset Variability and Regional Cultural Traditions

ISBN 978 1 4073 0700 8

© S LeBlanc and the Publisher 2010

The author's moral rights under the 1988 UK Copyright,
Designs and Patents Act are hereby expressly asserted.

All rights reserved. No part of this work may be copied, reproduced, stored,
sold, distributed, scanned, saved in any form of digital format or transmitted
in any form digitally, without the written permission of the Publisher.

BAR Publishing is the trading name of British Archaeological Reports (Oxford) Ltd.
British Archaeological Reports was first incorporated in 1974 to publish the BAR
Series, International and British. In 1992 Hadrian Books Ltd became part of the BAR
group. This volume was originally published by Archaeopress in conjunction with
British Archaeological Reports (Oxford) Ltd / Hadrian Books Ltd, the Series principal
publisher, in 2010. This present volume is published by BAR Publishing, 2016.

Printed in England

BAR titles are available from:

                BAR Publishing
                122 Banbury Rd, Oxford, OX2 7BP, UK
 EMAIL   info@barpublishing.com
 PHONE   +44 (0)1865 310431
   FAX   +44 (0)1865 316916
                www.barpublishing.com

The process of tradition making always occupies space or matter, (...) and practices are always novel and creative, in some ways unlike those in other times or place.

Pauketat
A New Tradition in Archaeology

ABSTRACT

This research addresses the issue of variability within the Middle Dorset (2000-1100 B.P.) culture on the island of Newfoundland and on the island of Saint-Pierre in the French Archipelago of Saint-Pierre and Miquelon. Practice theory provides the conceptual framework to interpret variability and it is argued that the variability expressed in the Middle Dorset material record reflects the existence of distinct regional traditions. The comparative study of specific aspects of the lithic technology at eight Middle Dorset sites identified a strong process of regional specialization in the technological practices of these Palaeoeskimo people. Raw material use-patterns indicate a strong reliance on regionally available raw materials. Stylistic analysis also identifies discrete stylistic trends. Endblades take an emblematic role as most sites produced distinct and recognizable endblade types. With a few exceptions, the data reveal a high degree of technological homogeneity within individual sites and scarce evidence of contact between sites. At a larger scale, the evidence also indicates faint contact between Newfoundland/Saint-Pierre and Labrador Middle Dorset groups. I suggest that the distinct regional technological practices reflect traditions of discrete territorially-defined social groups, much like the historical *–muit* groups in the Arctic. The picture I am proposing for the Newfoundland/Saint-Pierre region is one of a number of contemporaneous Middle Dorset groups, each living in discrete territories with their own technological traditions and specific developmental histories.

ACKNOWLEDGMENTS

First and foremost I would like to extend my sincere gratitude to my supervisor Dr. Raymond Le Blanc who invited me to undertake my doctoral studies at the University of Alberta. Over the years, not only did he provide guidance and support but, along with his wife Sheila Greer, made me feel welcome in their home. I would like to thank my committee members Drs. Pamela Willoughby and Charles Schweger for their helpful instruction and advice. I would also like to thank my internal and external examiners, Drs. John England (Department of Earth and Atmospheric Sciences, University of Alberta) and Robert McGhee (Canadian Museum of Civilization) for their comments, suggestions and a challenging and stimulating defense. Thank you to the members and staff at the Department of Anthropology for their assistance, specifically Gail Matthew and Harvey Friebe.

Funding for this research was provided by a number of sources: Faculty of Graduate Studies, University of Alberta; Province of Alberta; Andrew Stewart Memorial; Izaac Walton Killam; Human Resources Division, Government of Newfoundland and Labrador (through Baccalieu Trail Heritage Corporation); Department of Tourism, Culture and Recreation, Government of Newfoundland and Labrador; Institute of Social and Economic Research, Memorial University of Newfoundland; Smallwood Centre for Newfoundland Studies; Canadian Circumpolar Institute; Canadian Museum of Civilization; Fonds pour la Formation de Chercheurs et l'Aide à la Recherche; Miawpukek Band, Conne River; Education Nationale de France; Collectivité Territoriale de Saint-Pierre et Miquelon; Direction Territoriale de la Jeunesse et des Sports.

The geological component of my research was a true work of collaboration and I am thankful to the following: Sean O'Brien, Drs. Ian Knight and Stephen Colman-Sadd from the Geological Survey of Newfoundland and Labrador; Paul Dean, Director, Johnson Geo Center, St. John's; Dr. John Waldron (Earth and Atmospheric Sciences, University of Alberta; Dr. Mario Coniglio (Earth Sciences, University of Waterloo); and now retired Dr. Robert K. Stevens. Petrographic descriptions and microphotographs were done by Dr. Sherif A. Awadallah at the Department of Earth Sciences, Memorial University of Newfoundland.

I would like to thank the members of the Carrefour Culturel Saint-Pierrais and Jean-Louis Rabottin for their help in setting up the project in Saint-Pierre and for their friendship. Rosiane de Lizaraga, director of l'Arche Musée-Archives of Saint-Pierre, provided assistance and logistic support. For facilitating access to the Newfoundland archaeological collections I am grateful to Dr. Priscilla Renouf from Memorial University, Elaine Anton and Lori Balson from the The Rooms, Provincial Museum, and Martha Drake, Delphina Mercer, Stephen Hull and Ken Reynolds from the Department of Tourism, Culture and Recreation, Government of Newfoundland and Labrador. I would like to thank my colleagues Tim Rast, Dr. John Erwin and Laurie Mclean for bouncing ideas about rocks and style.

I cannot express enough gratitude to both my field crews from Saint-Pierre and Dildo Island. Their dedication, hard work and cheerful personalities made our time in the field most enjoyable.

At one point or another, Franca Boag, Eric Damkjar, and J. A. Tuck helped with content and/or editorial comments. Drs. Murielle Nagy and Shirleen Smith have officially been granted the title of personal editors. Stephen Fouquet and Marsha Mickalyk provided help with photographs and initiated me to Photoshop. Andrea Hiob, the fabulous and indispensable Andrea, drew all maps and illustrations.

I am grateful to all and truly apologetic if I have forgotten anyone. I alone am responsible for the ideas and interpretations expressed in this research.

TABLE OF CONTENTS

Chapter 1.	INTRODUCTION	1
Chapter 2.	BACKGROUND AND THEORETICAL FRAMEWORK	2
	Palaeoeskimo Culture History: an Overview	2
	Newfoundland/Labrador and Saint-Pierre and Miquelon Palaeoeskimo Culture History	2
	The Newfoundland Dorset Concept	4
	Variability in the Arctic Record: a Review	5
	Culture History	5
	Binfordian Functionalist Paradigm	6
	Cultural/Ecology Paradigm: the *Core Area* Model and the Regional Variant Theory	6
	A Social Approach to Variability: Practice Theory	7
	The Case Study	8
Chapter 3.	LITHIC RAW MATERIAL USE-PATTERNS	10
	Geological Setting	10
	An Island is Born	10
	Newfoundland Geological Zones	11
	Humber Zone (Western Zone)	11
	Central Zone	12
	Avalon Zone (Eastern Zone)	12
	Petrographic Analysis	12
	Research Methods	12
	Results	13
	Phillip's Garden Site (Port au Choix) – Newfoundland Northwest Coast	13
	Cape Ray Site – Newfoundland Southwest Coast	15
	Anse à Flamme Site – Newfoundland South Coast	16
	Anse à Henry Site – Saint-Pierre	18
	Dildo Island Site – Trinity Bay	19
	Shamblers Cove Site – Bonavista Bay	20
	Swan Island Site – Notre-Dame Bay	22
	Pittman Site – White Bay	23
	Summary	24
Chapter 4.	THE STYLISTIC EVIDENCE	27
	Research Methods	27
	Regional Stylistic Description	27
	Phillip's Garden Site (Port au Choix) – Newfoundland Northwest Coast	27
	Cape Ray Site – Newfoundland Southwest Coast	30
	Anse à Flamme Site – Newfoundland South Coast	33
	Anse à Henry Site – Saint-Pierre	34
	Dildo Island Site – Trinity Bay	35
	Shamblers Cove Site – Bonavista Bay	39
	Swan Island Site – Notre-Dame Bay	40
	Pittman Site – White Bay	43
	Summary	45
Chapter 5.	SUMMARY: TOWARDS A DEFINITION OF REGIONAL TRADITIONS	48
	Newfoundland Northwest Coast	48
	Newfoundland Southwest Coast	48

	Newfoundland South Coast and Saint-Pierre	48
	Trinity Bay	49
	Bonavista Bay	49
	Notre-Dame Bay	49
	White Bay	50
Chapter 6.	**CONCLUSION**	51

APPENDICES 53
    Appendix 1-Site Descriptions 53
    Appendix 2-Radiocarbon Dates 58
    Appendix 3-Thin Section Descriptions 59

REFERENCES CITED 70

LIST OF FIGURES

Figure 1	Timeline of Newfoundland and Saint-Pierre and Miquelon prehistory.	3
Figure 2	Map showing archaeological site locations discussed in the text.	5
Figure 3	The genesis of the island of Newfoundland.	11
Figure 4	Autochthonous and allochthonous rocks of the Humber Zone, western Newfoundland.	13
Figure 5	Distribution of the Marystown Group and correlative volcanic rocks, eastern Newfoundland and equivalent Saint-Pierre formations.	17
Figure 6	Distribution of the Musgravetown Group volcanic rocks (Bull Arm Formation) and Conception Group sedimentary rocks, eastern Newfoundland.	21
Figure 7	Bay of Exploits Caradocian Shales and Cherts, central Newfoundland.	22
Figure 8	Endblade Length/Width/Thickness Ratios.	46
Figure 9	Summary of Regional Traditions.	49

LIST OF TABLES

Table 1	Phillip's Garden Samples (Port au Choix) – Summary of Thin Section Descriptions.	14
Table 2	Phillip's Garden (Port au Choix) Material Type Frequencies.	15
Table 3	Cape Ray Samples– Summary of Thin Section Descriptions.	15
Table 4	Cape Ray Material Type Frequencies.	16
Table 5	Anse à Flamme Samples – Summary of Thin Section Descriptions.	16
Table 6	Anse à Flamme Material Type Frequencies.	17
Table 7	Anse à Henry Samples – Summary of Thin Section Descriptions.	18
Table 8	Anse à Henry Material Type Frequencies.	18
Table 9	Dildo Island Samples – Summary of Thin Section Descriptions.	19
Table 10	Dildo Island Material Type Frequencies.	20
Table 11	Shamblers Cove Material Type Frequencies	21
Table 12	Shamblers Cove Samples – Summary of Thin Section Descriptions.	21
Table 13	Swan Island Samples – Summary of Thin Section Descriptions.	22
Table 14	Swan Island Material Type Frequencies.	23
Table 15	Pittman Material Type Frequencies.	23
Table 16	Pittman Samples – Summary of Thin Section Descriptions	24
Table 17	Summary Raw Material Use-Patterns: Regional Versus Exogenous/Miscellaneous.	25
Table 18	Selected Attributes for Stylistic Artifact Analysis.	27

Table 19	Phillip's Garden Typical Endblade Metric Attributes.		28
Table 20	Phillip's Garden Endscraper Metric Attributes by Types.		29
Table 21	Cape Ray Typical Endblade Metric Attributes.		31
Table 22	Cape Ray Endscraper Metric Attributes by Types.		32
Table 23	Anse à Flamme Typical Endblade Metric Attributes.		34
Table 24	Anse à Henry Typical Endblade Metric Attributes.		34
Table 25	Dildo Island Typical Endblade Metric Attributes.		36
Table 26	Dildo Island Endscraper Metric Attributes by Types.		38
Table 27	Shamblers Cove Typical Endblade Metric Attributes.		39
Table 28	Swan Island Typical Endblade Metric Attributes.		40
Table 29	Swan Island Endscraper Metric Attributes by Types.		42
Table 30	Pittman Typical Endblade Metric Attributes.		43
Table 31	Pittman Endscraper Metric Attributes by Types.		44
Table 32	Summary – Endblade Attributes by Sites.		47
Table 33	Endscraper Type Frequencies by Sites.		47

LIST OF PHOTOS

Photo 1	Phillip's Garden (Port au Choix) typical endblades.		28
Photo 2	Phillip's Garden (Port au Choix) miscellaneous endblades.		28
Photo 3	Phillip's Garden (Port au Choix) selected endscraper sample.		29
Photo 4	Cape Ray Type 1 endblades.		30
Photo 5	Cape Ray short endblades (Type 2).		30
Photo 6	Cape Ray miscellaneous endblades.		30
Photo 7	Cape Ray selected endscraper sample.		31
Photo 8	Cape Ray selected endscraper sample.		32
Photo 9	Anse à Flamme endblades.		33
Photo 10	Anse à Henry endblade type.		34
Photo 11	Dildo Island ground endblades (Type 1).		35
Photo 12	Dildo Island endblades (Types 2 and 3).		35
Photo 13	Dildo Island elongated ground endblades (Type 4).		35
Photo 14	Dildo Island short endblades (Type 5).		36

Photo 15	Dildo Island miscellaneous endblades.	37
Photo 16	Dildo Island quartz crystal endscrapers.	37
Photo 17	Dildo Island miscellaneous endscrapers.	37
Photo 18	Shamblers Cove typical endblades.	39
Photo 19	Shamblers Cove miscellaneous endblades.	40
Photo 20	Swan Island typical endblades.	40
Photo 21	Swan Island miscellaneous endblades.	40
Photo 22	Swan Island selected endscraper sample.	41
Photo 23	Swan Island selected endscraper sample.	41
Photo 24	Swan Island endscraper reduction sequence.	42
Photo 25	Pittman typical endblades.	43
Photo 26	Pittman miscellaneous endblades.	43
Photo 27	Pittman selected endscraper sample.	44
Photo 28	Pittman selected endscraper sample.	44
Appendix 3 -	Microphotographs of thin sections.	67

CHAPTER 1. INTRODUCTION

This study explores the issue of variability within the Middle Dorset (2000- 1100 B.P.) culture on the islands of Newfoundland and Saint-Pierre in the French archipelago of Saint-Pierre and Miquelon. Middle Dorset variability is examined within the conceptual framework of practice theory which offers an interpretative lens through which the variability observed in the material record is viewed as reflecting distinct regional traditions.

The research stems from archaeological fieldwork in Trinity Bay, Newfoundland (LeBlanc 1997a, 1998, 1999) and on the island of Saint-Pierre (LeBlanc 1997b, 2000a, 2001, 2003a, 2004, 2005). Comparison of the material from these two areas with other Dorset material from Newfoundland/Labrador or the Canadian Arctic is clearly indicative of variability within the Dorset cultural tradition. A long-held view in Arctic archaeology is that the Dorset culture maintained a pattern of cultural homogeneity throughout the entire Dorset sphere (Greenland, Canadian Arctic, Newfoundland/Labrador, Saint-Pierre and Miquelon), with very little change occurring through time (Fitzhugh 1997: 398; Maxwell 1976b). The notion of a homogeneous "Newfoundland Dorset" culture (Harp 1964; Linnamae 1975; Maxwell 1976b) is a reflection of this general concept: "the remarkable six century changelessness of style and technology on the island of Newfoundland" (Maxwell 1976b:5) epitomizes this view of the Newfoundland Dorset culture.

However, as more research has accumulated on Newfoundland Dorset, which is strictly confined to the Middle Dorset period, it is becoming increasingly clear that the idea of a homogeneous "Newfoundland Dorset" culture is no longer tenable (Erwin 2001; Robbins 1985, 1986; Simpson 1986). Instead, the generic "Newfoundland Dorset" culture appears to be much more dynamic than previously believed. This is indicated by the uniqueness of different regional expressions of the Middle Dorset culture throughout the islands of Newfoundland and Saint-Pierre. For instance, Dorset material from a number of regions (Cape Ray, Port au Choix, White Bay, Notre-Dame Bay, Bonavista Bay, Trinity Bay, the Newfoundland south coast and Saint-Pierre) clearly establishes that there is a strong process of regionalization at work. This regional variability is expressed not only in terms of raw material choices but also in artifact design.

The variability expressed within Middle Dorset material culture in such a limited geographical area is intriguing and is at the centre of this inquiry. In considering the Newfoundland/Saint-Pierre example, the larger question that needs to be addressed is the significance of this variability; this is the focus of the research.

At the theoretical level, practice theory provides the framework to interpret Middle Dorset variability and, in particular "for understanding ancient technology as social practices" (Dobres 2000: 49). In essence, I argue that the different regional expressions observed in the material record reflect regional technological practices embedded in individual and specific cultural traditions. Using a case study, the main objective of this research is to demonstrate the existence of Middle Dorset regional groups in Newfoundland and in Saint-Pierre.

To explore this hypothesis, I examine the material patterning from eight Middle Dorset sites in Newfoundland and Saint-Pierre and Miquelon. Specifically, two sets of data are analysed: raw material use-patterns and artifact style.

These data will allow me to:
1- Provide an empirical description of Middle Dorset raw material use-patterns and artifact design in the different regions.
2- Identify idiosyncratic technological practices within those regions.
3- Propose a definition of the different regional expressions.

Chapter 2 offers a summary of Palaeoeskimo culture history, a brief review addressing the issue of Paleoeskimo variability in Arctic literature and the presentation of my theoretical framework. Chapter 2 also introduces the case study. The succeeding chapters deal principally with data: Chapter 3 focuses on geological sourcing and raw material use-patterns; Chapter 4 presents data bearing on stylistic patterning. Chapter 5 synthesizes the data and presents a definition for each of the regional traditions. Chapter 6 contains a discussion and conclusion.

CHAPTER 2. BACKGROUND AND THEORETICAL FRAMEWORK

PALAEOESKIMO CULTURE HISTORY: AN OVERVIEW

The North American Arctic and Greenland represent one of the last frontiers colonized by the human species. The arid and extreme conditions of this environment required extraordinary adaptation from the first explorers who ventured into this new territory. The precise homeland of those newcomers remains unclear, but most researchers agree on an Alaskan or Siberian origin. The Denbigh Flint Complex discovered in northwest Alaska is generally proposed (Dumond 1987) as the North American ancestor of what archaeologists have named the Arctic Small Tool tradition (ASTt) (Irving 1957). As indicated by its name, the ASTt is characterized by the small size of its lithic tools which are finely fashioned by pressure retouch.

Between 5000 and 4500 B.P., the Arctic Small Tool tradition sequence developed differently in Alaska and the Canadian Arctic/Greenland. In Alaska and the Bering region, it follows the Palaeo-Arctic Tradition and includes the Denbigh Tradition, which in time, is replaced by a number of manifestations – Choris, Norton, Ipiutak and Birnirk – eventually leading to Thule and modern Alaskan Eskimos (McGhee 1996:22).

In the Canadian Arctic and Greenland, Arctic Small Tool tradition relatives are known as Palaeoeskimo. The Palaeoeskimo sequence is divided into Early Palaeoeskimo (4500 to 2500 B.P.) and Late Palaeoeskimo (2500 to 500 B.P.) periods. The first period includes cultures such as Independence I, Pre-Dorset, Groswater/Saqqaq and Independence II (also called Dorset I) in Greenland. At about 4500 B.P., Independence I groups may have been the first to initiate an eastward expansion from Alaska. They traveled a northern route, across the High Arctic, and rapidly spread throughout much of the Canadian Arctic, Greenland, and northern Labrador. Indicative of the fast pace of expansion, some of the earliest Independence 1 radiocarbon dates are from northern Greenland (Knuth 1984: 140). Around 3500 B.P., these people were succeeded by Pre-Dorset, and then by Groswater/Saqqaq groups who came to occupy the entire Canadian Arctic, Greenland, the Labrador coast as well as the islands of Newfoundland and Saint-Pierre in the French Archipelago of Saint-Pierre and Miquelon.

The Late Paleoeskimo period refers exclusively to the Dorset culture. Following the Groswater example, the Dorset period is also one of maximum expansion and Dorset sites are found throughout the Canadian Arctic, Labrador/Newfoundland/Saint-Pierre and Greenland. The Dorset period is divided into a number of phases, each of which is not necessarily represented in every region of the Arctic. Radiocarbon dates also vary from one region to the other. For instance, in reference to western Ungava, Plumet (2002 Tuvaaluk/web) distinguishes Early Dorset (2000 to 1600 B.P.), Middle Dorset (1600 to 1300 B.P.), Recent Dorset (1300 to 600 B.P.) and Late Dorset (until 450 B.P.) On the other hand, as we shall see below, the Newfoundland/Labrador Dorset sequence displays a tripartite division with slightly different dates.

The timing and reasons for the disappearance of the Dorset culture is a matter of debate. After more than 3000 years of successful adaptation to a constantly changing Arctic environment, they were replaced by Thule culture immigrants from Alaska, the ancestral culture of today's Inuit. There is no shortage of speculation on the fate of the Dorset culture and their disappearance remains at the center of an animated debate. It is beyond the scope of this study to raise the issue but the main arguments put forward include the following: they were exterminated or assimilated by their Thule successors; forced into retreat by the advance of Indians, Inuit and Europeans; perished from Europeans (including Greenlandic Norse) diseases; contributed to the genetic pool of the Sadlermiut; vanished due to local or regional extinction prior to the arrival of Thule, or were decimated by worsening climatic conditions (Friesen 2000; Hayes *et al.* 2005; McGhee 1996, 2000, 2004; Park 1993, 2000, 2008; Plumet 1996; Odess *et al.* 2000; Sutherland 2000a and b; Sutherland and McGhee 1997).

Newfoundland/Labrador and Saint-Pierre and Miquelon Palaeoeskimo Culture History

In Newfoundland, Labrador and Saint-Pierre and Miquelon, the Palaeoeskimo sequence follows a trajectory similar to that observed in the Canadian Arctic including Early Palaeoeskimo and Late Palaeoeskimo traditions (Figure 1). The Early Palaeoeskimo Tradition lasted about 2000 years, between 4000 and 2100 B.P., and comprises the Independence 1 (4000 to 3500 B.P), Pre-Dorset (3500 to 2800 B.P.) and Groswater (2800 to 2100 B.P.) cultures (Tuck and Fitzhugh 1986). Shortly after 4000 B.P. (3800 B.P., Rose Island, Saglek Bay [Tuck 1975:57]), the first Palaeoeskimos to enter Labrador share a close affiliation with the Independence 1 culture of the High Arctic and Greenland (Tuck n.d: 100-104) and appear to have been confined to northern Labrador (Cox 1978; Tuck n.d., 1975). Beginning around 3500 B.P., their Pre-Dorset successors gradually initiated a southward migration along the Labrador coast to occupy, between 3000 and 2800 B.P., most of central and southern Labrador including the Québec Lower North Shore and the island of Newfoundland. In Newfoundland, hint of a Pre-Dorset presence was found at the Cow Head site on the west coast (Tuck 1978). However, evidence documenting this period remains sparse in Newfoundland (Tuck n.d.: 105) and as yet unknown in Saint-Pierre. This may be because Independence 1 and Pre-Dorset people were not alone in these areas at that time. Indeed, Maritime Archaic people were already present in southern Labrador by 9000 B.P. and well established in central and northern Labrador between 4000 and 3500 B.P. (Tuck and Fitzhugh 1986: 163). They

Chapter 2. Background and Theoretical Framework

Amerindian Occupation	Date	Palaeoeskimo Occupation
Maritime Archaic (5000-3200 B.P.)	5000 B.P.	
	4500 B.P.	
	4000 B.P.	
	3500 B.P.	
	3000 B.P.	Early Palaeoeskimo (3500-2100 B.P.)
	2500 B.P.	Groswater (2800-2100 B.P.)
	2000 B.P.	
Recent Indian (2000-500 B.P.) Cow Head (2000-1200 B.P.) Beaches (1600-900 B.P.) Little Passage (900-500 B.P.)	1500 BP	Late Palaeoeskimo Middle Dorset (2000-1100 B.P.)
	1000 B.P.	
	500 B.P.	
	0	
Beothuk (500 B.P.-1829 AD)	500 AD European Contact	
	1000 AD	
	1500 AD	
	2000 AD	

Figure 1. Timeline of Newfoundland and Saint-Pierre and Miquelon prehistory.

had reached the islands of Newfoundland and adjacent Saint-Pierre by 5000 B.P.

The emergence of the Groswater culture between 2800 and 2100 B.P. constitutes a period of dramatic population growth and maximum expansion for Paleoeskimo people in this region. Groswater sites are found virtually everywhere from the northern tip of Labrador to as far south as the island of Saint-Pierre. This sudden population influx coincides with the demise of the Maritime Archaic, which had vanished by 3200 B.P. For the next 1200 years or so, until the appearance of the Recent Indian culture around 2000 B.P., Groswater people had had the region to themselves, except for the period around 2500 B.P. when the Late Palaeoeskimo Dorset culture made its appearance in northern Labrador.

Following Cox's (1978) tripartite division, the Dorset culture is divided into Early (2500-2000 B.P.), Middle (2000-1100 B.P.) and Late Dorset (1100-650 B.P.). Its trajectory follows closely that of its predecessor, the Groswater. It first appeared in northern Labrador around 2500 B.P., then, over centuries, gradually expanded southward into central and southern Labrador to finally reach the islands of Newfoundland and Saint-Pierre around 2000 B.P. fully replacing the Groswater. The Dorset culture ended eventually around 650 B.P. in northern Labrador (Tuck and Fitzhugh 1986: 166).

Although Dorset sites are found throughout Newfoundland/Labrador, their distribution varies over time. Early and Late Dorset sites are limited to northern Labrador. As yet, no sites from these periods have been reported in central and southern Labrador or on the island of Newfoundland (Tuck and Fitzhugh 1986:165). In contrast, Middle Dorset sites have a wide geographic distribution, and shortly after 2000 B.P., there is a rapid southward migration along the Labrador coastline and onto the islands of Newfoundland and Saint-Pierre. Despite the large number of Middle Dorset sites in northern Labrador and Newfoundland, relatively few are reported from the central and southern Labrador/Québec Lower North Shore coasts (Jordan 1986: 137; Pintal 1998: 149; Tuck n.d: 116), possibly because of the presence of Recent Indian groups in this intervening area (Tuck n.d.: 116). Remarkably, this period of Dorset florescence in Newfoundland coincides with a period of population contraction in Arctic Canada and Greenland; indeed, much of these regions were abandoned by Palaeoeskimo people for most of the Middle Dorset period (Helmer 1996; Jensen 2005; Jordan 1986; Maxwell 1985; McGhee 1976).

On the island of Newfoundland, the Middle Dorset population began to wane around 1200-1100 B.P. and appeared to follow a retracting pattern that brought them back into Labrador and finally to northern Labrador, where the last of their descendants, the Late Dorset people, disappeared from the archaeological record around 650 B.P.

In Newfoundland, Middle Dorset site distribution overlaps with that of the preceding Groswater culture. Sites are located along the entire coastline including the island of Saint-Pierre. The best known of these is the large Phillip's Garden site in Port au Choix, northwestern Newfoundland, where nearly 70 house-depressions have been identified (Harp 1964; Hodgetts *et al.* 2003; Renouf 1986, 1987, 2006). The Cape Ray site on the southwest coast (Fogt 1998; Linnamae 1975), the Stock Cove (Robbins 1985) and Dildo Island (LeBlanc 1997a, 1998, 1999, 2003b) sites in Trinity Bay, as well as the spectacular soapstone quarry at Fleur de Lys (Erwin 2001, 2005; Nagle 1982), are also among the most significant Middle Dorset sites on the island.

Dating of the Middle Dorset occupation of the island is confidently positioned between 1970 ± 60 B.P. at Phillip's Garden (Renouf 2006) and 1090± 80 B.P. at the Bordeaux II site (Linnamae 1975).

Distinguishing features of the Middle Dorset technology in Newfoundland include: finely triangular tip-fluted[1]

---

[1] Tip-fluting of endblades is characteristic of the Early and especially Middle Dorset cultures in the Late Palaeoeskimo period. The technique consists of longitudinal removal of one or two thin, asymmetrical and elongated flakes from the distal end of the point. Generally, the endblade presents on one of its face (usually, the dorsal face) a longitudinal median ridge between two fluting scars (Plumet and Lebel 1997).

endblades[2] bearing straight or concave bases. Most are finely chipped but grinding is prevalent in some regions; the resultant fluting spalls[3]; a wide variety of bifaces, both symmetric and asymmetric, some of which are multi-notched; small to tiny thumbnail endscrapers; large quantities of microblades; an extensive ground industry including tabular burin-like-tools[4], spatulate or chisel-like-tools made of slate or nephrite, beveled slate knives or scrapers; grinding stones; flat-based rectangular soapstone lamps and vessels; gouged or scratched-in holes marking the disappearance of the drill. Raw materials appear to be of local origin, mainly cherts and rhyolites. Quartz crystal is commonly used to fashion microblades and endscrapers. Slate and nephrite are also used in tool making.

The organic technology, either bone, antler or ivory, includes a series of harpoon heads (closed-socket, self-tipped or slotted); bilaterally barbed fishing spears; sled runner shoes; foreshafts; various types of handles; needles; pressure flakers and, a series of anthropomorphic and zoomorphic figurines representing bears, seals and other animals. The Middle Dorset period is also marked by the appearance of residential agglomerations consisting of several houses. The Phillip's Garden site in Port au Choix with its many dwellings is certainly the most striking example.

As noted above, the florescence of the Middle Dorset period in Newfoundland corresponds with a virtual abandonment of most Canadian Arctic regions[5] (Jordan 1986: 144) and Greenland (Jenson 2005: 100) by Palaeoeskimo people. This apparent gap in the Palaeoeskimo occupational sequence in most of the Arctic and this sudden influx into a so-called marginal area has led scholars (Maxwell 1976a) to formulate the *Core Area* concept, a demographic model of depopulation and emigration/colonization of regions outside the core area. In general terms, the *Core Area* centers around the Foxe Basin and the shores and islands of the Hudson Strait (Maxwell 1985: 50-51). From there, it is argued that populations would have expanded into marginal (fringe) areas during favourable times and retreated back to the core area when environmental conditions worsened *(Ibid.)*. Layered onto or superimposed on the Newfoundland/Labrador Dorset situation this scenario was extremely convenient and came to justify as we shall see below the development of the Newfoundland Dorset concept.

The Newfoundland Dorset Concept

Although Howley (2000, Plate xxi) illustrated a few Dorset objects in 1915, the first archaeological evidence of this material on the island of Newfoundland was recovered by Diamond Jenness[6] (1928, 1929), during a coastal survey between the Bay of Exploits and White Bay (Figure 2). At the time, Jenness interpreted his finds as belonging to the Beothuk Indians "under strong Cape Dorset influence" (Tuck and Fitzhugh 1986: 161). Subsequent work by Wintemberg (1939, 1940) and Harp (1964) located several Dorset sites on the Newfoundland west coast. In comparison to other Dorset material from elsewhere in the Arctic, the newly discovered material from Newfoundland was perceived as distinctive and the concept of *Newfoundland Dorset Eskimo* was formulated (Harp 1964). The new designation and its variants: *Newfoundland Dorset* (Linname 1975), *typical Newfoundland Dorset* or *Early Dorset* (Bishop n.d.) remained in use up until Fitzhugh (1972) defined a distinct *Groswater Dorset* culture in Hamilton Inlet, Labrador. At that point, it became clear that the alleged distinctiveness of the so-called *Newfoundland Dorset* resulted from the intrusive presence of previously unrecognized Groswater elements. Once the distinction was made and Groswater and Dorset artifacts were sorted out, it became apparent that *Newfoundland Dorset* was remarkably similar to Middle Dorset from the Labrador coast (Tuck n.d: 118). On that basis, Tuck and Fitzhugh (1986: 165) finally suggested that the more generic term Middle Dorset replace all previous appellations on the island of Newfoundland.

With this issue apparently resolved, the concept of a *Newfoundland Dorset* nevertheless lasted for a while longer. On the basis of its distinctive and uniform features, Dorset material known from the island was still considered unique in comparison with other Arctic Dorset assemblages. As Linnamae (1975: 74-83) reports, several traits present in *Newfoundland Dorset* assemblages are absent from Arctic collections. This still appears to hold true but it must be cautioned that Middle Dorset elsewhere is poorly described and, therefore, does not allow a thorough comparison.

On the other hand, the notion of uniformity or homogeneity of the *Newfoundland Dorset* does not appear to have persisted. Robbins (1985: 11) judiciously notes that at the time the *Newfoundland Dorset* concept was formulated only data from the Newfoundland west coast were available. However, the concept was applied

---

[2] In Palaeoeskimo cultures, endblade, also called harpoon endblade, refers to a pointed stone tool inserted at the distal end of a harpoon head, to provide a piercing edge. Harpoons are usually associated with sea mammal hunting.

[3] Fluting spalls are thin, asymmetrical and elongated flakes resulting from endblade tip-fluting. They are distinguishable from other flake types by a number of criteria such as: elongated triangular shape with a straight or, in most cases, a slanting base; the inner face is unworked and shows a distal bulb of percussion, the outer face is flaked; the spall presents distinct lateral edges; one of which is thick and blunt, the opposite one, thin and sharp (Collins 1956).

[4] The tabular burin-like-tool is generally considered a distinctive feature of the Newfoundland Middle Dorset assemblage. From my own observation, I would, however, concur with Linnamae (1975: 74) and argue that burin-like-tools are rather infrequent in the Newfoundland collections I have examined for this study.

[5] In a recent publication Odess (2005) reports two Middle Dorset occupations on Baffin Island dating between 2100-1700 B.P. for the first one and, 1470 to around 1370 B.P. for the second.

[6] In 1925, Canadian anthropologist Diamond Jenness was the first to define the Dorset culture, from a Cape Dorset artifact collection, Baffin Island.

Chapter 2. Background and Theoretical Framework

Figure 2. Map showing archaeological site locations discussed in the text.

to the entire island because, it seems, there was no argument against it. In 1985, in the midst of accelerated research around the island (Trinity Bay [Evans 1982; Robbins 1985]; Notre-Dame Bay [Pastore 1981]; Bonavista Bay [Carignan 1975]), Robbins argued against this apparent homogeneity and clearly demonstrated the existence of three regional expressions of Middle Dorset in Newfoundland. Subsequent work by Simpson (1986) on the Port au Port Peninsula, Erwin (2001) at Fleur de Lys and LeBlanc (2000b) in Trinity Bay reinforces Robbin's assertion.

VARIABILITY IN THE ARCTIC RECORD: A REVIEW

In Palaeoeskimo research, the issue of variability has essentially been addressed in the realms of (1) culture history, (2) the Binfordian functionalist paradigm, and (3) the cultural/ecology paradigm. For many years, these have been the pre-eminent models in explaining variability in the Arctic record. A brief review and discussion follows.

Culture History

For many years, variability in the Arctic Small Tool tradition (ASTt) has been one of the dominant issues in Palaeoeskimo research. In an attempt to order Arctic data, variability among the different Early Palaeoeskimo components (Independence I, Saqqaq and Pre-Dorset) was used to establish either temporal relationships and/or cultural affiliation. Differences among archaeological components were then integrated within an evolutionary framework and interpreted in terms of cultural change through time. For instance, the issue of the relationship between Independence 1 and Pre-Dorset has been tackled by many researchers. The classic example is McGhee's (1976) Port Refuge cultural sequence where he was able to isolate chronologically, spatially and stylistically, Independence 1 components from those of Pre-Dorset. In McGhee's interpretation, Independence 1 people preceded Pre-Dorset people on Devon Island. A similar conclusion was reached by Schlederman (1978) for Ellesmere Island. On Somerset Island, Bielawski (1988) argued conversely that there is little evidence allowing for either a temporal or spatial distinctiveness between Independence I or Pre-Dorset. Other scholars (Maxwell 1985) have regarded Independence I as a contemporaneous variant of the *Core Area* Pre-Dorset, and Helmer (1991: 308) argues that the Icebreaker Beach complex on North Devon Island "represents a transitional stage typologically linking the Independence 1 and Pre-Dorset occupations of the High Arctic." A similar debate has focused around the Greenlandic Saqqaq variant. While some considered Saqqaq as being a late development of Independence 1 culture (McGhee 1976), others saw both as archaeological variants of the same culture (Elling 1996). Plumet (1996: 28) viewed Saqqaq and the Canadian Arctic Pre-Dorset as two regional facies of the same cultural formation. Other studies have also identified a "Transitional" phase (Independence II and Groswater) as making the link between the Early Palaeoeskimo and the later Dorset period (Maxwell 1985; Renouf 1994). This "Transitional" concept has not won general acceptance among researchers and several have expressed doubt about the applicability of cultural-historical relationship to this "Transitional" phase (Nagy 1994; Ramsden and Tuck 2001; Tuck and Fitzhugh 1986).

From the examples discussed above, it is clear that variability in itself did not constitute the focus of research. Variability was indeed recognized, but the initial problem did not lie in its understanding *per se*; instead, the expressed variability seems to have provided the means for the establishment of historical relationships among the different Palaeoeskimo assemblages. Working toward a developmental trajectory, the main objective was the positioning of the different cultural components within a temporal sequence. This approach emphasises cultural continuity where the different cultures are seen as part of a continuum each culture gradually evolving into the next one. In cases where cultural continuity could not be firmly established, as for Saqqaq and Pre-Dorset for instance, variability was explained in terms of regional variants and linked to different environmental settings. Within the limits of such cultural-historical assumptions (and certainly avoiding the issue of possible contemporaneity of the different archaeological components) no attempts were made to explain these regional variants; either they were considered as just that, regional variants, with no further explanations, or they were considered as anomalies (Arnold 1980: 424; Le Blanc 1994).

Binfordian Functionalist Paradigm
Resolutely entrenched in the Binfordian functionalist paradigm (Binford 1983), a number of studies have focused on the relation between archaeological assemblages and seasonal and/or subsistence activities. These studies examine intra- and inter-site patterning using data such as architecture, spatial organization, settlement patterns, and faunal and artifact distribution. The equation made is that variability expressed in one or any of these categories reflects difference in subsistence and seasonal patterns. For example, using data from Lake Harbour, Baffin Island, Maxwell (1980) interprets the co-occurrence of relative frequencies of artifact types and dwelling types in seasonal terms. Similarly, Jordan (1980) looking at Avayalik Island in northern Labrador, interprets variability in house forms and associated features as being seasonally and/or functionally related.

One of the inherent problems with the functional approach is that all categories do not share the same potential for assessing seasonal and functional differences. For instance, if site location and faunal evidence are generally considered as reliable indicators of seasonality, the season/function relationship weakens when dealing with dwelling types and tool assemblages. A simple but striking example of this is that in Arctic archaeology, tent rings are generally assumed to represent summer occupation whereas more substantial structures, such as semi-subterranean dwellings, represent colder season occupation. This makes sense, but does it mean that Independence I people, for which only tent rings have been described, did not have winter dwellings? By the same token, is it correct to assume that the absence of substantial Dorset dwellings in the Lake Harbour record necessarily indicates that the Dorset people must have had their winter houses on the ice at the floe edge (Maxwell 1980)? The latter example may seem extreme but does illustrate that seasonal/functional inferences are not always supported by data but are often elaborated from negative evidence.

The problem becomes even more acute when functional significance is attributed to artifacts. While in some cases, it is relatively safe to associate individual artifact types with specific activities, for instance harpoon endblades with sea-mammal hunting, the picture is more complex when functional significance is assigned to clusters of artifact types. In such cases, a direct relationship is made between artifact type frequencies and the activity presumably conducted at a site. Using functional categories (grouping), archaeologists are led to believe that they can infer individual site function when in fact, what the process really reveals is the frequency of different objects at a particular site. The main problems in using the functional argument are: firstly, the functional categories used by Arctic archaeologists are by and large pseudo-functional (*i.e.*, inferred function); rarely are formal use-wear studies conducted to verify assumed tool function. Secondly, functional studies rarely go beyond the individual site level and therefore, I would argue, only become effective in a comparative relationship and integrated within a broader regional context. At best, these comparative studies only indicate degrees of similarity or difference among sites; what they fail to indicate is the reason for the differences. Furthermore, and more importantly, this approach limits "technology to things and relations among things such that people often drop out of the picture together" (Dobres and Hoffman 1994: 230).

Cultural/Ecology Paradigm: the *Core Area* Model and the Regional Variant Theory
In Palaeoeskimo research, ecological models have developed within the context of the *Core Area* model (Maxwell 1976a). In this model, explanations for regional variability are formulated within a biogeographical and ecological framework reflecting adaptation to specific environmental conditions. Geographically, the core area corresponds to the region stretching from northern Baffin Island through Foxe Basin, northern Hudson Bay and Hudson Bay shores and islands. For this area, the model argues for a continuous and gradual *in situ* cultural development throughout the entire 4000 year period of Palaeoeskimo occupancy. This uninterrupted sequence of occupation is seen as resulting from the ecological and therefore economical stability in resource exploitation within this specific area (Fitzhugh 1997: 404). Expansions outside the core area are believed to have occurred during favourable climatic and ecological regimes *(Ibid.*: 402). During such periods, emigrants from the core moved out to explore and settle unknown marginal areas such as the High Arctic, Greenland, Newfoundland and Labrador. This expansionism can be summarized as follows:

Migration out of the core area → Adaptation
to new environmental conditions →
development of regional traits → isolation
→ either local extinction or retreat back to
the core area

It is within the limits of this model that explanations for variability were provided; regional variation either proceeded from geographical isolation or local environmental conditions or a combination of both. This is how, for example, the Greenlandic Saqqaq was distinguished from the Canadian Arctic Pre-Dorset. Both groups were contemporaneous but presented different cultural traits resulting from their respective regional environmental settings. Similarly, the unique character of the *Newfoundland Dorset* was in turn envisioned as an adaptive response to the subarctic environment (Fitzhugh 1976: 103; Harp 1969/70: 123), and/or resulting from geographical isolation (Cox 1978: 113; Fitzhugh 1976; Harp 1969/70; Linnamae 1975: 93). Even, Robbins' (1985: 139) interpretation of Middle Dorset regionalism as a response to different regional ecologies is tainted by the *Core Area* model.

This brief review of the Arctic literature has shown that archaeological variability has been addressed in culture-historical, functional and ecological terms. The discussion highlighted some of the limits of each approach. The chief feature emerging from the discussion is a perception of diversity that leads to the interpretation of different archaeological components in terms of "cultural isolates." Specifically obvious in the culture-historical and ecological models, we are led to imagine individual cultures existing in strict isolation. Either the different archaeological components are separated in time and assumed to represent different cultures sharing an historical relationship or, according to the *Core Area* model, cultural variability proceeds from geographical isolation. Barth's (1969:11) statement that: "This history has produced a world of separate peoples, each with their culture and each organized in a society which can be legitimately isolated for description as an island in itself" typifies this view. Such a perspective leaves very little place for synchronic differentiation of groups of people.

Returning to the Middle Dorset tradition on the island of Newfoundland and in Saint-Pierre, the question of temporal or spatial variability is not so acute. Radiocarbon dating firmly positions the different regional variants within the same interval between 2000 and 1100 B.P. As for climatic and environmental variables, every region was subject to the same climatic conditions during the Middle Dorset period, and although faunal resources may not have been uniformly distributed in time throughout the islands, the same resources were generally available in the different regions. Thus, it appears that in the study area cultural-historical or ecological approaches to cultural diversity are not necessarily appropriate and that the source of variability may need to be sought in some other direction. I have to be clear here that, by no means am I rejecting any of the other approaches, all were useful and complementary; I am simply proposing another reading of the problem.

Until now and perhaps because of the pre-eminence of the models discussed above, underlying socio-correlates of variability in the Arctic record have been overlooked, and rarely has the process of variability been considered to result from socio-cultural factors. Sutherland (1996) suggests that Palaeoeskimo variability could be approached in terms of local populations comparable to the mosaic of historic Arctic –*muit* groups. Considering the case at hand, this particular idea is appealing and this is perhaps how we might want to envision Middle Dorset variability in Newfoundland and Saint-Pierre. If Middle Dorset variability can be viewed and interpreted as reflecting the existence of regional groups, bands or societies, new insights and possibly an alternative explanation could be brought forward.

A SOCIAL APPROACH TO VARIABILITY: PRACTICE THEORY

Abandoning strictly historical, functionalist, and neo-evolutionist (adaptationalist) interpretations, I would like to re-examine Middle Dorset variability within the conceptual framework of practice theory. This approach incorporates concepts such as community of practice, local traditions and ethnic identity, and offers an interpretative lens through which the variability observed in the material record is interpreted as reflecting distinctive cultural traditions. My approach thus explicitly equates material culture and cultural identity. Such an approach is challenging at the theoretical level but practice theory is an important conceptual and theoretical avenue holding promise in making such a link.

A series of papers explore exhaustively this complex body of theory (Bourdieu 1972, 1980; Dietler and Herbich 1998; Dobres 2000; Dobres and Hoffman 1994, 1999; Dobres and Robb 2000; Dornan 2002; Emerson and McElrath 2001; Hodder 2000; Lemonnier 1992, 1993; Pauketat 2001a; Schlanger 1991; Shanks and Tilley 1987; Stark 1998). Practice theory has undergone a series of permutations and has fully developed, in the aftermath of Bourdieu's English translation of *Esquisse d'une théorie de la pratique* (1972) in 1977 and *Le Sens Pratique* (1980) in 1990, into agency theory under the pens of British and American scholars (cf., Dornan 2002). This reformulation is most significant but is, in my view, often articulated in an unduly complex jargon that is at times difficult to comprehend.

For the sake of clarity, I am following the French tradition and am articulating my discussion within the bounds of practice theory, avoiding the lexicological semantics of agency theory. As a starting point, I wish to return to the foundational work of Marcel Mauss and tease out some of his key concepts, which as we shall see, laid the ground work upon which practice theory was originally elaborated. I am essentially proposing a deconstruction exercise and in doing so hope to deliver a simple and coherent description that captures the essence and makes comprehensible the basic elements underlying that theory.

Solidly anchored in the French tradition of *techniques and culture,* contemporary practice theory can be traced back to the seminal work of Marcel Mauss (1935) *Les Techniques du Corps (The Notion of Body Techniques -* 1979*)* in which he sets out to demonstrate how body techniques (*i.e.,* body gestures and every aspect of action on the matter) both reflect and condition social traditions. As Durkheim's student, Mauss implements Durkheim sociology that considers "social facts as *things"* and uses the notion in reverse, stating that "things are social" (Schlanger 1991: 121) and further proposes that technology is a *total social fact.* According to Mauss, technology is social to the core and has to be understood in relation to the collective social body and the enframing traditions within which it is produced, reproduced and transmitted. Technology is not practiced in a cultural vacuum (Dobres and Hoffman 1999: 213); it is material, concrete, practiced collectively, tacitly and by habits (Schlanger 1991: 128). In *The Notion of Body Techniques,* Mauss (1979: 101) introduces the concept of *habitus*, a fundamental concept later brought forward by Bourdieu (1972, 1980) in formulating his theory of practice. Essentially, *habitus* refers to the society's structure, which at once is conditioned and conditions social motivations, behaviours, and consequently ultimately affects material culture patterning. Dietler and Herbich (1998: 246-248) provide a clear and succinct summary of this complex concept. Thus *habitus* is the product of a unique set of circumstances (history, physical constraints, individual and collective practices, values, perceptions and significance, etc...), which more or less guarantee the conformity of those practices and their constancy through time (Bourdieu 1980: 91).

Mauss (1947) insists that technology needs to be examined as it unfolds; that is, along every stage of its fabrication, from raw material to the finished object. It is crucial to comprehend *les enchaînements organiques* or the sequence of gestures and behaviours and the inherent process of decision-making made at each stage of production. A close examination of this sequence of actions "engenders a near microscopic view of cultural process" (Pauketat 2001b: 11) bringing to light how tools were made and used, which set of actions were used, which decisions were made in the process of tool making. In Mauss, we can clearly identify the source of Leroi-Gourhan's (1964) later concept of *chaîne opératoire*.

According to Mauss, technology is human in nature, therefore arbitrary and characterized by its infinite variety that is particular and specific to every society (Schlanger 1991: 118, 125). Mauss (1935) defines technology as an action that is effective and traditional (*acte traditionel efficace*). He argues that technology is a reasoned (*raisonné*) practice, individually and collectively. To be effective, technology ultimately results from a series of consensual choices about what is meaningful and what works for them. Technological choice means the ability to choose between a number of possible alternatives (Lemonnier 1993:7). During this sorting out, choices are going to be enacted at each step throughout the entire technological process. These choices are obviously guided by physical/natural constraints (raw material availability, the intended function of the object, etc.), but they are also, and mostly, made within a specific social context (frame of reference or *habitus*). It is through the *habitus* that not only technological practices develop and are reproduced but this *habitus* also shapes the cultural perceptions of the limits of the possible in patterns of choices (Dietler and Herbich 1998: 238, 246). Those cultural perceptions otherwise referred to as "social representations" (Lemonnier 1992: 6) or "mental traditions" (Leroi-Gourhan 1973) are ultimately what shape the technology, the technological traditions, and for Mauss (1979:104), "there is no technique and no transmission in the absence of tradition."

Thus, in reference to Mauss, technology is first and foremost a social act. It is arbitrary and a reasoned practice involving individual and communal choices. These choices result in style or technological practices generated in a specific social context, *the habitus*. To summarize, the crux of that matter is that: "Acting individually, but within a social context, these individuals create communities of practice that in their multiple interactions we might envision as creating traditions" (Emerson and McElrath 2001).

This is the framework within which I situate my research. Using the Newfoundland/Saint-Pierre example I am seeking communities of practice, cultural traditions or to use Leroi-Gourhan (1973) terminology: *des Milieux techniques partagés*.

As an illustration of how the notions of style, practice and tradition are enacted let me bring forward a current example from the Newfoundland northwest coast. On the Northern Peninsula, people have built their garbage containers using abandoned wooden cable spools. The cables were used and are still being used to drag fishing nets, while the spools left behind have been used in the construction of trash containers. Dragger fishery started in Port au Choix in the late 1960s early 1970s and by the early 1980s a large number of empty spools had accumulated. Concomitant with the heyday of the dragging fleet in the early 1980s, local communities were incorporated and garbage collection was instituted; before that people had been responsible for the disposal of their own trash. Garbage collection was a new reality imposing specific constraints: garbage was now being picked up only once a week and had to be protected from animals, mainly seagulls. Set within this specific historical and social context, it is at this time that local residents began to use the ends of cable spools to construct containers in which to keep their garbage; they were creating a new local tradition. To this day, this vernacular tradition is in use in most communities on the Northern Peninsula, creating a community of practice.

In this research, the term tradition is put forward specifically to refer to a set or body of distinctive cultural features shared by a defined cultural community: such traits can include technology, typology, architecture, settlement and subsistence patterns and others. Returning specifically to the Tuck and Fitzhugh (1986: 162) definition, the term tradition "is taken to mean the persistence of a cultural pattern whose distinctive features … form a cohesive body of customs traceable through time and space."

THE CASE STUDY

I propose to explore the issue of "cultural traditions" by means of an extended case study. The research focuses on recognition of spatially defined local traditions in the Middle Dorset period (2000 to 1100 B.P.) cultural assemblages on the island of Newfoundland and the island of Saint-Pierre in the French Archipelago of Saint-Pierre and Miquelon. The Newfoundland/Saint-Pierre example is extremely amenable to this type of study for a number of reasons. Firstly, Middle Dorset regional variants have already been clearly recognized and described (Erwin 2001; LeBlanc 2000b; Robbins 1985, 1986; Simpson 1986). Secondly, the variability observed in such a limited geographical region offers an ideal scale to observe the process of tradition-making. Thirdly, the study area also provides a controlled temporal framework. Contrasting with other Arctic regions where there is evidence of Early, Middle and Late Dorset occupations, only Middle Dorset people reached the islands of Newfoundland and Saint-Pierre. Finally, in dealing with Middle Dorset variability in Newfoundland it is difficult to bring forward climatic or environmental considerations. Although the latter factors might have prompted the migration onto the island, they provide no explanation regarding the different regional expressions. Thus, the highly regional and temporally limited aspects of the Newfoundland/Saint-Pierre case offer extraordinary potential to increase the resolution and examine tradition-making at close range.

In order to obtain data relevant to the issue of practices, traditions and identity I examine archaeological collections from eight sites in Newfoundland and Saint-Pierre and Miquelon: Phillip's Garden, Cape Ray, l'Anse à Flamme, l'Anse à Henry, Dildo Island, Shamblers Cove, Swan Island and Pittman (Figure 2). Appendix 1 provides a summary description of those sites; radiocarbon dates for the Middle Dorset components at these sites are available in Appendix 2. These specific sites were selected for a number of reasons: (1) their spatial distribution provides a broad geographical coverage of the island; (2) they contain artifact assemblages unequivocally diagnostic of the Middle Dorset culture (style, context and date); and (3) the assemblages, when possible, were sufficiently abundant at each site as to be statistically significant.

The research presented is based on practice theory and its primary goal is to identify patterns in the technological practices at each site. I adopt an analytic method that proceeds from the most elementary and most material aspect of material culture to build an empirical corpus of technical facts or traits. I chose to explore technological patterning according to two axes: raw material use-patterns and artifact style. Due to generally poor preservation conditions this study focuses only on the lithic component of the assemblages. Endblades, endscrapers and microblades constitute the artifact categories considered for analysis on the basis of their shared and non-ambiguous respective function (*i.e.*, endblades are used similarly by all Dorset hunters).

Once the database was established, I explored the variants among the sites. This was done not solely to demonstrate the presence or absence of particular traits among the different assemblages but to illustrate conformity in technological practices within regions. This case study is predicated on the hypothesis that Middle Dorset groups settled in specific regions where they developed their own regional technological traditions. Therefore, my expectation is to find distinctive regional expressions, each exhibiting conformity in style and in lithic raw material use-patterns.

The purpose here is to demonstrate that one is inclined to do what one does in certain ways, at different places, because of one's experiences in a specific social setting (Pauketat 2001b: 4); the variants become therefore socially significant and bring to the fore the link between technical phenomena and social reality (Lemonnier 1983: 17).

CHAPTER 3. LITHIC RAW MATERIAL USE-PATTERNS

Lithic raw material use-patterns comprise the first set of data examined in my investigation of Middle Dorset regional technological practices. The objective pursued is threefold and involves: (1) the identification and characterization of specific raw material types (2) the localization of their geological provenience, (3) the evaluation of their respective quantitative importance in the archaeological assemblages.

In order to understand the geographical distribution of the Newfoundland rocks it is necessary to provide some content concerning the mechanisms behind their formation. Thus, the first section of this chapter provides a background discussion relating to rock formation and the geological setting of the island of Newfoundland. Following this brief discussion, the method and results of the raw material analysis are presented.

GEOLOGICAL SETTING

An Island is Born

It is generally accepted that the island of Newfoundland is divided into three main geological zones: the Humber Zone, the Central Zone and the Avalon Zone. The rocks in each of these zones display sharp contrasts in lithology, stratigraphy, and mineral assemblages. They also exhibit structural, faunal and geophysical differences (Williams 2001: 2-5). The formation and the spatial distribution of these rocks result from tectonic activity which for millions of years set the stage for the present day geological setting of Newfoundland.

Newfoundland geology can be summarized in terms of the formation and the destruction of an ancient ocean. The story begins at a time prior to 650 million years ago (late Proterozoic), when the Canadian Shield and all of the Earth's landmasses were part of one super-continent. Shortly after 650 million years ago, this super-continent began to break apart along an ancient ridge to form two separate continents: Laurentia (North American plate) to the west and Gondwana (Eurasian/African plate) to the east. The separation of these two landmasses created a large valley (rift) that filled with water to eventually become by 540 million years ago (Early Paleozoic) the thousand kilometer wide Iapetus Ocean (Figure 3). For over a hundred million years, sediments eroded from the land, washed offshore and accumulated to form large continental shelves at the margins of these newly formed continents (Burzynski and Marceau 1995: 21).

During that time, the climate along the Laurentian coast was tropical, as it lay about 15 degrees south of the equator (Knight 1989: 63) and in the warm waters of the Iapetus Ocean abundant life forms developed. Calcium-carbonate rich mounds of coral-like algae, crustaceans, mollusks, planktonic animals and other organisms lived, died, and slowly blanketed the ocean-floor (Burzynsky and Marceau 1995: 21). Cambrian and Ordovician limestone beds formed in the warm shallow coastal waters and in time, the fossil-rich sediments of the continental shelves extended hundreds of kilometres offshore to create kilometer-thick carbonate banks (*Ibid.*). Occasionally, fragments of the shelves would collapse and tumble down the continental slope, sending shell-rich sediments into the deep ocean basin. During the same time period, sandstones and shales formed along the Gondwana margin. The fauna and flora were significantly different reflecting the prevailing colder conditions on that side of the Iapetus Ocean (Atlantic Geoscience Society 2001: 78-79).

In the Early Ordovician (500-450 million years ago), the mantle convection currents reversed and the continents on each side of the Iapetus Ocean began to move towards each other again (Burzynski and Marceau 1995: 24) (Figure 3). In order to accommodate the tremendous compressive forces involved, one of the plates moved beneath the other oceanic or continental plate (Staff of Asarco Inc., and Abitibi-Price 2001: 7). This process is called subduction; the process by which it is induced is still not fully understood, but it is generally believed that, between the continental crust that is relatively light, and the denser, therefore heavier oceanic crust, it is the latter that will yield (Colman-Sadd and Scott 1994). In this way, the subducted oceanic crust was progressively dragged down eastward to immense depths into the mantle where it was melted by high temperatures. The magma thus formed started making its way up to the surface, bubbling up through the overlying solid rocks to finally erupt as volcanic lava (Burzunski and Marceau 1995: 24). By about 490 million years ago, a volcanic island-arc had risen from the ocean floor above the subduction zones. Remnants of this volcanic arc are today preserved in the Ordovician volcanic and intrusive rocks of Notre-Dame Bay, central Newfoundland (*Ibid.*; Colman-Sadd and Scott 1994).

As the Iapetus Ocean floor continued to be consumed by subduction, the two continental plates progressively converged causing continental-shelf sediments, continental slope deposits, portions of the oceanic floor, oceanic crust and upper mantle (ophiolites) to be transported westward on top of the old continental Laurentian margin (Burzynski and Marceau 1995: 24; Hodych, King and Neale 1989: 11; Ryan 1983: 3). The movement ended when the base of the volcano island-arc jammed against the edge of the continental Laurentian margin (Burzynski and Marceau 1995: 24).

Chapter 3. Lithic Raw Material Use-Patterns

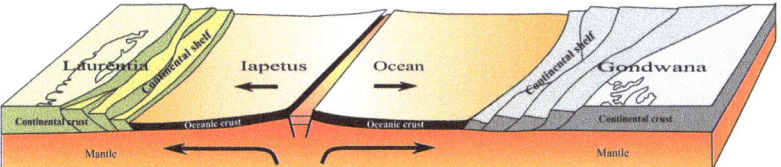
Super-continent break apart to form two separate continents: Laurentia and Gondwana. Opening of the Iapetus Ocean.

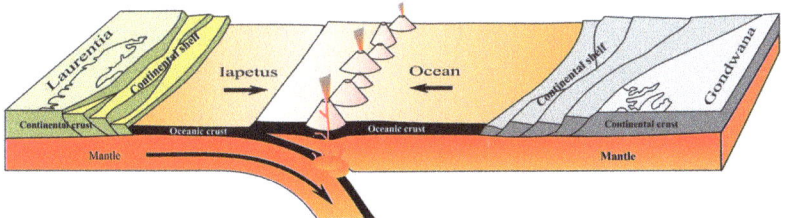
Subduction moves continents towards each other and volcanic island arc rises from the ocean above the subduction zone.

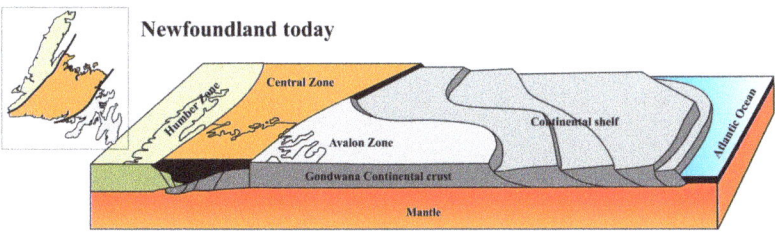
Laurentia and Gondwana collide to form the island of Newfoundland.

Figure 3. The genesis of the island of Newfoundland (after Colman and Sadd 1994).

By 410 million years ago, Laurentia and Gondwana had collided forming a huge, new supercontinent: Pangaea. From the force of the collision emerged a massive mountain chain that included the entire Appalachians. Pangaea lasted until Early Jurassic time (200 million years ago) then broke apart to give way to the present Atlantic Ocean. This time the break did not occur exactly along the same line followed by the earlier Iapetus rift but further to the east, leaving fragments of the Eurasian/African plate (Gondwana) still attached to the North American plate (Laurentia).

These tectonic episodes of ocean formation and destruction resulted in the setting of three distinct geological regions (Figure 3): to the west, the Humber Zone consists of Laurentian continental-shelf and oceanic floor sediments and oceanic crust and upper mantle rocks; central Newfoundland was left with remnants of the Iapetus oceanic floor and a volcanic island-arc; the Avalon Zone, to the east, is a fragment of Gondwana left attached to central Newfoundland, as it tore off from Pangaea (*Ibid.*: 28).

Newfoundland Geological Zones
Humber Zone (Western Zone)
The Humber Zone, also called the Western Zone, represents the eastern continental margin of the Laurentian Plate (Ancient North America) and is composed of autochtonous and allochtonous rocks. Autochthonous refers to "*in place*" rocks and includes: (1) the Precambrian crystalline basement, remnants of the old Canadian Shield that split apart during the Iapetus opening episode. The main lithologies are gneisses, schists and granites that now constitute the core of the Great Northern Peninsula (Williams *et al.* 1996: 24) and; (2) the Carbonate Sequence that consists of shallow to progressively deeper marine sediments formed on the Laurentian continental-shelf also referred to as the carbonate-shelf. The Carbonate Sequence is sub-divided into the Labrador, Port au Port, St. George and Table Head groups. Most of the rocks in the sequence are carbonate rocks (calcium carbonate and/or calcium magnesium carbonate), predominantly limestones (hardened carbonate bank) and dolomite[7] with minor sandstone and shale (Williams 2001:20). Associated fauna includes tribolites, brachiopods and Midcontinent conodonts (Williams *et al.* 1996: 23). Microscopic fossils such as mineralized conodonts, sponge spicules and radiolarians are also present. However, the latter are not always well preserved in these limestones; the turbidity induced by waves and tides abrades the smaller fossils and "flushes them into the deeper water. In addition, the high level of biologic activity makes these tiny particles excellent food for the many filter feeding organisms which inhabit this setting" (*Ibid.*: 15).

Allochthonous refers to rocks that were transported great distances by tectonic movements following their original formation. Referred to as the Humber Arm Allochthon, these rocks formed to the east, far from shore in a much deeper ocean setting at the base of the continental slope and abyssal plain of the Iapetus Ocean (*Ibid.*: 8). As the plates moved towards one another, these sediments were thrust onto the ancient continental margin of Laurentia. The Humber Arm Allochthon is principally composed of deep marine sedimentary rocks of the Cow Head and Curling Groups (ocean floor sediments) and of ophiolites, derived from the oceanic crust and underlying mantle. The Cow Head and Curling Groups (Humber Arm Supergroup) are dominated by shales, deep water

---
[7] Dolomization is the process by which limestone is converted into dolomite rock by "replacing a portion of the calcium carbonate with magnesium carbonate" (Parker 1997: 82).

limestones, organic conglomerates, megabreccia and sandstones (*Ibid.*: 11 and 31). Formed at great water depth, rocks of these groups are characterized by a lack of oxygen, fine texture and an abundant deep water microscopic flora and fauna including chitinozoa, acritarchs and conodonts, radiolarians and silicious sponge spicules (James and Stevens 1986: 38; Williams *et al.* 1996: 12-13). With the exception of graptolites, macrofossils are generally rare in those sediments (Williams *et al.* 1996: 11). The Ophiolite Sequence includes ocean floor sediments, oceanic crust rocks (pillow lavas and sheeted dykes) and, ultramafic rocks characteristic of the earth's mantle (Burzynski 1999: 48; James and Stevens 1986: 7; Williams *et al.* 1996: 31).

Central Zone
The Central Zone consists of a mix of thick, strongly deformed volcanics, these being remnants of the volcanic island arcs, as well as Ordovician oceanic crust and upper mantle (ophiolites), which are remnants of the Iapetus Ocean sea-floor (Hodych, King and Neale 1989: 11). The Central Zone is subdivided into the Dunnage Zone (including the Notre-Dame and Exploits Subzones) and the Gander Zone. Each of these zones has distinctive rocks and faunal assemblages due to their proximity to either the Gondwana or Laurentian margins of the Iapetus Ocean during the early Ordovician period (Williams *et al.* 1996: 22). The Dunnage Zone is characterized by its abundant volcanics, deep water sedimentary rocks, ophiolite suites and *mélange* (Williams 1995: 139). The sedimentary rocks include greywackes, slates, cherts and minor limestones (*Ibid.*; Williams 2001: 61). Fossiliferous units display deep water microfossils such as conodonts (Kean 1989: 43) and radiolarians, remnants of the Cambro-Ordovician Iapetus depositional episode (Paul Dean, pers. comm. 2001). It should be noted, however, that radiolarian preservation is often obliterated in those sediments due to the recrystallization process that followed the volcanic episodes (*Ibid.*). The Gander Zone is characterized by granitic intrusions, deep marine metamorphosed sandstone, shale and a few conglomerate beds and volcanic rocks (Williams 2001: 86; Blackwood 1989: 33). In places metamorphism has progressed to schist and gneiss (Colman-Sadd and Scott 1994). These rocks are unfossiliferous (Williams *et al.* 1996: 22).

Avalon Zone (Eastern Zone)
The Avalon Zone includes the Avalon, Bonavista and Burin Peninsulas of eastern Newfoundland. The thick sequence of rocks of the Avalon Zone "reflects a long history of volcanism, marine and terrestrial sedimentation" (King 1989: 17). The oldest rocks were deposited below the sea and consist of well preserved late Precambrian volcanics (pillow basalt, volcanic lava and ash). Over a long period of time, these were covered by successive layers of volcanic ash and lava and deep marine sediments that include tuffaceous siltstone and sandstone. Those in turn, were overlain by minor volcanics, shales and sandstones deposited as alluvium in riverbeds and shallow marine deltas. Finally, shales, sandstones and a few limestones were deposited in the shallow seawater of the ancient Cambrian continental-shelf (Gondwana) (Colman-Sadd and Scott 1994).

PETROGRAPHIC ANALYSIS

Research Methods
On the island of Newfoundland, lithic raw material sourcing studies have been conducted on the Port au Port Peninsula (Simpson 1984; Nagle 1985) and in the Gros Morne National Park area (Nagle 1985)[8]. The information generated by these studies was significant, most especially in regard to the recognition of radiolarian fossils (*Ibid.*), which are clear fingerprints of Cambro-Ordovician sedimentary rocks of the Humber Zone. Unfortunately, however, that research did not yield reference collections to which archaeological samples could be compared. Indeed, neither archaeological nor geological research conducted in Newfoundland has produced any reference database to which archaeological material could be compared.

Without any available material, the first step of the research presented here was to create a basic raw materials reference collection. The common procedure in lithic sourcing studies is to compare geological samples of known origin with archaeological specimens. For this study, it was necessary to proceed in the reverse order and track down the geological provenience from the archaeological specimens. A thorough examination of the lithic artifact assemblages of the selected archaeological sites identified recurrent raw material types. Each raw material type was then identified in the debitage collection of the same sites and thin sections were prepared from the debitage samples so as not to destroy any formal tools.

Of the eight archaeological sites examined in this study, 58 debitage samples were selected to be thin sectioned. Petrographic description was carried out by Sherif A. Awadallah at the Department of Earth Sciences, Memorial University of Newfoundland. The descriptions are strictly qualitative, based on visual and microscopic data. Colour, texture, fracture, luster and translucency were noted. Colour is determined using the Rock-Color Chart from the Geological Society of America (The Rock-Color Chart Committee 1995); texture is qualified in terms of aphanitic, coarse grain or granular; luster is described as dull, medium or glossy; translucency as opaque or translucent. Structure is described as being massive (homogeneous), banded or laminated. The thin sections were examined using a petrographic microscope under natural and polarized light, the latter to identify minerals. Each thin section was micro-photographed in black and white, and in colour under plain and polarized light at magnification of 20, 100 or 200. Complete descriptions are presented in Appendix 3.

---

[8] Research devoted to sourcing lithic raw materials is far more developed in Labrador (e.g., Blackman and Nagle 1983; Fitzhugh 1972; Gramly 1978; Lazenby 1980; Loring 2002; McCaffrey 1989; Nagle 1984, 1986).

Chapter 3. Lithic Raw Material Use-Patterns

In order to establish the sample's geological provenience, individual hand specimens, thin sections, photographs and petrographic descriptions were presented to the following geologists: Stephen Colman-Sadd, Ian Knight and Sean O'Brien from the Geological Survey of Newfoundland and Labrador; Paul Dean, Director, Johnson Geo Center, St. John's; Dr. John Waldron, Department of Earth and Atmospheric Sciences, University of Alberta; and Dr. Mario Coniglio, Department of Earth Sciences, University of Waterloo. Their observations focused mainly on colour, depositional modes (texture/structure), and presence/absence of fossils and diagnostic minerals. These determinations, combined with data extracted from the geological literature, made it possible, in most cases, to link conclusively the different raw material samples to a specific rock group or formation. Appendix 3 provides the detailed description of individual thin section, a summarized version is included in tables throughout this chapter.

Following identification, the raw material debitage samples were compared with artifact collections from each of the archaeological sites, which included the complete collection of endblades, endscrapers and microblades. However, at sites where the integrity of the archaeological context was equivocal (survey collection, multi-component sites), only the endblades were considered. In those contexts, the distinction between Groswater and Middle Dorset endscrapers and/or microblades remained unclear. Also, at sites where artifact inventories were too large to be handled within the scope of this study, only a selected sample of artifacts was retained for analysis. For example, at the Cape Ray site only the artifacts collected during the 1997 excavation (Fogt 1998) of a Middle Dorset dwelling were analysed. Similarly, at the Phillip's Garden site in Port au Choix site where, at least, 70 Middle Dorset dwellings are reported (Hodgetts *et al.*, 2003: 107) only the data from Midden Feature 2 were included in the study. The large artifact collection from Dildo Island Middle Dorset - House 2 prompted the decision to confine the analysis to the clearly defined cultural layers (2A and 3 - see LeBlanc 2003b). The comparative analysis produced a record of the artifact raw material type frequencies for each of the sites.

The sourcing of quartz crystal was not attempted in the present study. In the Newfoundland context, the exercise would have been inconclusive as veins of quartz crystal are common to all major tectonic zones and can be found in virtually any part of the island

As a word of caution, one has to keep in mind that the results presented here are a reflection of the current status of geological research and that the detailed geological mapping of the island of Newfoundland is constantly being refined.

Results
Phillip's Garden Site (Port au Choix)
Newfoundland Northwest Coast
From the Phillip's Garden site (Figure 4) eight samples were thin sectioned (PG-1 to 8 - Table 1). Petrographic analysis divides the samples into two groups: (1) cherts from the Cow Head Group and, (2) replacement cherts from the Carbonate Sequence. The Cow Head Group is composed "of a series of late Cambrian to Early Middle-Ordovician deep marine limestones and shales with carbonate conglomerates and megabreccias" (Williams *et al.* 1996: 31). Cherts are most common in the Ordovician part of the sequence that coincides with the appearance of radiolarians and siliceous sponge spicules (James and Stevens 1986: 38). The replacement cherts formed within the relatively shallow waters of the continental-shelf (or carbonate-shelf). Lithologies are predominantly limestones (hardened carbonate rocks) and dolostones

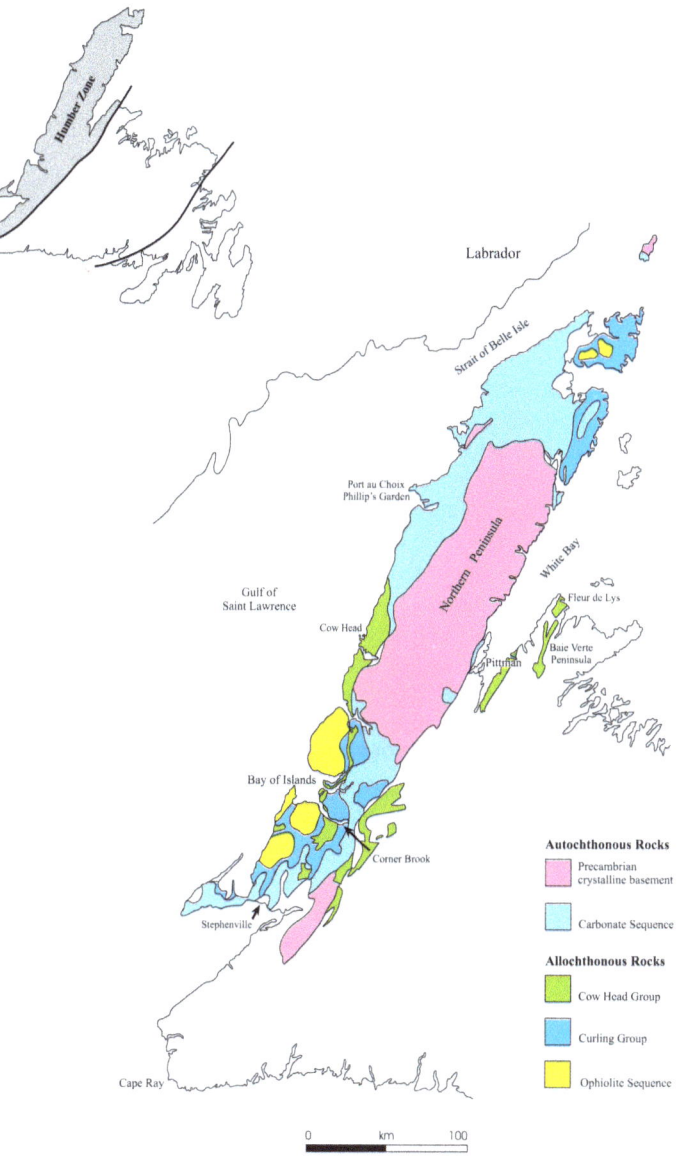

Figure 4. Authochonous and allochthonous rocks of the Humber Zone, western Newfoundland (after Knight, James, and Williams 1995).

Sample	PG-1	PG-2	PG-3	PG-4	PG-5	PG-6	PG-7	PG-8
Colour	Black	Brown	Green	Blue grey	Dark blue-green	Dark blue and grey	Dark blue and grey	Dark blue and grey
Texture	Aphanitic	Aphanitic	Aphanitic	Aphanitic	Aphanitic	Aphanitic	Aphanitic	Aphanitic
Fracture	Conchoidal	Conchoidal	Conchoidal	Conchoidal	Conchoidal	Conchoidal	Conchoidal	Conchoidal
Luster	Glossy	Glossy	Glossy	Glossy	Glossy to dull	Glossy to dull	Glossy to dull	Glossy to dull
Translucency	Opaque but translucent along the edges	Semi-transparent	Opaque	Semi-transparent	Opaque	Opaque but translucent along the edges	Opaque but translucent along the edges	Opaque
Structure	Massive	Massive	Well laminated	Massive except for few fractures	Well laminated	Well laminated	Laminated	Well laminated
Fossils	Sponge spicules Ghosts of radiolarian	-	Sponge spicules Ghosts of radiolarians	-	Sponge spicules Radiolarians	Sponge spicules Radiolarians	Sponge spicules Radiolarians	Sponge spicules Ghosts of radiolarians
Mineral	Pyrite	Dolomite rhombs	Pyrite and rare carbonates	Dolomite rhombs	Dolomite rhombs	Rare carbonate rhombs	Rare carbonate rhombs	Pyrite Rare carbonate and dolomite rhombs
Other features	-	-	-	-	Chalcedony	Chalcedony	Chalcedony	Chalcedony
Origin	Cow Head Group	Carbonate Sequence	Cow Head Group	Carbonate Sequence	Cow Head Group	Cow Head Group	Cow Head Group	Cow Head Group

Table 1. Phillip's Garden Samples (Port au Choix) - Summary of Thin Section Descriptions.

with minor sandstone and shale (Williams 2001: 20). Cow Head Group and Carbonate Sequence replacement cherts are well exposed in western Newfoundland and the Port au Choix Peninsula is in fact, literally sitting on the carbonate-shelf (Figure 4).

Samples PG-2 and 4 are identified as replacement cherts from the Carbonate Sequence of either the St. George or the Port au Port Groups (J. Waldron, pers. comm. 2001). The Carbonate Sequence is uniform throughout the west coast and trying to tie these cherts to one of these groups could prove to be a futile exercise (*Ibid.*). Sample PG-2 is brownish in colour; PG-4 is blue-grey and both show an aphanitic texture resembling European gunflint. The fracture is conchoidal. Luster is glossy to dull; translucency ranges between opaque and semitransparent while the edges are translucent. Structure is massive; PG-4 shows a few fractures. No fauna was identified. Both samples show well developed dolomite rhombs, which is consistent with a Carbonate Sequence provenience. Both samples exhibit rounded cortex that is characteristic of nodular chert in limestone from the carbonate-shelf (*Ibid.*).

Samples PG-5, 6 and 7 are identical. Their colours alternate from one lamina to the other, between black, grey and dark blue grey. All three samples have an aphanitic texture, with a fracture that is conchoidal to irregular, and a glossy to dull luster. The core portion of the samples is opaque; the clay-rich grey laminae are translucent along the edges. The structure is strongly laminated. All samples contain abundant well preserved radiolarians and sponge spicules. The silica in some of the radiolarians is chalcedony. The fauna argues for a deep water Ordovician assemblage characteristic of the Cow Head Group.

Samples PG-1, 3, and 8 share similar features. Sample PG-1 is black, PG-3 and 8 are dark blue-green. All three present an aphanitic texture and a conchoidal fracture. The luster is glossy to dull; translucency is mainly opaque, but sample PG-1 is slightly translucent along the edges. PG-1 structure is massive; PG-3 and 8 are well laminated. All samples contain sponge spicules and either flattened radiolarians or radiolarian ghosts (ill-preserved radiolarians). Pyrite is present in all three samples. Chalcedony is visible in PG-8. PG-3 and 8 show limited trace of carbonate. The provenience of these samples is not as easy to establish and a number of elements have to be considered. On the one hand, traces of carbonate and specifically dolomite rhombs in PG-8 could be elements arguing in favour of a Carbonate Sequence origin. On the other hand, the presence of radiolarians as well as pyrite, indicative of an anaerobic environment (I. Knight, pers. comm. 2001), suggest a deep marine environment that is in line with a Cow Head origin. In addition, PG-3 shows a specific configuration in which the spicules are all aligned to each other suggesting that they fell through the water-column (*Ibid.*). Thus, combined, the fauna, mineralogy and deposition mode strongly argue for a Cow Head Group origin.

Archaeological Data

The archaeological data from Phillip's Garden indicates that the raw materials originating from the west coast (Humber Zone) were exploited. Table 2 shows that cherts from the Cow Head Group and the Carbonate Sequence dominate. Quartz crystal was also used in good proportion for the fabrication of microblades (32%). The use of exogenous raw materials is extremely rare: a single endblade is made of quartzite originating form Ramah Bay in northern Labrador; three other specimens are made of Caradocian chert and Marystown Group rhyolite.

Chapter 3. Lithic Raw Material Use-Patterns

Raw material	Endblades		Endscrapers		Microblades	
	N	%	N	%	N	%
Cow Head Group						
PG-1	8	8.9	8	9.2	25	16.1
PG-5, 6, 7	35	38.9	11	12.6	29	18.7
Misc. Cow Head	5	5.6	5	5.8	5	3.2
Subtotal	48	53.4	24	27.6	59	38.0
Carbonate Sequence						
PG-2	15	16.7	29	33.3	27	17.4
PG-4	1	1.1	25	28.7		
Subtotal	16	17.8	54	62.0	27	17.4
Caradocian chert						
SW-2					1	0.6
SW-5	1	1.1				
Subtotal	1	1.1			1	0.6
Marystown Group						
AF-3			1	1.2		
Subtotal			1	1.2		
Ramah Quartzite	1	1.1				
Quartz crystal			1	1.2	49	31.6
Miscellaneous	24	26.7	7	8.1	19	12.3
Grand total	90	100.1	87	100.1	155	99.9

Table 2. Phillip's Garden (Port au Choix) Material Type Frequencies.

These lithic types will be discussed later in this chapter. The dichotomy between the use of Cow Head chert and Carbonate Sequence chert is worth mentioning. While Cow Head chert is used intensively in the manufacture of endblades (54%), Carbonate Sequence chert is preferred in the production of endscrapers (62%). In fact, a number of expedient blade/flake/microblade endscrapers exhibit the rounded cortex of carbonate-shelf pebbles. As reported earlier, the Port au Choix Peninsula sits on the the carbonate-shelf (Figure 4) where raw materials are largely available, notably in the form of pebbles. The closest acquisition area for Cow Head cherts is located 70 km to the south. Quartz crystal is ubiquitous in all tectonic zones

Cape Ray Site – Newfoundland Southwest Coast
Seven rock samples (C. Ray 1 to 7 - Table 3) from the Cape Ray site (Figure 4) were thin sectioned and identified as belonging to the Cow Head Group on the basis of the presence of well preserved radiolarians.

All Cape Ray samples are aphanitic in texture and present conchoidal to sub-conchoidal fractures. They come in a variety of colours ranging from beige to beige-rose, blue-grey and reddish brown. Luster goes from dull to highly glossy. Translucency is mostly opaque; one sample (C. Ray-1) is slightly translucent along the edges. Structure is generally homogeneous showing some fractures in a few cases. Radiolarians are visible with a hand lens.

Thin section analysis points out to high silica content in the form of cryptocrystalline and microcrystalline quartz constituting the groundmass. Carbonates are present in the form of rhombohedral (or rhombic) crystals. Fossils include radiolarians and sponge spicules.

Archaeological Data
At Cape Ray, Cow Head Group chert clearly dominates all tool categories (Table 4). Carbonate Sequence chert occurs in smaller amounts (< 4%) whereas quartz crystal make-up 32 percent of the microblade assemblage. The use of exogenous raw materials is rare and only Marystown Group rhyolite (AF-3) was identified in the endscraper category. Cow Head chert does not occur at Cape Ray, as the site is located slightly to the south of the Humber Zone (Figure 4). The nearest location to acquire Cow Head Group chert is ca. 130 km to the north.

Sample	C. Ray-1	C. Ray-2	C. Ray-3	C. Ray-4	C. Ray-5	C. Ray-6	C. Ray-7
Colour	Blue grey and beige	Beige rose	Beige and blue-grey	Reddish-brown	Pale green and blue	Blue grey	Blue grey and mottled brown
Texture	Aphanitic	Aphanitic	Aphanitic	Aphanitic	Aphanitic	Aphanitic	Aphanitic
Fracture	Conchoidal	Sub-conchoidal	Conchoidal to sub-conchoidal	Conchoidal to sub-conchoidal	Conchoidal	Conchoidal	Conchoidal
Luster	Dull to glossy	Dull	Dull	Dull to slightly glossy	Dull to glossy	Dull to glossy	Dull to glossy
Translucency	Opaque but slightly translucent along the edges	Opaque	Opaque	Opaque	Opaque	Opaque	Opaque
Structure	Massive except for fractures	Laminae and fractures	Massive except for fractures	Massive showing parallel laminae	Massive except for fractures	Massive with abundant fractures	Massive
Fossils	Radiolarians Sponge spicules	Radiolarians	Radiolarians	Radiolarians	Radiolarians	Radiolarians	Radiolarians
Mineral	Carbonate rhombs Pyrite	-	Carbonate grains and rhombs	Hematite	Carbonate grains	Carbonate rhombs	Carbonate grains and rhombs
Origin	Cow Head Group	Cow Head Group	Cow Head Group	Cow Head Group	Cow Head Group	Cow Head Group	Cow Head Group

Table 3. Cape Ray Samples - Summary of Thin Section Descriptions.

Raw material	Endblades N	Endblades %	Endscrapers N	Endscrapers %	Microblades N	Microblades %
Cow HeadGroup						
Ray 1					82	15.7
Ray 2	5	2.5	4	2.1	41	7.9
Ray 3	61	30.8	2	1.0	31	6.0
Ray 4	2	1.0	4	2.1	9	1.7
Ray 5	1	0.5	17	8.8	1	0.2
Ray 6	80	40.4	63	32.5	66	12.7
Ray 7	11	5.6	25	12.9	29	5.6
PG-6			8	4.1	7	1.3
Misc. Cow Head	35	17.7	38	19.6	50	9.6
Subtotal	195	98.5	161	83.1	316	60.7
Carbonate Sequence						
PG-2			7	3.6	6	1.2
PG-4					2	0.4
Subtotal			7	3.6	8	1.6
Marystown Group						
AF-3			11	5.7		
Subtotal			11	5.7		
Quartz crystal			7	3.6	168	32.2
White quartzite	1	0.5				
Miscellaneous	2	1.0	8	4.1	29	5.6
Grand total	198	100.0	194	100.1	521	100.1

Table 4. Cape Ray Material Type Frequencies.

Anse à Flamme Site – Newfoundland South Coast

Six samples (Table 5) from the l'Anse à Flamme site (Figure 5) were thin sectioned. Sample (AF-2) is a radiolarian chert originating from the Cow Head Group. The remaining samples belong to formations of the Marystown Group on the Burin Peninsula (Figure 5). The Marystown Group consists mainly of suites of Precambrian volcanic flows and volcanistics rocks (Williams, O'Brien, King and Anderson 1995: 229) and extends from the southern end of the Burin Peninsula to Bonavista Bay (Figure 5).

Samples AF-1a and b are identified as rhyolite of the Marystown Group. This rhyolitic tuff is completely silicified, resembling a volcanic breccia (Aubert De La Rue 1951: 53). Visually, the rock is aphanitic presenting a conchoidal to sub-conchoidal fracture. The background matrix exhibits a yellow-beige colour and multiple purplish veins; mauve-brown veins and spots appear throughout the samples. Silvery metallic mineral inclusions are visible along fractures. The luster is dull and translucency opaque. The structure shows well-defined laminae and numerous fractures.

Microscopic analysis shows laminae indicative of an extrusive type of rock (volcanic flow). Under polarized light, the silvery mineral inclusions appear as red earthy recrystalized minerals: specular hematite, also known as Alaska Diamond (S. O'Brien, pers. comm 2001).

This mineralogy is quite distinctive and is only reported in a specific area between Monskstown and Swift Current in the northern part of the Burin Peninsula (*Ibid.* 2006) (Figure 5). In Saint-Pierre, rhyolite exhibiting specular hematite also outcrops in the equivalent Trépied Formation on Grand Colombier Island (Jean-Louis Rabottin 1999).[9]

Sample AF-2 is a radiolarian chert from the Cow Head Group. It is aphanitic and has a conchoidal fracture. Colour is blue-grey with occasional purple stains; one

---

[9] The Burin Peninsula and Saint-Pierre and Miquelon share a similar geology. Similar geological formations bear different names in Newfoundland and Saint-Pierre whether they were mapped by Newfoundland or French geologists.

Sample	AF-1a, b	AF-2	AF-3	AF-4a, b
Colour	Yellow beige	Blue	Medium grey	Light Pink
Texture	Aphanitic	Aphanitic	Aphanitic	Aphanitic
Fracture	Conchoidal	Conchoidal	Conchoidal	Irregular to sub-conchoidal
Luster	Dull	Glossy	Dull to glossy	Dull
Translucency	Opaque	Opaque	Opaque	Opaque
Structure	Laminated with fractures	Massive except for fractures	Massive except for fractures	Massive with fractures
Fossils	-	Radiolarians Sponge spicules	-	-
Mineral	Specular hematite	Carbonate	Non identified opaque minerals	Piedmontite
Origin	Marystown Group rhyolite / Saint-Pierre equivalent: Trépied Formation rhyolite on Grand Colombier Island	Cow Head Group	Marystown Group tuff	Marystown Group, Hare Hills Formation rhyolite / Saint-Pierre equivalent: Cap Rouge Formation rhyolite

Table-5. Anse à Flamme Samples - Summary of Thin Section Descriptions.

Chapter 3. Lithic Raw Material Use-Patterns

exposed to the surface. Microscopic examination documented the presence of piedmontite, a manganese rich epidote (S. O'Brien, pers. comm. 2001). Piedmontite is an uncommon mineral only reported in the Hare Hills Tuffs formation of the Marystown Group on the Burin Peninsula (*Ibid.* 2006) and in the equivalent Cap Rouge Formation at the northern tip of the island of Saint-Pierre (Rabu and Chauvel 1993: 49) (Figure 5).

Archaeological data

Since both Dorset and Groswater artifacts were recovered during excavations at the l'Anse à Flamme site, only the diagnostic Dorset endblades are discussed (Penney 1984). Rhyolites from the Marystwon Group (AF-1, 3, and 4) constitute 48% of the artifact collection; Cow Head Group cherts, 21%; Conception Group cherts 17%; and miscellaneous cherts, 14% (Table 6)

The raw materials used at l'Anse à Flamme do not match the geology in the immediate surrounding of the site, which is mostly granite. Marystown Group rhyolites are available within 75-100 km of the site on the Burin Peninsula (Figure 5). Cherts from the Conception Group, described later in this chapter, and the Cow Head Group would have been acquired either around the Avalon Isthmus and/or Bonavista Bay (Figure 6) or the Newfoundland west coast (Figure 4), respectively. A

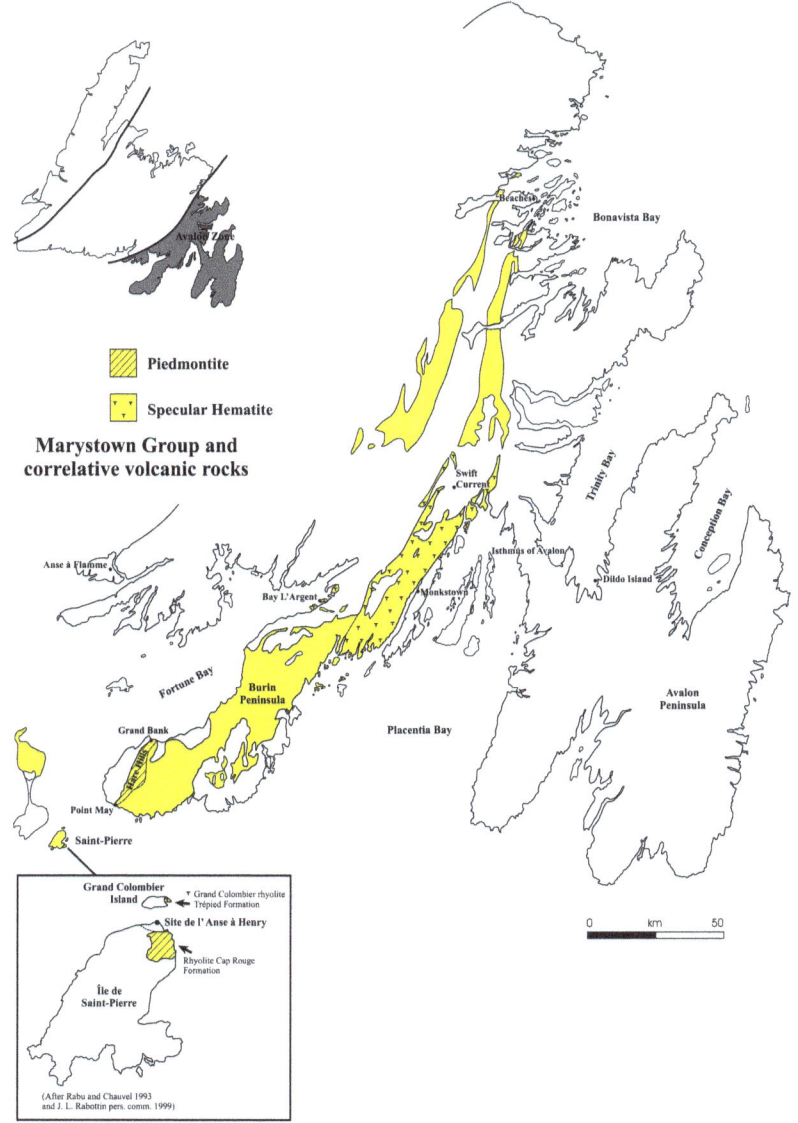

Figure 5. Distribution of Marystown Group and correlative volcanic rocks, eastern Newfoundland (after Coldman-Sadd and Scott 1994) and equivalent Saint-Pierre formations

end of the sample is beige-grey. The luster is glossy and translucency opaque. Its structure is homogeneous except for fractures. Microscopic analysis shows well preserved radiolarians.

AF-3 is a tuffaceous type of rock. It is aphanitic and shows a conchoidal fracture. Colour is medium grey. Luster is dull to glossy; translucency is opaque. Microscopic analysis reveals small amounts of earthy hematite. Although it cannot be attributed to a specific formation, this type of lithology is common in the Marystown Group on the Burin Peninsula (S. O'Brien, pers. comm. 2001).

AF-4a and b are felsic volcanic rocks, most probably rhyolites. Grain size is aphanitic and fracture is conchoidal. Luster is dull; translucency is opaque. Structure is laminated (volcanic flow). The colour varies from a bright light pink to a dull darker purplish pink. The pink colouration of the rock is due to the presence of hematite which oxidizes when the volcanic rocks are

Raw material	Endblades N	%	Endscrapers*	Microblades
Marystown Group				
AF-1	8	27.6		
AF-3	3	10.3		
AF-4	3	10.3		
Subtotal	14	48.3		
Cow Head Group				
Misc. Cow Head	6	20.7		
Subtotal	6	20.7		
Conception Group				
Dil-11	5	17.2		
Subtotal	5	17.2		
Miscellaneous	4	13.8		
Grand total	29	100.0		

*As the control of the context was equivocal at this site solely the endblades were considered in the analysis.

Table 6. Anse à Flamme Material Type Frequencies.

strong case for the use of locally available raw materials is not as easy to establish at the l'Anse à Flamme site. The small size of the artifact sample (25 endblades) may have affected the results.

Anse à Henry Site– Saint-Pierre
Four samples from the l'Anse à Henry site, on the island of Saint-Pierre (Figure 5), were thin sectioned (Table 7). Petrographic analysis indicates similarity to the l'Anse à Flamme samples AF-1 and AF-4. Sample AH-1 is identified as Grand Colombier rhyolite from the Trépied Formation (Figure 5) it is identical to l'Anse à Flamme sample AF-1. Samples AH-2, 3, and 4 are all Cap Rouge Formation rhyolites, identical to l'Anse à Flamme sample AF-4.

Archaeological Data
At l'Anse à Henry, raw material analysis is restricted to diagnostic Middle Dorset endblades as a distinct Dorset component has yet to be isolated. Most of the Dorset material at this site was recovered from test pits or found mixed within Recent Indian components. Local Cap Rouge and Grand Colombier rhyolites comprise 25% and 8% of the endblade sample, respectively (Table 8). Exogenous cherts from the Conception Group are the most frequent lithology (42%). This lithology is found at least 200 km from the site (Figure 6) and is discussed in the net section. Cap Rouge and Grand Colombier rhyolites (Marystown equivalents) occur within 2 km of l'Anse à- Henry (Figure 5).

Raw material	Endblades N	Endblades %	Endscrapers*	Microblades
Cap Rouge rhyolite (AH-2, 3, 4)	6	25.0		
Subtotal	6	25.0		
Gd Colombier rhyolite AH-1	2	8.3		
Subtotal	2	8.3		
Cow Head Group				
Misc. Cow Head	1	4.2		
Subtotal	1	4.2		
Conception Group				
Dil-1	4	16.7		
Dil-6	1	4.2		
Dil-8	1	4.2		
Dil-11	4	16.7		
Subtotal	10	41.8		
Caradocian chert				
SW-6	1	4.2		
Subtotal	1	4.2		
Miscellaneous	4	16.7		
Grand total	24	100.2		

*Only endblades were analysed at the l'Anse à Henry site. Middle Dorset material was recovered during survey and endscraper or microblade affiliation to either Groswater or Middle Dorset could not be comfortably asserted.

Table 8. Anse à Henry Material Type Frequencies.

Sample	AH-1	AH-2	AH-3	AH-4
Colour	Yellow beige	Pinkish beige	Pinkish beige	Pinkish beige
Texture	Aphanitic	Aphanitic	Aphanitic	Aphanitic
Fracture	Irregular and fractured	Irregular to conchoidal	Irregular	Irregular to conchoidal
Luster	Glossy to dull	Dull	Dull	Dull
Translucency	Opaque	Opaque	Opaque	Opaque
Structure	Mostly massive but faintly laminated	Massive with fractures	Massive except for few fractures	Massive except for few fractures
Fossils	-	-	-	-
Mineral	Specular hematite	Piedmontite	Piedmontite	Piedmontite
Other features	-	-	-	-
Origin	Trépied Formation rhyolite on Grand Colombier Island. Newfoundland equivalent : Marystown Group rhyolite	Cap Rouge Formation rhyolite. Newfoundland equivalent: Marystown Group, Hare Hills Formation rhyolite	Cap Rouge Formation rhyolite. Newfoundland equivalent: Marystown Group, Hare Hills Formation rhyolite	Cap Rouge Formation rhyolite. Newfoundland equivalent: Marystown Group, Hare Hills Formation rhyolite

Table 7. Anse à Henry Samples - Summary of Thin Section Descriptions.

Chapter 3. Raw Material Use-Patterns

Dildo Island –Trinity Bay

Twelve samples (Table 9) from the Dildo Island site (Figure 6) were thin sectioned. All samples were identified as being from the Conception Group (S. O'Brien pers. comm. 2001). The Conception Group is dominated by green to grey siliceous sedimentary rocks. The abundance of tuff and other volcanic detritus within the rocks suggests sedimentation contemporaneous with volcanism (King 1990: 29). Within the Conception Group, the sea-green, siliceous volcanisclastic sedimentary rocks of the Drook Formation (*Ibid.*: 30) are compatible with the lithology of the samples from the site. The Conception Group occurs throughout the Avalon Peninsula; it also extends northward from the bottom of Placentia Bay (including Long Island) to Bonavista Bay (Figure 6).

The samples exhibit aphanitic texture with irregular but conchoidal fracture. Lustre is dull; translucency is opaque. Structure is mainly massive although a few samples show faint laminations. All samples, except for two (Dil-4 and 5), exhibit a whitish-beige or brownish-beige weathering rind (4 to 33 mm thick) that can be chalky on occasion. Fresh-cut surfaces display a blue-grey (battleship) colour. This distinctive colour combined with the whitish-brownish/beige weathering constitutes a clear Conception Group signature (S. O'Brien, pers. comm. 2001). Microscopically, both the very fine grain tuffaceous texture and the fine lamination point to distal volcanic import into the sediments (*Ibid.*).

Archaeological Data

Endblade, endscraper and microblade raw materials exhibit a strong bimodal pattern (Table 10). Conception Group chert constitutes 98% of the endblades, while quartz crystal dominates both endscrapers (88%) and microblades (96%). Minute quantities of Cow Head and Caradocian cherts, Ramah quartzites as well as Marystown Group and Bull Arm Formation (description follows) rhyolites suggest restricted contact outside the region.

Conception Group chert is unavailable in the immediate area of Dildo Island but occurs, if one were to travel on foot, within a 25 km range along the inner west side of Conception Bay and on the Avalon Isthmus, at the head of Placentia Bay (Figure 6). By water, the closest location is Sunnyside at the head of Bull Arm. At the Stock Cove site in Sunnyside, Robbins (1985: 157) reports that Dorset people were using large quantities of this weathered chert.

Sample	Dil-1	Dil-2	Dil-3	Dil-4	Dil-5	Dil-6	Dil-7	Dil-8	Dil-9	Dil-10	Dil-11	Dil-12
Colour	Weathering rind: whitish-beige Inner core: blue-grey (battleship)	Weathering rind: brownish-beige Inner core: blue-grey (battleship)	Weathering rind: whitish-beige Inner core: blue-grey (battleship)	Blue-grey (battleship)	Blue-grey (battleship)	Weathering rind: light blue-grey Inner core: blue-grey (battleship)	Weathering rind: greenish-beige Inner core: blue-grey (battleship)	Weathering rind: greenish-beige Inner core: blue-grey (battleship)	Weathering rind: light blue-grey Inner core: blue-grey (battleship)	Weathering rind: brownish-beige Inner core: blue-grey (battleship)	Weathering rind: brownish-beige Inner core: blue-grey (battleship)	Weathering rind: whitish-beige Inner core: blue-grey (battleship)
Texture	Aphanitic	Aphanitic	Aphanitic	Aphanitic	Aphanitic	Aphanitic	Aphanitic	Aphanitic	Aphanitic to slightly granular	Aphanitic	Aphanitic	Aphanitic
Fracture	Irregular but conchoidal	Irregular but conchoidal	Irregular but conchoidall	Conchoidal	Conchoidal	Conchoidal	Irregular but conchoidall	Irregular but conchoidal	Irregular but conchoidal	Conchoidal	Irregular but conchoidal	Irregular but conchoidal
Luster	Dull	Dull	Dull	Dull	Dull	Dull	Dull	Dull	Dull	Dull	Dull	Dull
Translucency	Opaque	Opaque	Opaque	Opaque	Opaque	Opaque	Opaque	Opaque	Opaque	Opaque	Opaque	Opaque
Structure	Massive except for fractures	Massive but shows laminae	Massive with minor fractures	Massive	Faint laminae	Massive	Massive except for small black spots	Massive except for fractures	Laminae	Massive	Massive with minor fractures	Massive with minor fractures
Fossils	-	-	-	-	-	-	-	-	-	-	-	-
Mineral	-	-	-	-	-	-	-	-	-	-	-	-
Other features	Thin weathering rind	Thick weathering rind (4 to 34 mm)	Thin weathering rind	-	-	Thin weathering rind	Thin weathering rind	Thin weathering rind	Weathering in process	Weathering in process	Medium weathering rind (up to 5mm)	Medium weathering rind (up to 10mm)
Origin	Conception Group	Conception Group	Conception Group	Conception Group	Conception Group	Conception Group	Conception Group	Conception Group	Conception Group	Conception Group	Conception Group	Conception Group

Table 9. Dildo Island Samples - Summary of Thin Section Descriptions.

	Endblades		Endscrapers		Microblades	
Raw material	N	%	N	%	N	%
Conception Group						
Dil-1	342	36.5	2	0.5	9	0.9
Dil-2	23	2.5				
Dil-3	68	7.3	5	1.1	5	0.5
Dil-4	13	1.4				
Dil-5	16	1.7				
Dil-6	17	1.8			2	0.2
Dil-7	99	10.6			5	0.5
Dil-8	40	4.3	3	0.7	2	0.2
Dil-9	20	2.1				
Dil-10	21	2.2				
Dil-11	197	21.0	1	0.2	9	0.9
Dil-12	58	6.2			4	0.4
Subtotal	914	97.6	11	2.5	36	3.6
Bull Arm Formation						
SH-1	1	0.1	2	0.5		
SH-2			4	0.9		
SH-5	2	0.2			1	0.1
SH-6					1	0.1
Subtotal	3	0.3	6	1.4	2	0.2
Caradocian Chert						
SW-2	3	0.3	1	0.2		
SW-3			1	0.2		
SW-5	1	0.1				
SW-6			1	0.2		
SW-8	2	0.2				
Subtotal	6	0.6	3	0.6		
Marystown Group						
AF-1			2	0.5		
Subtotal			2	0.5		
Cow Head Group						
Misc. Cow Head	1	0.1	11	2.5	2	0.2
Subtotal	1	0.1	11	2.5	2	0.2
Ramah Quartzite	1	0.1	1	0.2		
Quartz crystal			395	88.4	962	96.0
White quartzite	1	0.1				
Miscellaneous	11	1.2	18	4.0		
Grand total	937	100.0	447	100.1	1002	100.0

Table 10. Dildo Island Material Type Frequencies.

Shamblers Cove Site–Bonavista Bay
Since no debitage was kept from the excavation at Shamblers Cove (Tuck 1983) raw material samples representative of this site's artifacts were obtained from the Beaches site, 35 km to the southwest (Figure 6). Six debitage samples from the Beaches site were thin sectioned (Table 12). All samples were identified as rhyolite from the Bull Arm Formation of the Musgravetown Group (S. O'Brien, pers. comm. 2001). The Bull Arm Formation is described mainly as subaerial volcanic flows (lava and ash) and pyroclastic rocks (O'Brien and King 2005: 109) erupted from mainly onshore volcanoes (Colman-Sadd and Scott 1994). It consists of red, buff and grey, flow-banded rhyolite intercalated with minor ash-flow tuff and rhyolite breccia (O'Brien and Knight 1988: 197). The Bull Arm Formation has a wide geographical distribution. In Bonavista Bay, the formation is found on each side of the Bloody Reach fault (western belt, eastern belt) as well as on the eastern side of the bay. A narrow strip extends north of Bull Arm to the area around Musgravetown. It also outcrops in Trinity Bay around Bull Arm and the Avalon Isthmus and in Placentia Bay (Figure 6).

The samples display an aphanitic to slightly granular texture. The fracture is irregular but mostly conchoidal to sub-conchoidal. The lustre is dull with the exception of SH-2 which is slightly glossy; translucency is opaque. Structure is massive showing faint lamination and some fractures. Colours vary from light blue/grey on the weathered samples (SH-3, 4, 5, 6) to dark blue/black-grey (SH-1, 2).

Microscopic inspection supports a volcanic origin as most samples show a cryptocrystalline or micro- to cryptocrystalline groundmass. The faint lamination observed in most samples is consistent with a volcanic throw (pyroclastic) of ash-tuff origin. The lithology is classified as rheoignimbrite (S. O'Brien, pers. comm. 2001) a flow banding silicic volcanic rock formed "on the slope of a volcanic crater, that has developed secondary flowage due to high temperatures" (Parker 1994). The granular texture of some of the samples is indicative of recrystallization possibly during metamorphism (S. O'Brien, pers. comm. 2001). Two distinctive minerals characteristic of a metamorphic mineral assemblage were also identified. Samples SH-1, 3, and 5 contain sericite, which is a fine grain mineral member of the mica family (S. O'Brien, pers. comm. 2001). Together with quartz, sericite is consistant with the low-grade regional metamorphism typical of this part of Bonavista Bay (O'Brien and Knight 1988: 202) Riebeckite, an amphibole, is also present in all samples. This mineral, responsible for the blue tinge of all samples, is common in rocks with a peralkaline geochemistry formed in rift environments (S. O'Brien, pers. comm. 2005). To summarize, the Bull Arm Formation rhyolite is distinguishable on the basis of four specific criteria: (1) the silicious nature of the rock, (2) the nature of its banding (flow banding–rheoignimbrite); (3) the presence of riebeckite; and (4) the presence of sericite.

Archaeological Data
Archaeological data analysed at this site comprises only endblades. The Shamblers Cove Middle Dorset material was collected from five excavation areas (1, 5, 7, 8 and 9) and test pit 6 (see Appendix 1). Since Groswater material was also obtained at some of these loci, only the diagnostic Dorset endblades are included in this study.

Endscapers and microblades were deliberately left out as

Chapter 3. Raw Material Use-Patterns

their cultural affiliation to either Dorset or Groswater could not be determined with certainty.

The geology of the Shamblers Cove area is mostly granites. Raw materials suitable for knapping are accessible to the south in the Bull Arm Formation about 25km from the site and in the Conception Group about 35 km from the site. This is mirrored in the endblade composition: 53%, Bull Arm Formation rhyolite and 13%, Conception Group chert (Table 11). It is also relevant to note that raw materials of unidentified origins are also represented in significant proportions (33%).

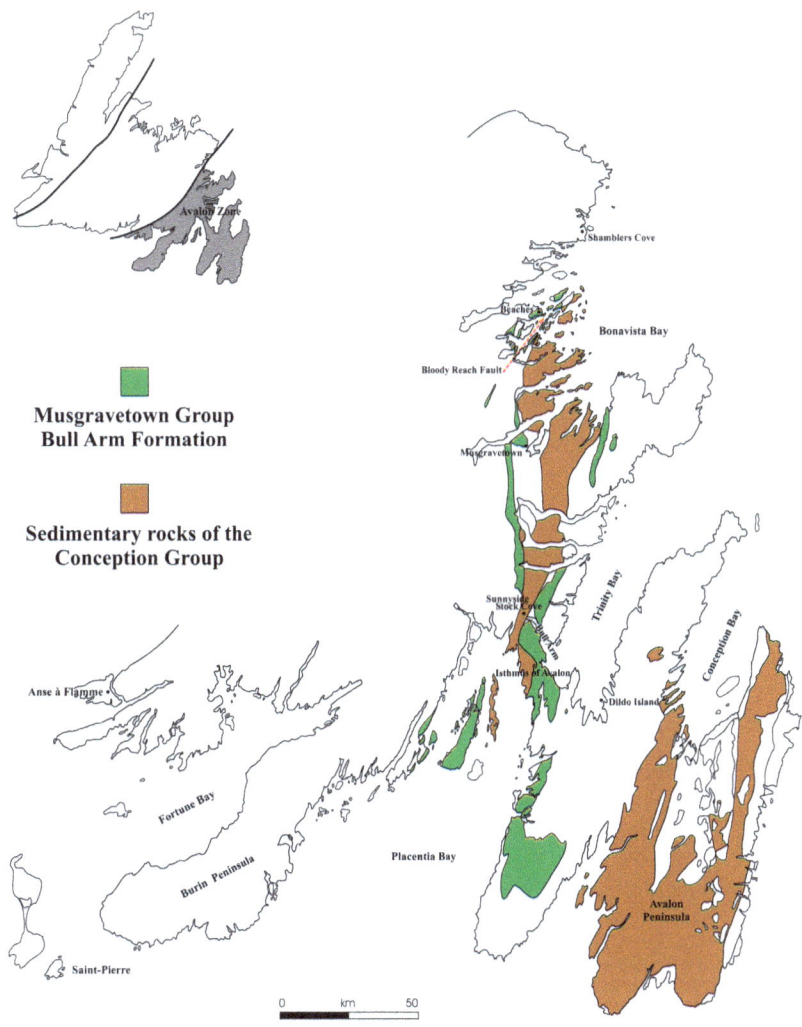

Figure 6. Distribution of Musgravetown Group, volcanic rocks (Bull Arm Formation) and Conception Group sedimentary rocks, eastern Newfoundland (after Coldman-Sadd and Scott 1994).

Raw material	Endblade N	Endblade %	Endscraper N	Endscraper %	Microblade N	Microblade %
Bull Arm Formation						
SH-1	6	10.0				
SH-2	1	1.7				
SH-3	3	5.0				
SH-4	9	15.0				
SH-5	8	13.3				
SH-6	5	8.3				
Subtotal	32	53.3				
Conception Group						
Misc. DIL	8	13.3				
Subtotal	8	13.3				
Miscellaneous	20	33.3				
Grand total	60	99.9				

*Because of the multi-component nature of this site, the endscrapers and microblades were left out of the study as their cultural affiliation to either Groswater or Dorset was impossible to determine.

Table 11. Shamblers Cove Material Type Frequencies.

Sample	SH-1	SH-2	SH-3	SH-4	SH-5	SH-6
Colour	Dark blue and grey	Dark grey	Light blue-grey	Light blue-grey	Light blue-grey	Light blue-grey
Texture	Aphanitic	Aphanitic	Aphanitic	Slightly granular	Slightly granular	Aphanitic
Fracture	Irregular but conchoidal	Irregular but sub-conchoidal	Irregular but conchoidal	Irregular but sub-conchoidal	Irregular but sub-conchoidal	Irregular but sub-conchoidal
Luster	Dull	Dull to glossy	Dull	Dull	Dull	Dull
Translucency	Opaque	Opaque	Opaque	Opaque	Opaque	Opaque
Structure	Massive showing crude laminae and fractures	Massive with faint laminae	Massive	Massive with faint laminae and fractures	Massive with faint laminae and fractures	Massive with faint laminae and fractures
Fossils	-	-	-	-	-	-
Mineral	Sericite Riebeckite Rare carbonates	Riebeckite	Sericite Riebeckite	Riebeckite	Sericite Riebeckite	Riebeckite
Origin	Musgravetown Group Bull Arm Formation rhyolite	Musgravetown Group Bull Arm Formation rhyolite	Musgravetown Group Bull Arm Formation rhyolite	Musgravetown Group Bull Arm Formation rhyolite	Musgravetown Group Bull Arm Formation rhyolite	Musgravetown Group Bull Arm Formation rhyolite

Table 12. Shamblers Cove Samples - Summary of Thin Section Descriptions.

Swan Island Site – Notre-Dame Bay

Eight samples from the Swan Island site (Figure 7) were thin sectioned (Table 13). Samples SW-1 and 4 are identified as Conception Group chert. Both display a brownish-beige weathering rind surrounding a blue-grey (battleship) core, aphanitic texture, and a curved to conchoidal fracture. Luster is dull to glossy; translucency is opaque. The samples are mostly massive in structure even though SW-1 is faintly laminated and SW-4 shows rare fractures. Unidentified opaque minerals were observed under microscopic examination.

SW-2, 3, 5, 6, 7, and 8 belong to the mid-Ordovician Caradocian cherts and shales (or argillite) of the Exploits Group (P. Dean, pers. comm. 2001). The dominant lithologies include: "black, red and green chert, cherty argillite, slate and shale, with thin to thick interbeds of tuff, greywacke and carbonate" (Dean and Meyer 1982: 175). The Caradocian cherts formed in deep seawater (Colman-Sadd and Scott 1994) and are remnants of Iapetus Ocean floor material. They are highly fossiliferous (Dean 1978: 113), containing radiolarians. The latter are difficult to observe as they often have been obliterated by the recrystalization process during metamorphism (P. Dean, pers. comm 2001). Caradocian cherts have a widespread distribution in Notre-Dame Bay and occur at the heads of

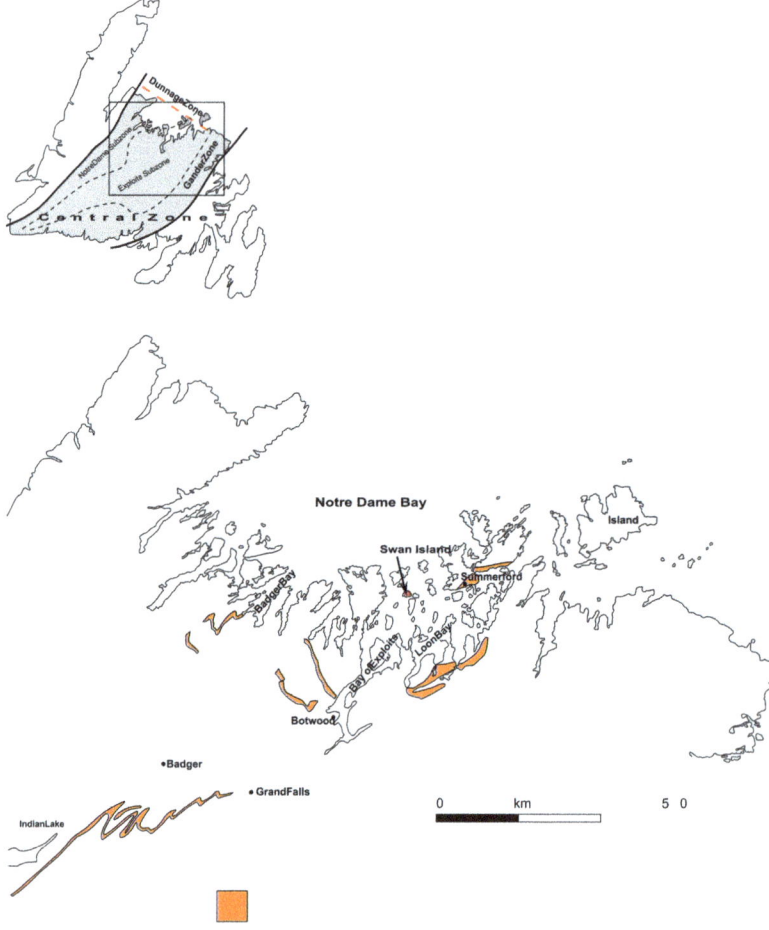

Bay of Exploits Caradocian Shales and Cherts

Figure 7. Bay of Exploits Caradocian Shales and Cherts, central Newfoundland (after Coldman-Sadd and Scott 1994).

Sample	SW-1	SW-2	SW-3	SW-4	SW-5	SW-6	SW-7	SW-8
Colour	Brownish-beige outer weathering Blue-grey (battleship) inner core	Green-grey	Green-grey	Brownish-beige outer weathering Blue-grey (battleship) inner core	Green-grey	Green-grey	Green-grey	Green-grey
Texture	Aphanatic	Aphanatic	Aphanitic to granular	Aphanatic	Aphanitic to granular	Aphanitic to granular	Aphanitic to granular	Aphanitic to granular
Fracture	Irregular to curved	Curved	Curved to conchoidal	Curved to conchoidal	Curved to conchoidal	Curved to conchoidal	Curved to conchoidal	Curved to conchoidal
Luster	Dull to glossy	Dull to glossy	Dull to glossy	Dull to glossy	Dull to glossy	Dull to glossy	Dull to glossy	Dull to glossy
Translucency	Opaque	Opaque	Opaque	Opaque	Opaque	Opaque	Opaque	Opaque
Structure	Massive to faintly laminated	Highly fractured	Massive except for minor fractures	Massive with rare fractures	Massive with fractures	Faintly laminated	Massive with minor fractures	Massive
Fossils		Sponge spicules	Sponge spicules and broken ornaments from radiolarians		Sponge spicules	Sponge spicules	Sponge spicules and broken ornaments from radiolarians	Sponge spicules and broken ornaments from radiolarians
Mineral	Unidentified opaques			Unidentified opaques		Pyrite Calcite		
Other features	Weathering rind up to 4mm			Thin weathering rind				
Origin	Conception Group Sample identical to Dil-2	Bay of Exploits Caradocian cherts	Bay of Exploits Caradocian cherts	Conception Group Sample identical to Dil-4	Bay of Exploits Caradocian cherts	Bay of Exploits Caradocian cherts	Bay of Exploits Caradocian cherts	Bay of Exploits Caradocian cherts

Table 13. Swan Island Samples - Summary of Thin Section Descriptions.

Badger Bay and Loon Bay, south of Badger, to the northwest of Botwood, and in the Summerford area (Figure 7).

Samples SW-2, 3, 5, 6, 7, and 8 are green-grey in colour, aphanitic to granular in texture, and present a curved to conchoidal fracture. Luster is dull to glossy; translucency is opaque. Structure goes from massive to highly fractured. Pyrite and calcite are present in SW-6. Sponge spicules and/or broken ornaments from radiolarians (radiolarian spikes) have been observed microscopically in all thin sections.

Archaeological Data
All artifact categories are dominated by Caradocian cherts of the Exploits Group (73-78% - Table 14). These cherts are available within 25 km of the site (Figure 7).

Cherts from the Carbonate Sequence, Cow Head Group, Conception Group as well as Bull Arm Formation rhyolites and quartz crystal were used but in negligible amounts.

Pittman Site – White Bay
Seven samples from the Pittman site (Figure 4) were thin sectioned (Table 16). Sample Pit-1 is black and presents an aphanitic texture and a conchoidal fracture. Luster is glossy and translucency is opaque. The structure is massive except for some fractures. Microscopic analysis shows a microcrystalline to cryptocrystalline groundmass containing carbonate inclusions and carbonate grains some of which have rhomb shapes (dolomite rhombs). Ghosts of radiolarians, visible in part of the thin section, indicate a Cow Head Group origin.

Raw material	Endblades N	Endblades %	Endscrapers N	Endscrapers %	Microblades N	Microblades %
Caradocian chert						
SW-2	18	21.7	17	13.8	43	13.3
SW-3	7	8.4	2	1.6	42	13.0
SW-5	3	3.6	5	4.1	11	3.4
SW-6	23	27.7	48	39.0	107	33.1
SW-7	1	1.2	4	3.3	11	3.4
SW-8	13	15.7	19	15.5	23	7.1
Subtotal	65	78.3	95	77.3	237	73.3
Cow Head Group						
PIT-1	1	1.2				
PG-1	1	1.2			1	0.3
PG-5			1	0.8		
Misc. Cow Head			6	4.9	11	3.4
Subtotal	2	2.4	7	5.7	12	3.7
Carbonate sequence						
PG-2			1	0.8		
Subtotal			1	0.8		
Bull Arm Formation						
SH-1	1	1.2				
SH-2			1	0.8		
SH-3	2	2.4	1	0.8		
SH-4						
SH-5	1	1.2	1	0.8		
Subtotal	4	4.8	3	2.4		
Conception Group						
Dil-7					1	0.3
Dil-11	1	1.2				
SW-1			1	0.8	17	5.3
Subtotal	1	1.2	1	0.8	18	5.6
Pit-2a	2	2.4				
	1	1.2	1	0.8	1	0.3
Quartz crystal					16	5.0
Miscellaneous	8	9.7	15	12.2	39	12.1
Grand total	83	100.0	123	100.0	323	100.0

Table 14. Swan Island Material Type Frequencies.

Raw material	Endblades N	Endblades %	Endscrapers N	Endscrapers %	Microlades N	Microlades %
Caradocian chert						
SW-2	3	2.4	3	2.2	4	1.2
SW-3					4	1.2
SW-5	1	0.8	1	0.7	4	1.2
SW-6	1	0.8	5	3.7	8	2.4
SW-8			3	2.2	3	0.9
Subtotal	5	4.0	12	8.8	23	6.9
Cow Head Group						
PIT-1	28	22.6	19	13.9	78	23.2
PG-1			2	1.5		
PG-3			1	0.7		
PG-5, 6, 7	1	0.8	2	1.5	7	2.1
Misc. Cow Head	4	3.2	22	16.1	10	3.0
Subtotal	33	26.6	46	33.5	95	28.3
Carbonate sequence						
PG-2	1	0.8	8	5.8	3	0.9
PG-4	1	0.8	2	1.5	3	0.9
Subtotal	2	1.6	10	7.3	6	1.8
Marystown Group						
AF-1			1	0.7		
AF-3			2	1.5		
Subtotal			3	2.2		
Conception Group						
PIT-5			2	1.5		
Subtotal			2	1.5		
Bull Arm Formation						
SH-1			1	0.7		
Subtotal			1	0.7		
Pit-2 (unknown)	47	37.9	10	7.3	19	5.7
Ramah	1	0.8			4	1.2
Quartz crystal			3	2.2	45	13.4
Quartzite	4	3.2	11	8.0	21	6.3
Miscellaneous	32	25.8	39	28.5	123	36.6
Grand Total	124	99.9	137	100.0	336	100.2

Table 15. Pittman Material Type Frequencies.

Sample	Pit-1	Pit-2 a, b	Pit-3	Pit-4	Pit-5	Pit-6
Colour	Black	Dark to light grey	Green-grey	Green-grey	Whitish beige	Green-grey
Texture	Aphanitic	Aphanitic to granular	Aphanitic to granular	Aphanitic	Granular	Aphanitic
Fracture	Conchoidal	Irregular to conchoidal	Conchoidal	Curved to conchoidal	Irregular to curved conchoidal	Irregular to conchoidal
Luster	Glossy	Dull to slightly glossy	Dull to glossy	Dull to glossy	Dull to earthy	Dull to glossy
Translucency	Opaque	Translucent along the edges, otherwise opaque	Opaque	Opaque	Opaque	Opaque
Structure	Massive except for fractures	Massive but show faint laminae in light colour part	Massive except for fractures	Massive except for fractures	Mostly massive with faint laminae	Mostly massive
Fossils	Ghosts of radiolarians		Sponge spicules Radiolarians	Sponge spicules Radiolarians		Rare radiolarians
Mineral	Dolomite rhombs	Carbonate grains Carbonate rhombs Pyrite	-	Carbonate	Some carbonate grains	-
Other features		Chalcedony	-	-	-	-
Origin	Cow Head Group	Possibly Carbonate Sequence	Bay of Exploits Caradocian chert same as SW-3	Bay of Exploits Caradocian chert same as SW-2	Conception Group Similar to Dildo samples	Bay of Exploits Caradocian chert same as SW-2

Table 16. Pittman Samples - Summary of Thin Section Descriptions.

Samples Pit-2a and Pit-2b are respectively dark grey/anthracite and light grey in colour. Both are aphanitic to granular in texture resembling quartzite.

The fracture is conchoidal to irregular; luster dull to.lightly glossy; and translucency opaque except along the edges of samples. The structure is mostly massive although faint laminae appear in the light coloured ection of the sample. Carbonate rhombs are present in both Pit-2a and b; in Pit-2b some of the cavities are filled with carbonate partially replaced by chalcedony. Scattered dark opaque minerals, possibly pyrite, also concentrate in cavities. The provenience of these two samples remains unknown; none of the geologists involved in the present research were able to assign an origin for the samples. The presence of dolomite rhombs could argue for a Carbonate Sequence origin but geologists familiar with the Humber Zone have never encountered similar material during the course of their studies (I. Knight, pers. comm. 2001; J. Waldron, pers. comm. 2002).

Pit-3, 4 and 6 share similar characteristics and have been identified as Caradocian cherts of the Exploits Group. All three samples are green-grey in colour, some of them show a thin grey-beige weathered surface. The texture varies from aphanitic to granular. Fracture is curved to conchoidal. Luster is dull to glossy; translucency is opaque. Structure is massive, except for few fractures. Under plain light, high power microscope reveals the presence of sponge spicules and radiolarians.

Sample Pit-5 shows a thick weathering rind (7 to 10 mm), whitish-beige in colour surrounding a blue-grey (battleship) inner core. It is granular in texture; the fracture goes from irregular to curved/conchoidal. The luster is dull to earthy; translucency is opaque. Structure is massive with faint laminae. This sample is identical to Trinity Bay-Dildo Island samples and belongs to the Conception Group.

Archaeological Data

The Pittman site exhibits a wide range of raw materials in each tool category (Table 15). Three raw material types occur with greatest frequency: Pit-2 of uncertain origin (6-38%); Cow Head Group chert (27-33%); and miscellaneous cherts (25-36%). Cow Head cherts are accessible within 10 km of the site on Baie Verte Peninsula (Figure 4). Other raw material types such as Marystown and Bull Arm Formation rhyolites; Caradocian, Conception Group and Carbonate Sequence cherts, Ramah quartzite, quartzite and quartz crystal were used in limited quantities.

SUMMARY

The objectives pursued in this chapter were to review the geological setting of the island of Newfoundland and to identify Middle Dorset raw material use-patterns in the eight regions under study. Fifty-eight raw material samples were thin sectioned; of them eight raw material types[10] were identified and linked to specific geological formations. In most cases, these data indicate that Middle Dorset people were using raw materials available locally. For instance, the Phillip's Garden, Cape Ray, Dildo

---

[10] Quartz crystal, Ramah quartzite, white quartzite, and miscellaneous raw material types were tabulated but not analysed petrographically.

Chapter 3. Lithic Raw Material Use-Patterns

Island, Swan Island and Shamblers Cove sites show a pattern indicative of a high reliance on regional[11] raw materials (Table 17). A similar pattern was not observed at the Pittman, l'Anse à Flamme and l'Anse à Henry (Saint-Pierre) sites and strong inferences about the utilization of regional raw materials cannot be made at this point. Provisional explanations will be provided in Chapter 5.

---

[11] Following Desrosiers and Rahmani (in press), in this study, a given raw material is qualified as regional when the distance between a site and the closest lithic procurement source lies within 100–150 km. Exogenous is reserved for source areas located beyond that range. For a more detailed discussion on that terminology, see Plumet 1994.

Raw Material	Endblades %	Endscrapers %	Microblades %
PHILLIP'S GARDEN			
Regional subtotal	71.2	89.6	55.4
Cow Head Group	53.4	27.6	38.0
Carbonate sequence	17.8	62.0	17.4
Quartz crystal	–	1.2	31.6
Exogenous and miscellaneous subtotal	28.9	9.3	12.9
	100.1	100.1	99.9
CAPE RAY			
Regional subtotal	98.5	86.7	62.3
Cow Head	98.5	83.1	60.7
Carbonate sequence	–	3.6	1.6
Quartz crystal	–	3.6	32.2
Exogenous and miscellaneous subtotal	1.5	9.8	5.6
	100.0	100.1	100.1
DILDO ISLAND			
Regional subtotal	97.6	2.5	3.6
Conception Group	97.6	2.5	3.6
Quartz crystal	–	88.4	96.0
Exogenous and miscellaneous subtotal	2.4	9.0	0.4
	100.0	99.9	100.0
SWAN ISLAND			
Regional subtotal	78.3	77.3	73.3
Caradocian chert	53.3	–	–
Quartz crystal	–	–	5.0
Exogenous and miscellaneous ubtotal	21.7	22.7	21.7
	100.0	100.0	100.0
SHAMBLERS COVE			
Regional subtotal	66.6	–	–
Bull Arm Formation	53.3	–	–
Conception Group	13.3	–	–
Exogenous and miscellaneous subtotal	33.3	–	–
	99.9		

Table 17. Summary Raw Material Use-Patterns: Regional Versus Exogenous/Miscellaneous.

Raw Material	Endblades %	Endscrapers %	Microblades %
PITTMAN			
Regional subtotal	**28.2**	**40.8**	**30.1**
Cow Head Group	26.6	33.5	28.3
Carbonate sequence	1.6	7.3	1.8
Pit-2 unknown	**37.9**	**7.3**	**5.7**
Quartz crystal		**2.2**	**13.4**
Exogenous and miscellaneous ubtotal	**33.9**	**49.7**	**51.0**
	100.0	100.0	100.2
ANSE À FLAMME			
Regional subtotal	**48.3**	–	–
Marystown Group	48.3	–	–
Exogenous and miscellaneous ubtotal	**51.7**	–	–
Cow Head Group	20.7	–	–
Conception Group	17.2	–	–
Others	13.8	–	–
	100.0		
ANSE À HENRY			
Regional subtotal	**33.3**	–	–
Cap Rouge rhyolite	25.0	–	–
Grand Colombier rhyolite	8.3	–	–
Exogenous and miscellaneous ubtotal	**66.9**	–	–
Cow Head Group	4.2	–	–
Conception Group	41.8	–	–
Others	20.9	–	–
	100.2		

Table 17. (cont'd). Summary Raw Material Use-Patterns: Regional Versus Exogenous/Miscellaneous.

CHAPTER 4. THE STYLISTIC EVIDENCE

RESEARCH METHODS

Artifact style constitutes the second set of data examined in order to identify technological practices at a regional scale. In this chapter, I provide an empirical description of the artifact style for each of the Middle Dorset sites examined in this study. The stylistic analysis has been restricted to endblades and endscrapers. The large number of microblades, coupled with the tedious, perhaps impossible task of documenting microblade style beyond metric attributes, is beyond the scope of this research. The current analysis is designed to provide detailed description of the two selected artifact types and is conducted both qualitatively and quantitatively. Analysis is conducted on complete specimens or specimens complete enough to obtain maximum length/width/thickness information. Attributes considered in the endblade analysis are listed in Table 18. Quantitative data based on length/width/thickness ratios are also used to illustrate stylistic patterning.

Plagued with the inherent problem of their positioning in a maintenance/reduction sequence (Blades 2003; Dibble 1995; Morrow 1997; Shott 1995), a satisfactory classification system is difficult to implement with respect to endscraper typology. Indeed, the object or the "endscraper form" recovered in the archaeological record does not necessarily represent a discrete type but is more than likely only a static resultant at an arbitrary point along a continuum of reduction or *chaîne opératoire* (Dibble 1995). Using the terminology put forward in this study, one particular type may, for instance, be the precursor (elongated type) of a second type (contracting stem), which in turn through resharpening and eventual exhaustion, become a thumbnail endscraper (see Photo 23). A firm classification is also difficult to establish as endscraper categories are not mutually exclusive. To illustrate, an expedient endscraper fashioned from a random flake or a chert pebble may very well have a thumbnail-like morphology. Thus, one has to question into which categories these objects should be classified. To circumvent this issue, I have chosen a splitter approach in which the typologies are deliberately multiplied for the sake of clarity. At this point, the typologies proposed herein have only a descriptive value.

Selected attributes for endscraper analysis are listed in Table 18. Only the complete specimens were examined (or complete enough that metric measurements could be obtained). It is acknowledged that endscrapers fashioned on microblades might suffer under-representation as most of the specimens of this type were incomplete in the collections. Specific description of artifact style at the different archaeological sites follows.

Attributes	Endblades	Endscrapers
Outline morphology	x	x
Base shape	x	
Lateral edges shape	x	
Basal treatment	x	
Presence/absence tip-fluting	x	
Presence/absence of grinding	x	
Flaking patterns	x	
Cross-section	x	
Working edge convexity		x
Working edge angle		x
Hafting elements		x
Striking platform		x
Support		x
Length	x	x
Width	x	x
Thickness	x	x

Table 18. Selected Attributes for Stylistic Artifact Analysis.

REGIONAL STYLISTIC DESCRIPTION

Phillip's Garden Site (Port au Choix)
Newfoundland Northwest Coast
At the Phillip's Garden site in Port au Choix, the specimens selected for examination come from Feature 2, a midden associated with a Middle Dorset dwelling (Hodgetts *et al.*, 2003; Renouf 1986, 1987, 2006).

Endblades (n=30; Photos 1 and 2)
Of the 30 complete endblades analyzed, two types prevail: Type 1 includes 15 specimens that are generally broad and short (Photo 1a-f). They exhibit a basal concavity which can be quite pronounced and the lateral edges are slightly curvilinear (convex). Flaking quality varies from one specimen to another but the dorsal face generally shows medium to fine parallel opposed flaking; on the ventral surface, some objects show evidence of tip-fluting, others show fine, irregular or partial flaking. Basal treatment is bifacial and consists of the removal of a single or multiple longitudinal thinning flakes. A reversed V or U basal pattern is also observable on the dorsal face. There is no evidence of grinding. Cross-section is plano-convex. Type 2 includes nine small specimens (Photo 1g-j) that are shorter versions of Type 1. The only distinctive trait of Type 2 is that partial grinding is visible on two specimens. Metric values for Type 1 and 2 endblades are provided in Table 19.

Phillip's Garden endblades Type 1; n=15 (50%)

Metric attributes (mm)	Length	Width	Thickness	Ratio W/L	Ratio T/W
Mean	26.2	17.1	4.1	0.7	0.2
S.D.	3.9	1.2	0.7	0.1	0.0
Range	19.2–31.7	14.8–18.7	3–5.7	0.6-0.8	0.2-0.3

Base shape: Deeply concave
Tip-fluting scars: 6/15
Grinding: Absent
Serration: Absent
Cross-section: Plano-convex

Phillip's Garden enblades Type 2; n=9 (30%)

Metric attributes (mm)	Length	Width	Thickness	Ratio W/L	Ratio T/W
Mean	18	11.4	2.9	0.6	0.3
S.D.	2.1	1.0	0.4	0.0	0.3
Range	15.7–22.5	9.9–13.5	2.5–3.6	0.6-0.7	0.2-0.3

Base shape: Deeply concave
Tip-fluting scars: 2/9
Grinding: Partial on 2 specimens
Serration: Absent
Cross-section: Plano-convex

Table 32 at the end of this chapter provides a site-by-site comparative summary of the endblade attributes

Table 19. Phillip's Garden Typical Endblade Metric Attributes.

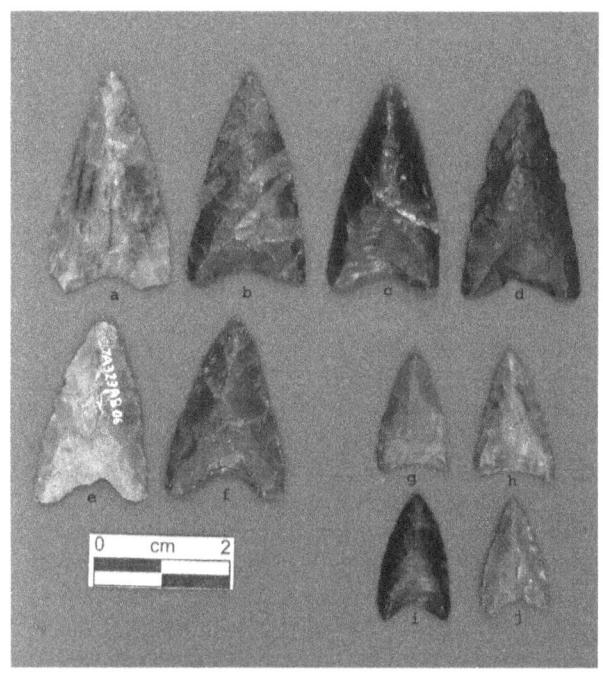

Photo 1. Phillip's Garden (Port au Choix) typical endblades: Type 1 (a-f); Type 2 (g-j).

Photo 2. Phillip's Garden (Port au Choix) miscellaneous endblades: Cape Ray style (a); Pittman style (b); elongated specimens (c-e).

Of the six remaining specimens, one thin, short and broad specimen is reminiscent of the typical Pittman site endblade (Photo 2b), the description of which is provided later. Despite the poor quality of the flaking, a second specimen bears a close resemblance to the endblades of the Cape Ray site as it is longer and narrower in outline (Photo 2a). Four small elongated specimens are atypical (Photo 2c-e); one of them is seemingly produced from a microblade.

Endscrapers (n=65; Photo 3)
The 65 complete endscrapers examined at Phillip's Garden (Feature 2) fall within five general categories (Table 20).

Triangular (n=8; Photo 3a-d)
Eight endscrapers constitute this group. They are triangular in outline with the proximal end tapering off to a point at the striking platform. The working edges

Type	N	%	Length			Width			Thickness		
			Mean	S.D.	Range	Mean	S.D.	Range	Mean	S.D.	Range
Thumbnail	26	40.0	16.8	2.9	10.6-13.7	15.4	1.9	11.8-19.9	4.5	1.0	2.8-7.1
Triangular	8	12.3	20.9	2.6	17.7-24.8	18.4	2.5	15.1-21.5	5.6	1.8	3.4-9.3
Flared-end	2	3.1	15.1	3.0	12.9-17.2	15.8	4.0	12.9-18.6	4.0	1.4	3.0-5.0
Elongated	6	9.2	26.0	1.7	23.4-28.3	16.9	1.2	14.8-18.3	5.3	0.9	4.5-6.9
Blade, flake and microblade	23	35.4	21.9	6.8	13.2-36.6	16.1	3.7	10.1-27.5	4.5	1.4	2.1-7.8
Total	**65**	**100.0**									

Table 20. Phillip's Garden Endscraper Metric Attributes by Types.

are moderately convex and thick, bearing a steep angle. Lateral edges are straight to slightly convex, showing generalized marginal retouches. In all cases, the dorsal surface has been carefully flaked. Most of the ventral face is intact; six specimens show removal of thin spalls in the vicinity of the percussion bulb.

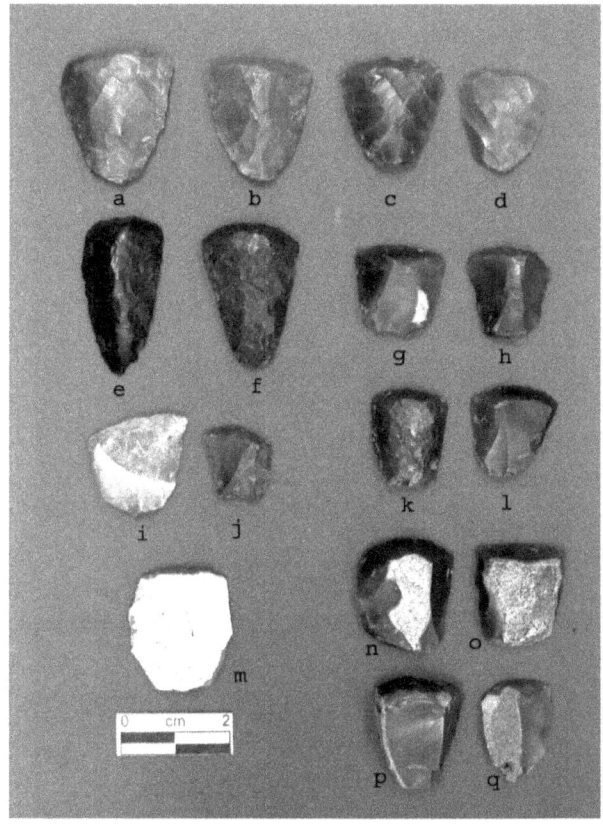

Photo 3. Phillip's Garden (Port au Choix) selected endscraper sample: triangular (a-d); elongated (e-f); thumbnail (g-h, k-l); flared-end (i-j); expedient endscrapers made from carbonate-shelf chert pebbles (m-q).

Thumbnail (n=26; Photo 3g-l)
Twenty-six specimens are defined as thumbnail endscrapers. Their morphology and size resembles one's thumbnail; that is, they are somewhat trapezoidal with a straight or rounded proximal end. They exhibit a convex distal end, which can either be symmetrical or asymmetrical (skewed). In most cases, the working edge is thick and abrupt, although it is thin and low on a few specimens. Dorsal flaking varies from fine and invasive to rudimentary; both lateral margins exhibit retouch. Most specimens are unifacial, although thin pressure flaking can occur near the percussion bulb on the ventral face. Though the shape remains essentially the same, some of the smallest specimens are clearly at the end of the reduction sequence and qualified as exhausted (or nubs).

Flared-end (n=2; Photo 3i-j)
Two endscrapers exhibit at their distal end a flared or expanding corner. The first specimen presents a working edge that is asymmetrical, slightly convex with a steep bevel angle; working edge on the second one is semi-abrupt. Dorsal retouch is fine and generalized in one specimen, crude on the second. Bilateral edge retouch affect both specimens. Ventral retouch is absent.

Elongated (n=6; Photo 3e-f)
Six specimens have an elongated somewhat triangular shape. Working edges are convex, generally thick and steep. Lateral edges are straight to slightly convex, tapering off to the proximal end which is pointed or slightly rounded. In all but one case, showing unilateral marginal retouches, both lateral edges are affected by continuous retouch. Dorsal flaking is generalized on all but one specimen. Ventral retouch is restricted to light thinning of the bulb of percussion. This endscraper type probably represents an earlier stage of the thumbnail and flared types described above.

Microblade, blade and flake endscrapers (n=23; Photo 3m-q)
Eleven endscrapers are expediently produced from Carbonate Sequence chert pebbles. Their shape varies from quadrangular to triangular; all are unifacial and bear a straight to slightly convex working edge with a semi-abrupt to low angle. The original flakes are essentially unaltered except for the careful preparation of the scraping edge and for partial lateral retouch on four of them. Evidence of their provenience is seen in the portion of the pebble's cortex that most of them retain.

Five endscrapers are also expediently fashioned on thick blade-like flakes. They are unifacial showing irregular and crude dorsal flaking. The working edge is thick and steep and in most cases convex. Three other specimens are rudimentary, produced on random-shaped flakes; their shape varies following the original flake morphology: sometimes tongue-shaped, sometimes elongated. Flaking is minimal affecting mostly the scraping edges; the latter are thin with a weak angle. Bilateral retouch is visible on two specimens. Three endscrapers are made at the distal end of microblades. They are unifacial, showing no evidence of flaking aside from the longitudinal scars resulting from prior microblades detachment on the dorsal face. The working edge is straight to convex and semi-abrupt. One endscraper has been fashioned on a biface thinning flake. It is small in size, thin, with a semi-abrupt and slightly convex working edge. It retains the striking detachment platform and bulb of percussion. Retouch is restricted to the dorsal face and consists of thin longitudinal pressure flaking and bilateral fine marginal retouch.

Cape Ray Site – Newfoundland Southwest Coast
Endblades (n=49; Photos 4 to 6)
Forty-nine complete endblades were examined at the Cape Ray site. Two main types can be distinguished. Cape Ray Type 1 is represented by 31 specimens. Although the general outline remains similar, its size varies (Photo 4). The base shows a well-defined concavity and the lateral edges are slightly convex. Cross-section is plano-convex. The dorsal retouch consists of medium to fine parallel opposed flaking. The ventral face shows, in most cases, a tip–fluting scar although a few specimens show fine to irregular flaking or remain virtually untouched. On both faces, basal treatment consists of the removal of longitudinal thinning flakes. Here again a reversed U or V pattern is replicated on the dorsal proximal end. At this specific location, partial grinding can be observed on 10 specimens. At this point, it remains difficult to assess if grinding was intentionally produced or if it results from the rubbing of this part of the endblade somewhere within the hafting socket.

Fourteen short endblades constitute Type 2 (Photo 5). Their shape varies from short and broad to slightly elongate; they generally exhibit a well-defined basal concavity. Three of them are expediently produced from flakes; a fourth is from a fluting spall. Flaking characteristics resemble closely those described for the larger specimens; the chief trait justifying their grouping in a category of their own is their small size. Refer to Table 21 for detailed metric attributes of Type 1 and 2 endblades.

In general, the two types defined at Cape Ray resemble somewhat the typical endblades from Phillip's Garden in Port au Choix. However, length/width/thickness ratios (Tables 19, 21 and Figure 8a and b at the end of this chapter) show slightly different clustering patterns attributed to the generally longer and narrower outline of the Cape Ray endblades.

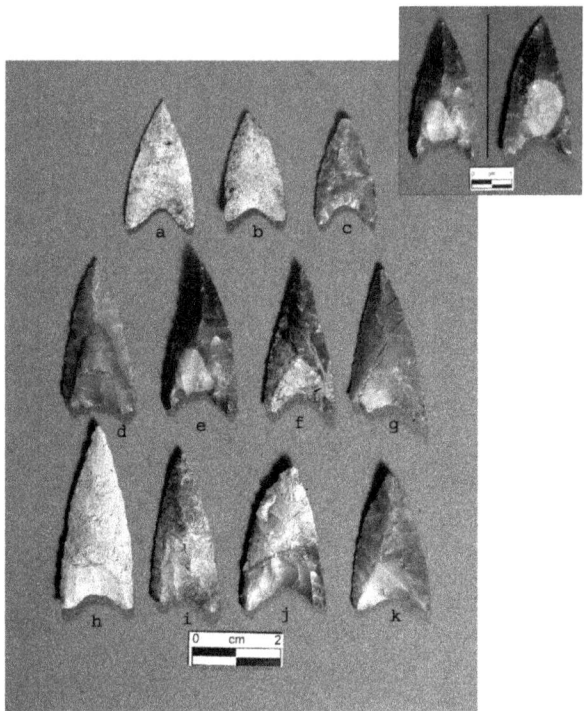

Photo 4. Cape Ray Type 1 endblades. In inset, dorsal and ventral faces of specimen e.

Photo 5. Cape Ray short endblades (Type 2).

Photo 6. Cape Ray miscellaneous endblades: Phillip's Garden (PAC) style (a); South coast style (b); Trinity Bay style (c); unknown (d).

Cape Ray endblades Type 1; n=31 (63%)

Metric attributes (mm)	Length	Width	Thickness	Ratio W/L	Ratio T/W
Mean	32.0	16.5	3.8	0.5	0.2
S.D.	3.9	1.6	0.6	0.1	0.0
Range	24.2-40.8	13.2-19.7	2.6-4.9	0.4-0.6	0.2-0.3

Base shape: Deeply concave
Tip-fluting scars: 20/31
Grinding: Partial on 10 specimens
Serration: Absent
Cross-section: Plano-Convex

Cape Ray endblades Type 2; n=14 (29%)

Metric attributes (mm)	Length	Width	Thickness	Ratio W/L	Ratio T/W
Mean	19.7	11.2	2.7	0.6	0.2
S.D.	2.5	1.1	0.5	0.1	0.0
Range	14.7-24.4	9.8-13.4	1.8-3.7	0.4-0.8	0.2-0.3

Base shape: Deeply concave
Tip-fluting scars: 3/14
Grinding: Partial on 1 specimen
Serration: Absent
Cross-section: Plano-convex

Table 21. Cape Ray Typical Endblade Metric Attributes

Of the four remaining endblades, one shares some similarities with Port au Choix specimens (Photo 6a); a second could possibly be at home in a south coast (Anse à Flamme or Saint-Pierre) assemblage (Photo 6b); a third one, partially ground on both faces hints at a Trinity Bay origin (Photo 6c). The last specimen fashioned from white quartzite is atypical and bears no resemblance with any known type (Photo 6d).

Endscrapers (n=148; Photos 7 and 8)
One hundred and forty-eight endscrapers were analysed at the Cape Ray site. The specimens are classified into nine broad categories (Table 22). A selected sample of the types discussed below is presented in Photos 7 and 8.

Triangular (n=10; Photo 7h-j)
This group includes 10 specimens with triangular outline and resemble closely those described at Port au Choix. The scraping edge is slightly convex to straight; one specimen has an asymmetrical working edge. Generally, the dorsal face is finely flaked and marginal retouch is bilateral. Ventral retouch consists of sporadic marginal retouch and/or thinning of the bulb of percussion. One specimen has a longitudinal flake removed from the base.

Thumbnail (n=54; Photo 8i-p)
Fifty-four endscrapers constitute this group. To avoid repetition, the specimens will not be described as they conform in all points to the definition provided for the Port au Choix thumbnail endscrapers.

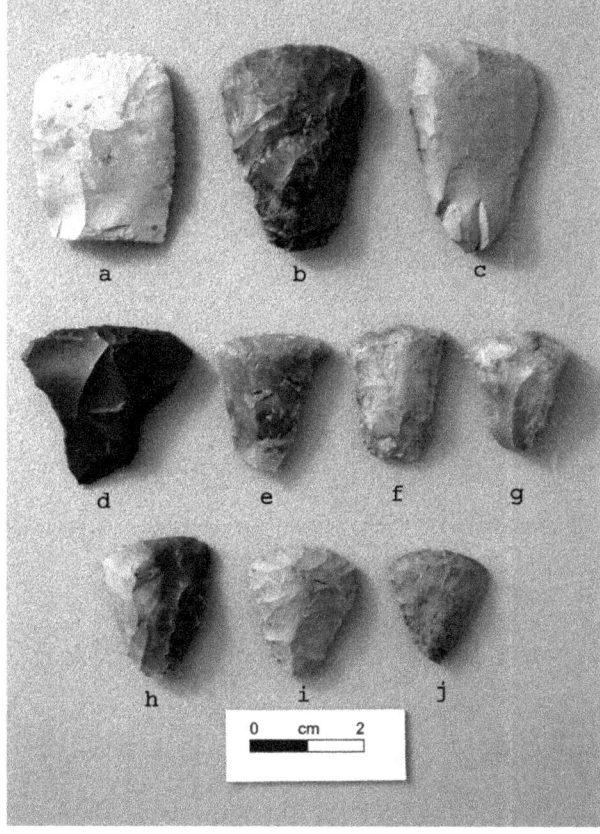

Photo 7. Cape Ray selected endscraper sample: tongue-shaped (a-c); flared-end (d-g); triangular (h-j).

Type	N	%	Length			Width			Thickness		
			Mean	S.D.	Range	Mean	S.D.	Range	Mean	S.D.	Range
Thumbnail	54	36.7	17.9	3.3	11.7-27.6	16.7	2.5	12.1-23.5	4.8	1.1	2.8-8.2
Triangular	10	6.8	20.4	3.7	15.0-27.0	17.8	2.2	15.1-21.0	5.0	1.2	2.8-6-5
Flared-end	9	6.1	20.2	3.4	15.0-26.3	19.0	4.2	15.5-29.8	4.9	1.4	2.7-6.9
Elongated	17	11.6	29.7	6.2	19.1-39.7	18.0	2.7	13.2-23.6	5.3	1.5	3.4-8.6
Contracting stem	15	10.2	24.9	3.4	18.4-31.5	18.8	1.9	15.6-23.7	5.6	1.5	3.7-8.9
Tongue-shaped	7	4.8	31.1	3.3	26.8-35.3	19.6	1.9	24.6-25.5	6.1	1.1	4.3-7.3
Disk and ovoid	4	2.7	24.9	0.6	21.1-25.6	19.1	2.6	16.6-22.8	5.2	1.3	4.0-6.7
Quadrangular	1	0.7	18.8	–	–	22.9	–	–	3.6	–	–
Blade, flake and microblade	30	20.4	19.8	4.8	11.3-29.0	14.0	2.8	8.0-20.6	3.6	0.8	2.4-5.8
Total	147	100.0									

Table 22. Cape Ray Endscraper Metric Attributes by Types.

Flared-end (n=9; Photo 7d-g)

Nine specimens exhibit distal flaring ends; six of which with a single-spur, the three others with double-spurs. Some researchers have classified single spur specimens within a category of their own: snub-nosed endscrapers (Fitzhugh 1972; Carignan 1975). Of the six single-spured specimens, five are produced on relatively thick and short flakes; the sixth specimen is made from a thin flake. Dorsal retouch varies from fine to expedient. Lateral retouch is unilateral or bilateral. Most of the ventral surface remains untouched; thin retouch is only observable at the proximal end or along a single lateral edge. Working edges are either slightly convex or straight and in most cases asymmetrical. Scraping edge angles range from steep, to semi-abrupt to low. Of the three double-spured specimens two are also fashioned on relatively short and thick flakes. They present a convex and steep working edge. Dorsal retouch is generalized; lateral edges are retouched bilaterally. The third specimen exhibits well-pronounced flaring distal corners and seems to have been produced expediently from a large and thin flake. Bilateral retouch along the edges has resulted in a well-defined hafting element.

Elongated (n=17; Photo 8a-d)

Seventeen specimens have an elongated/triangular shape. In most cases, the end product resembles the original flake blank from which it was made and the striking platform and bulb of percussion are visible at the proximal end. Working edges are moderately convex to straight with angles varying from abrupt, to semi-abrupt, to acute. Dorsal surface flaking is rudimentary in most specimens but three of them exhibit generalized fine dorsal retouch. Lateral edge retouch is either unilateral or bilateral. Most of the surface on the ventral side is intact with the exception of a few specimens showing partial unilateral edge retouch. Two specimens show intense flaking in the lower two-thirds of the object.

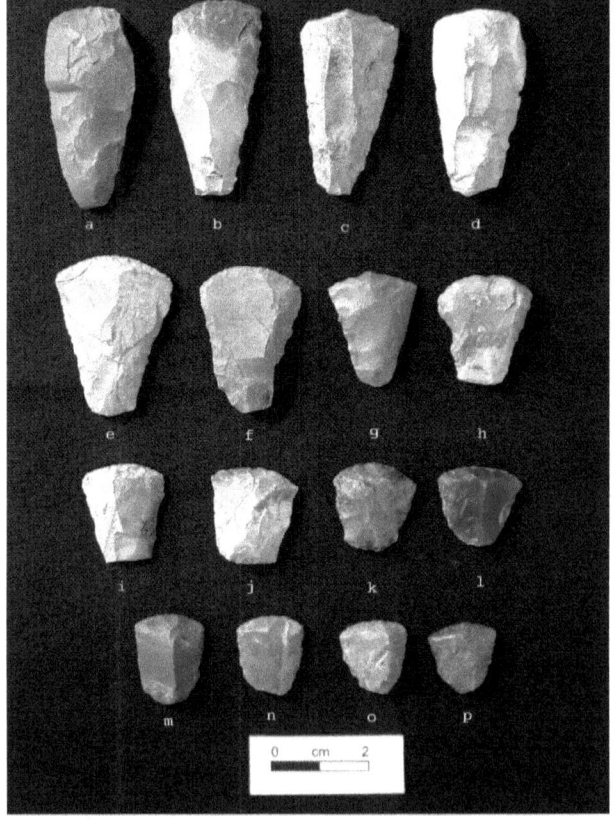

Photo 8. Cape Ray selected endscraper sample: elongated (a-d); contracting stem (e-h); thumbnail (i-p).

Contracting stem (n=15; Photo 8e-h)

Fifteen endscrapers constitute this group. They are characterized by the slight constriction of the lateral edges beginning shortly below the working edge. Although shorter, their somewhat elongated/triangular shape resembles the elongated types described above. The scraping edges are moderately convex; they can be thick or thin with bevel angles ranging from steep to acute. With the exception of two specimens that are more carefully crafted, dorsal flaking is generally rudimentary. Continuous bilaterally dorsal retouch occurs along the lateral edges, constituting the stem. Ventral retouch is scarce, occurring only in a discontinuous fashion along a single edge or near the proximal end.

Tongue-shaped (n=7; Photo 7a-c)
Seven specimens have a tongue shape and are produced on large flakes and present a wide distal end with a slightly convex to straight scraping edge and a semi-abrupt to low bevel angle. Dorsal retouch varies from generalized and fine to coarse. Bilateral marginal retouch is the norm. Of the seven specimens, ventral retouch is absent on two, minimal near the bulb of percussion on two, quite invasive on two and, on one specimen longitudinal flakes have been removed from the base. Two specimens are transversally truncated in their mid-sections. The remaining specimens retain the striking platform and bulb of percussion at the proximal end.

Disk-shape and ovate (n=4)
Three endscrapers are produced on ovoid flakes. They present a well-rounded scraping edge with a moderately low angle. Dorsal flaking is generalized on two specimens; the third one bears the scar left by the removal of a wide longitudinal flake. Marginal retouch affect both dorsal lateral edges. On all specimens, the ventral surface shows evidence of unilateral retouch. A fourth endscraper is fashioned on a disk-shaped flake. It has a thin and well-rounded working edge with a semi-abrupt angle. Dorsal retouch is irregular, continuous lateral retouch extends along both edges. Ventral surface is intact. All four specimens retain the striking platform and percussion bulb.

Quadrangular (n=1)
One short and broad specimen has a quadrangular outline. The working edge is slightly convex and presents a steep angle. Dorsal retouch is generalized and fine retouches affect both lateral margins. Ventral retouch is limited to thin pressure in the vicinity of the bulb of percussion.

Microblade, blade and flake endscrapers (n=30)
Eight endscrapers are fashioned on microblade fragments. Most of them are transversally truncated across their mid-sections; only one quartz crystal microblade is complete. Working edges, present at one extremity of the microblade, are slightly convex and can be asymmetrical; edge angle is semi-abrupt. Retouch is mainly restricted to the working edge, except for the complete quartz crystal specimen which displays continuous bilateral retouch. Two other specimens made on blade-like flakes share similar characteristics. Two small specimens are produced at the distal end of small biface thinning flakes. Eighteen others are made from irregular flakes. In terms of shape, the latter display a wide degree of variation ranging from quadrangular, triangular, thumbnail and irregular. Aside from the preparation of the working and perhaps sporadic lateral retouch, most of them show minimal dorsal and ventral retouch.

Anse à Flamme Site – Newfoundland South Coast Endblades (n=13; Photo 9)
Thirteen complete specimens were analysed. Harpoon endblades at l'Anse à Flamme do not appear to reflect the same stylistic homogeneity evident in the assemblages already discussed. Instead, the limited sample from the area gives the impression of heterogeneity in style, shape and craftsmanship. Two specimens bear some affinities with those of other sites: one resembles Trinity Bay (Photo 9k) as it is partially polished on both faces, and a second could be at home in a Cape Ray assemblage (Photo 9d). The only traits unifying the rest of the l'Anse à Flamme endblade collection are their relatively small size (Table 23) and the poorer quality of the flaking.

Photo 9. Anse à Flammme endblades. Cape Ray style ? (d); Trinity Bay style (k).

<u>**Endscrapers (=0)**</u>
No endscrapers were analyzed as the integrity of the site context was equivocal.

Typical Anse à Flamme (south coast) endblades; n=11 (84%)

Metric attributes (mm)	Length	Width	Thickness	Ratio W/L	Ratio T/W
Mean	22.3	12.8	4.0	0.6	0.3
S.D.	4.6	2.2	0.8	0.1	0.0
Range	15.7	9.7-17.1	3.0-5.4	0.5-0.7	0.3-0.3

Base shape: Slightly concave
Tip-fluting scars: 5/11
Grinding: Absent
Serration: Absent
Cross-section: Plano-convex

Table 23. Anse à Flamme Typical Endblade Metric Attributes.

Anse à Henry – Saint-Pierre
Endblades (n=14; Photo 10)

Of the 14 complete endblades examined, five Trinity Bay style endblades (Photo 10a-e), with their polished triangular facets and lateral edge serration, comprised part of the l'Anse à Henry assemblage. Another endblade, exhibiting ventral grinding, may have a Trinity Bay origin. Three specimens resemble Cape Ray Types 1 and 2 specimens (Photo 10i, l-m). One endblade is atypical (Photo 10f); its large size sets it apart from any other known specimen in Newfoundland. It is extremely long, exhibits a basal concavity and is fashioned from local Cape Rouge rhyolite. Dorsal retouch consists of fine parallel-opposed flaking in the upper ¾ of the object; the base has been thinned down by the removal of longitudinal flakes from the base. A median ridge, a remnant of tip-fluting, runs longitudinally in the upper half portion of the ventral face; the lower portion is retouched by parallel-opposed flaking. The cross-section is plano-convex. The four remaining endblades (Photo 10g-h, j-k), also made from locally available raw materials, vary stylistically.

Interestingly, none of the small endblade type has been recovered at l'Anse à Henry (Table 24). The endblade length/width/thickness ratios plots observed at l'Anse à Henry (Figure 8d) reveals some similarity with the one observed at the l'Anse à Flamme site (Figure 8c).

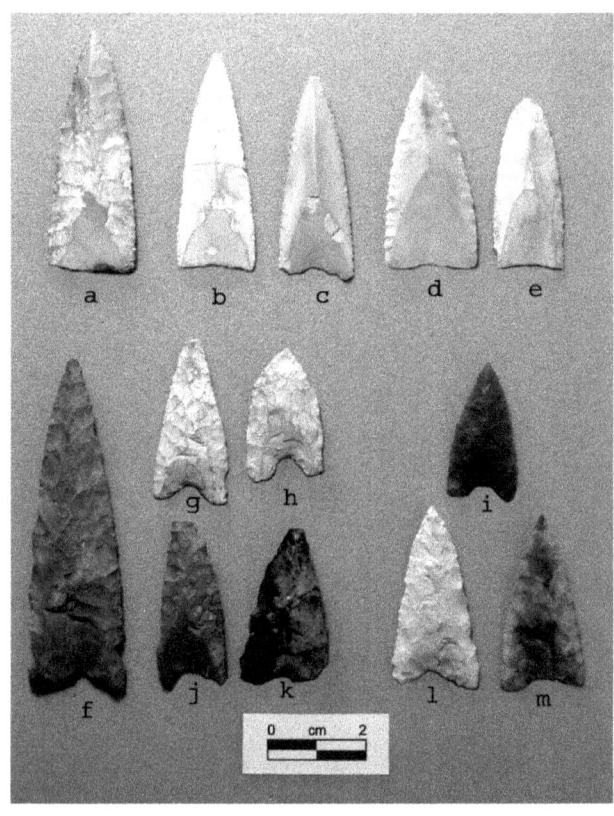

Photo 10. Anse à Henry endblade type (g-h, j-k). Trinity Bay style (a-e); Cape Ray style (i, l-m); unknown type (f).

Typical Anse à Henry (south coast) endblades; n=4 (29%)

Metric attributes (mm)	Length	Width	Thickness	Ratio W/L	Ratio T/W
Mean	30.1	15.5	4.5	0.5	0.3
S.D.	3.3	1.1	1.3	0.1	0.1
Range	25.2-32.4	14.3-16.8	3.4-6.4	0.4-0.6	0.2-0.4

Base shape: Deeply to slightly concave
Tip-fluting scars: 2/4
Grinding: Absent
Serration: Absent
Cross-section: Plano-convex

Table 24. Anse à Henry Typical Endblade Metric Attributes.

Chapter 4. The Stylistic Evidence

Endscrapers (n=0)
No endscrapers were analyzed. At the l'Anse à Henry site, Middle Dorset material was recovered during survey and endscraper affiliation to either Groswater or Middle Dorset could not be comfortably asserted.

Dildo Island Site – Trinity Bay
Endblades (n=233; Photos 11 to 15)
For Dildo Island, 233 complete endblades specimens were classified into five main types (Table 25). The trademark endblade, referred to here as Type 1, is made from Conception Bay Group chert varying in colour from battleship blue-grey to weathered whitish beige. It exhibits, on its dorsal face, three triangular polished facets; two of these are parallel and run laterally along a central ridge (remnant of tip-fluting), while the third facet covers the proximal end of the object. The ventral face either replicates the dorsal face or is ground flat. In any event, both faces are fully ground. The base is straight or slightly concave. Aside from grinding, the most remarkable feature is the extremely fine bilateral serration. Cross-section presents either a diamond or a triangular outline. Sixty specimens belong to this category. A selected sample is presented on Photo 11.

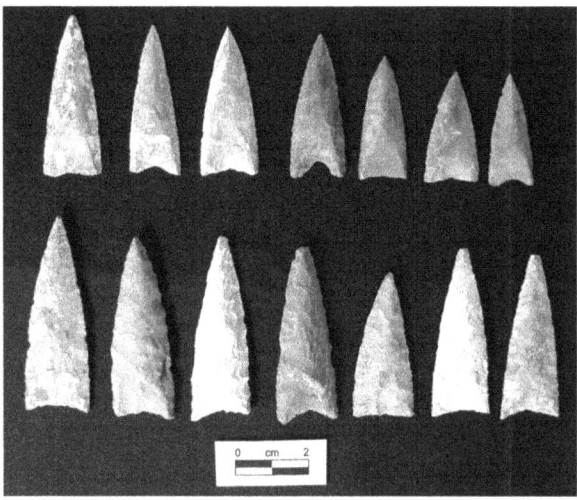

Photo 12. Dildo Island endblades (Types 2 and 3). First row: partially ground endblades (Type 2); second row: chipped endblades (Type 3).

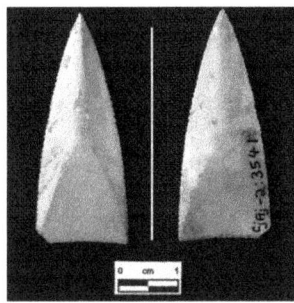

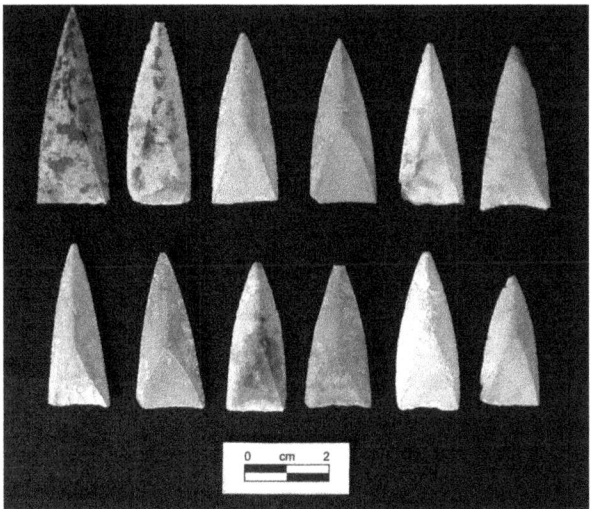

Photo 11. Dildo Island ground endblades (Type 1). Close up (dorsal/ventral) in inset.

Type 2 endblades include 60 specimens sharing more-or-less the same attributes as Type 1 except they are only partially as opposed to fully ground (Photo 12). For instance, some specimens may present the three ground triangular facets on a single face; other specimens may only exhibit grinding of the basal triangle or along one

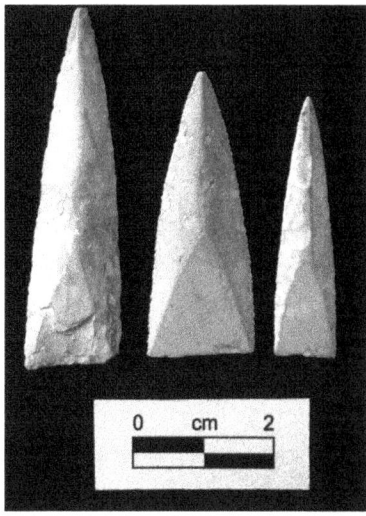

Photo 13. Dildo Island elongated ground endblades (Type 4).

side of the median ridge; others have a unifacial ground flat surface; still others, show irregular and scattered grinding patterns. In this category, many specimens exhibit a basal concavity and it is interesting to note that, in most instances, straight or straighter bases tend to co-occur with the dorsal grinding of the basal triangular facet as if basal grinding was obliterating proximal concavity.

Twenty-six endblades represent Type 3, which does not display grinding (Photo 12). They generally have a dorsal face finely fashioned by parallel-opposed flaking in the upper ¾ of the object; the base, generally slightly concave, is thinned by the removal of longitudinal flakes. The ventral face is either a replica of the dorsal face or exhibits a central ridge, related to the process of tip-fluting, extending from approximately the upper and lower ¼ of the endblade.

Aside from the presence/absence of grinding, the first three categories are somewhat similar in size and outline. At this point, it remains difficult to determine

Dildo Island endblades Type 1-2-3; n=146 (63%)

Metric attributes (mm)	Length	Width	Thickness	Ratio W/L	Ratio T/W
Mean	35.5	15.3	3.7	0.4	0.2
S.D.	5.6	1.6	0.6	0.1	0.0
Range	25.1-51-1	11.1-19.2	2.1-6.3	0.3-0.6	0.2-0.4

Base shape: Straight to slightly concave
Tip-fluting scars: 34/146
Grinding: Fully ground: 60; partially ground: 60; no grinding: 26
Serration: 93/146
Cross-section: Triangular or diamond-shaped

Dildo Island endblades Type 4; n=14 (6%)

Metric attributes (mm)	Length	Width	Thickness	Ratio W/L	Ratio T/W
Mean	49.2	15.3	3.9	0.3	0.3
S.D.	6.0	1.6	0.7	0.1	0.1
Range	40.9-60.1	13.0-19.2	3.0-5.1	0.2-0.4	0.2-0.3

Base shape: Straight to slightly concave
Tip-fluting scars: 2/14
Grinding: Fully ground: 7; partially ground: 5; no grinding: 2
Serration: 10/14
Cross-section: Triangular or diamond-shaped

Dildo Island endblades Type 5; n=67 (29%)

Metric attributes (mm)	Length	Width	Thickness	Ratio W/L	Ratio T/W
Mean	22.3	10.8	2.9	0.5	0.3
S.D.	5.1	1.7	0.5	0.1	0.1
Range	13.5-34.9	7.3-16.0	1.8-4.4	0.2-0.7	0.2-0.4

Base shape: Straight to slightly concave
Tip-fluting scars: 27/67
Grinding: Fully ground: 3; partially ground: 34; no grinding: 30
Serration: 23/67
Cross-section: Triangular or diamond

Table 25. Dildo Island Typical Endblade Metric Attributes.

if these categories constitute or should constitute a unique category in which the different endblades are more or less positioned along a production continuum that goes from chipped to completely ground endblades. Adopting this perspective, the chipped specimens could be viewed as unfinished endblades.

The 4th and 5th types include specimens sharing most of the characteristics described for Types 2 and 3. I have however classified them into discrete categories on the basis of their length: Type 4 (n=14) are noticeably longer, and Type 5 (n=67) noticeably shorter. Photos 13 and 14 present some of these specimens with their metric data presented in Table 25. Figure 8d shows a distribution reflecting a wide spectrum including these shorter and longer endblades.

Of the six remaining endblades, two specimens (Photo 15a-b) resemble closely those described at the Shamblers Cove site, in Bonavista Bay. A third specimen (Photo 15c) could possibly be at home in a Cape Ray assemblage. The last three specimens cannot be firmly associated with any types known in the study area.

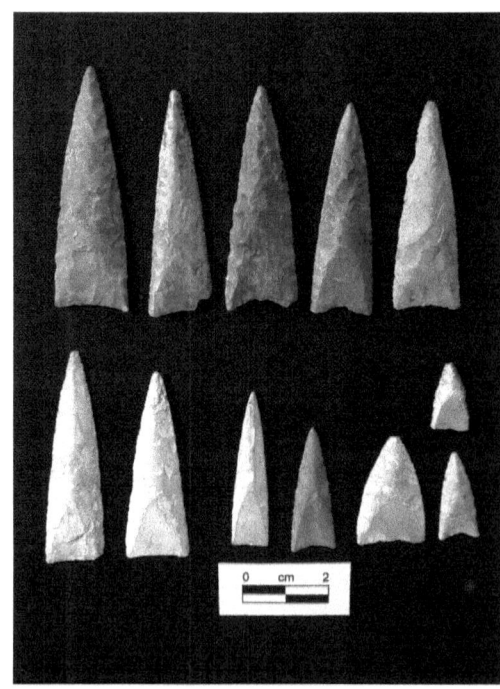

Photo 14. Dildo Island short endblades (Type 5).

Chapter 4. The Stylistic Evidence

Photo 15. Dildo Island miscellaneous endblades (d-f). Shamblers Cove style (a-b); Cape Ray style (c).

Endscrapers (n=161; Photos 16 and 17)
One hundred and sixty-one complete endscrapers from the Dildo Island site were examined. They are classified into 10 groups (Table 26).

Quartz crystal (n=118; Photo 16)
Small quartz crystal endscrapers (n=95) clearly outnumber any other type in this collection. The specimens are extremely small in size and produced

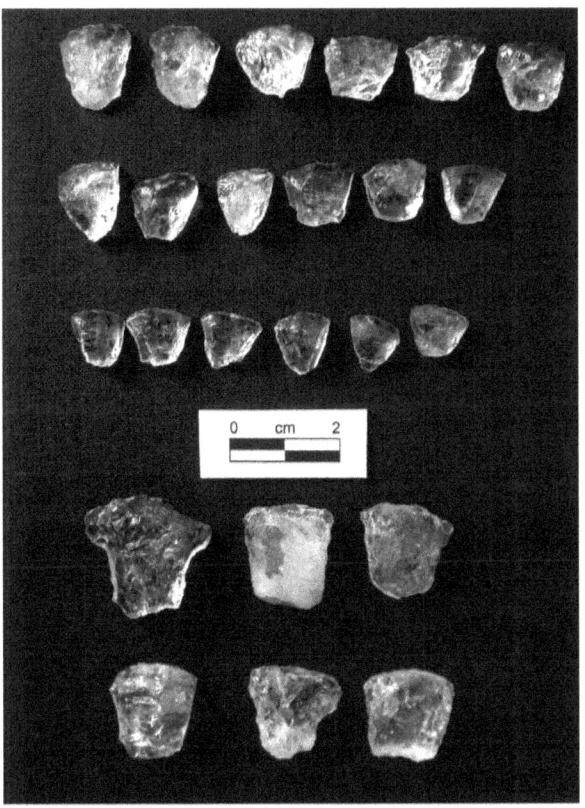

Photo 16. Dildo Island quartz crystal endscrapers.

either directly from quartz crystal cores (in their natural hexagonal shape) or remaining (discarded) quartz crystal microblade cores. Their small dimension is most certainly a reflection of the size of the cores. Their shape varies from quadrangular to triangular. All have a single working edge, which in most cases is convex; only a few specimens have straight to convex working edges. Edge angles are ranging from abrupt to semi-abrupt. On 11 specimens, the distal ends form pronounced single or double-spurs. Flaking is variable, ranging from rudimentary and irregular to completely absent. It affects mostly the dorsal face; in some cases, scars left from microblade removal remain visible; in others, the dorsal face retains the flat surface proper to natural hexagonal quartz crystals. Ventral faces are either intact, exhibit random flaking or rare microblade removal scars. Lateral edges are randomly retouched. Ninety-five endscrapers conform to this definition. Although slightly larger, 23 other quartz crystal specimens share similar attributes as those described above.

Triangular (n=1; Photo 17k)
One endscraper displays a quasi-equilateral triangular outline. It has a slightly convex (almost straight) working edge which is rather thick with a steep angle. Dorsal retouch is generalized; ventral retouch is present on one lateral edge. This specimen compares well with some described at the Port au Choix and Cape Ray sites.

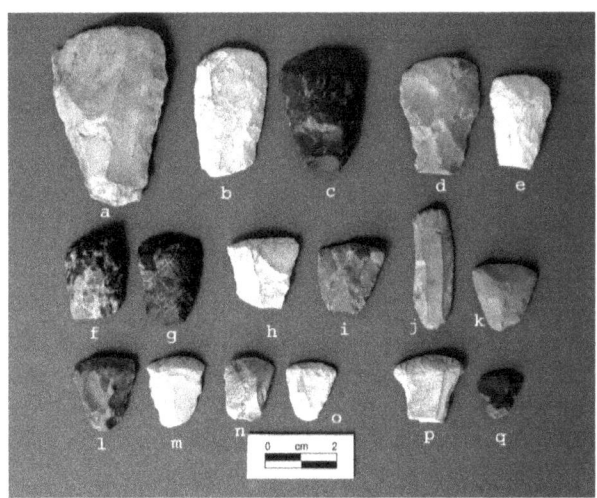

Photo 17. Dildo Island miscellaneous endscrapers: tongue-shaped (a-c); contracting stem (d-e); quadrangular (f-g); trapezoidal (h-i); blade (j); triangular (k); thumbnail (l-o); flared-end (p-q).

Thumbnail (n=13; Photo 17l-o)
Thirteen endscrapers belong to the thumbnail type described earlier. However, six of them are seemingly at the end of the maintenance/reduction sequence as they are reduced to a nub.

Flared-end (n=2; Photo 17p-q)
One endscraper has two spurs flaring at the working edge. The working edge is slightly convex and rather thick with a steep edge angle. Dorsal retouch is limited, affecting mostly the lateral margins; the ventral face is intact. Another small endscraper exhibits spurs or flared-ends mimicking the typical Groswater flared-endscraper (cf., Auger 1984, Plate VIII k-s; Fitzhugh 1972, Plate 65h; Renouf 1994, Fig. 8a and d). It is fashioned on a thin flake which still retains striking platform and bulb of percussion. Working edge is convex, relatively thick with a steep angle edge. Lateral edges are constricted to form a

Type	N	%	Length			Width			Thickness		
			Mean	S.D.	Range	Mean	S.D.	Range	Mean	S.D.	Range
Thumbnail	13	8.1	15.5	3.6	10.6-23.0	14.3	2.2	11.5-18.5	4.3	0.9	2.7-5.8
Triangular	1	0.6	17.9	–	–	13.5	–	–	3.7	–	–
Flared-end	2	1.2	30.1	25.0	12.4-47.7	21.7	13.7	12.0-31.4	6.5	4.9	3.0-10.0
Contracting stem	3	1.9	30.5	4.5	25.5-34.1	20.2	2.6	17.5-22.6	5.9	0.5	5.5-6.4
Tongue-shaped	4	2.5	20.7	5.8	16.3-29.0	18.3	3.3	15.0-21.7	5.1	1.2	3.5-6.5
Quadrangular	2	1.2	22.9	13.1	13.6-32.1	18.4	7.6	13.0-23.8	4.9	1.5	3.9-6.0
Trapezoidal	3	1.9	17.6	2.3	15.0-19.2	17.9	1.6	16.8-19.7	5.3	0.3	5.0-15.5
Shallow Bay	2	1.2	13.2	0.6	12.7-13.6	10.3	1.0	9.6-11.0	3.6	0.8	3.0-4.1
Quartz crystal	118	73.3	13.1	2.7	7.7-22.6	12.3	2.4	8-21.9	5.1	1.4	2-9.7
Blade, flake and microblade	13	8.1	15.1	6.0	9.7-31.9	10.4	3.1	8.0-18.0	3.2	1.5	2.0-7.0
Total	161	100.0									

Table 26. Dildo Island Endscraper Metric Attributes by Types.

distinct stem. Dorsal retouch consist mainly of lateral retouch; on the ventral surface, transversal thin flaking is visible on the bulb of percussion.

Contracting stems (n=3; Photo 17d-e)
Three endscrapers bear evidence of constriction along their lateral margins. One is fashioned on a tongue-shaped flake. It has a convex and moderately thin working edge with a weak edge angle. Dorsal retouch is irregular; grinding covers most of the ventral surface. Lateral edges of stem are bifacially retouched. The other two specimens, produced on shorter and thicker flakes, exhibit working edges slightly convex and thick with semi-abrupt angle. The dorsal face is affected by generalized retouch; fine pressure flaking extends along the margin of the stem. Ventral faces are intact on both.

Tongue-shaped (n=4; Photo 17a-c)
Four endscrapers are tongue-shaped. Fashioned on large expanding flakes, they often retain the percussion bulb and/or striking platform at the opposite end of the working edge. The working edge ranges from well-rounded to slightly convex; its angle is generally semi-abrupt although one specimen displays an acute angle. Dorsal flaking varies from crude to medium; the ventral face is intact in one case, unilaterally retouched in two specimens. The last specimen displays irregular retouch as well as partial grinding on its ventral surface.

Quadrangular (n=2; Photo 17f-g)
Two specimens have a quadrangular outline. The first one is fashioned on what appears to be an endblade preform, as the ventral face exhibits the central ridge characteristic of tip-fluting. Dorsal retouch is generalized including lateral margins. Working edge is slightly convex, asymmetric and thick; edge angle is steep. The second specimen has a straight and relatively thin working edge with a low angle. Dorsal retouch is mostly irregular but tends to be continuous along the marginal edges. Ventral face is retouched along one lateral edge

Trapezoidal (n=3; Photo 17h-i)
Three endscrapers present a trapezoidal outline. The working edge is, in the first case, slightly convex, straight in the second and, asymmetrical in the last. Thickness of scraping edge ranges from medium to thin; edge angle is either steep or semi-abrupt. Aside from fine bilateral retouch; dorsal flaking is generally rudimentary. Ventral surface remains intact in two specimens; unilateral edge retouch affects the third one.

Shallow Bay (n=2)
The collection also counts two tiny endscrapers which closely resemble those described as belonging to the pre-Dorset Shallow Bay Complex, originally defined by Tuck (pers. comm., 2001) at the Shallow Bay site in the Cow Head area on the Newfoundland west coast and later renamed as the Phillip's Garden West variant by Renouf (2005: 67, Fig. 7). Both specimens are unifacial, extremely small in size and have a scalene triangular outline. They are finely flaked on the dorsal face and present an asymmetric single working edge rather thick and slightly "pulled out" (*Ibid.*) to one side.

Microblade, blade and flake (n=13)
Nine specimens are fashioned at one end of quartz crystal microblades. One endscraper is produced on a chert microblade. The working edge is prepared at the distal end of the blade; it is relatively thick and abrupt. Striking platform and percussion bulb are visible at the opposite end. Dorsal surface retains a central scar left by the prior removal of a microblade; on this face continuous unilateral retouch affects one edge of the blade. The ventral surface is intact. Two endscrapers are fashioned on random shaped flakes. Both present a slightly convex and thin working edge with a semi-abrupt angle. On both dorsal faces, the central portion remains mostly intact; retouch is restricted to fine pressure flaking along the lateral margins. Ventral retouch consist of unilateral edge retouch on one specimen; the second one has been retouched on both lateral margins and on the bulb of

percussion. One endscraper is produced at the distal end of a small biface thinning flake.

Shamblers Cove Site – Bonavista Bay
Endblades (n=28; Photos 18 and 19)
From the Shamblers Cove site in Bonavista Bay 28 complete endblades were examined. The typical endblade (n=24) is generally slightly elongated, has straight to slightly curvilinear lateral edges and shows a slight to deeply concave base (Photo 18). The dorsal face exhibits fine parallel opposed flaking; the ventral face shows a median ridge, remnant of tip-fluting, running from the tip to anywhere between the upper and lower quarter of the object. The most noticeable features that set the Shamblers Cove endblades apart are their cross-section configuration and basal treatment. On the dorsal face, the thick plano-convex cross-section literally takes on the aspect of a "speed-bump" that culminates slightly under the mid-point of the object. Below that point, a transversal line marks the point where a unique longitudinal basal thinning flake ends (in a few cases only, longitudinal basal flakes are multiple). On the ventral face, the base is generally thinned out and shows the same longitudinal thinning process and the transversal line, which this time, ends up at the meeting point with the tip-fluting scar. Metric measurements are presented in Table 27.

Of the remaining four endblades, two share some affinities with Trinity Bay specimens as they exhibit a ground basal triangle (Photo 19a-b). The last two specimens stylistically diverge from the rest of the assemblage; the first one, chiefly on the basis of its small size (Photo 19d); the second, on the account of its relatively thin cross-section and of its basal treatment consisting of multiple thin longitudinal flakes (Photo 19c).

Endscrapers (n=0)
Because of the multi-component nature of this site, endscrapers were left out of the study as their cultural affiliation to either Groswater or Dorset was impossible to determine.

Photo 18. Shamblers Cove typical endblades. In inset, dorsal and ventral faces of first specimen on second row.

Typical Shamblers Cove endblades; n=24 (86%)

Metric attributes (mm)	Length	Width	Thickness	Ratio W/L	Ratio T/W
Mean	36.5	14.9	4.7	0.4	0.3
S.D.	6.4	1.8	0.9	0.1	0.1
Range	26.4-48.6	11.3-19.4	2.1-6.5	0.3-0.5	0.2-0.4

Base shape: Slightly concave
Tip-fluting scars: 23/24
Grinding: Absent
Serration: Absent
Cross-section: thick and plano-convex

Table 27. Shamblers Cove Typical Endblade Metric Attributes.

Photo 19. Shamblers Cove miscellaneous endblades. Trinity Bat type (a-b); unknown (c-d).

Swan Island Site – Notre-Dame Bay
Endblades (n=21; Photos 20 and 21)

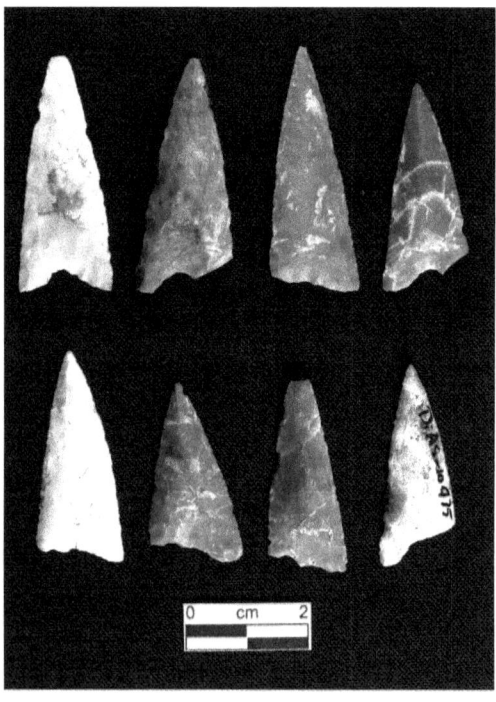

Photo 20. Swan Island typical endblades.

Twenty-one endblades were analyzed at the Swan Island site. The most common type (n=13) is generally long and slender (Photo 20 - Table 28) and bears straight to slightly curvilinear lateral edges. Basal concavity is either absent or not pronounced. The dorsal face is generally finely crafted whereas the ventral face shows the longitudinal ridge remnant of tip-fluting. The cross section is plano-convex and rather thick resembling the one observed on the Shamblers Cove specimens. Basal treatment, on both faces, consists of the removal of a single or multiple longitudinal basal thinning flakes.

Photo 21. Swan Island miscellaneous endblades: Shamblers Cove style (a-c); Cape Ray style (d); Phillip's Garden (PAC) style (e); miscellaneous short endblades (f-h).

Of the remaining eight specimens, three bear some affinities with Shamblers Cove endblades (Photo 21a-c). These include: a larger specimen rather crudely fashioned, reminiscent of Cape Ray (Photo 21d); and a short and broad specimen, although not as carefully

Typical Swan Island endblades; n=13 (62%)

Metric attributes (mm)	Length	Width	Thickness	Ratio W/L	Ratio T/W	
Mean	32.0	14.5	4.3	0.5	0.3	**Base shape**: Slightly concave to straight **Tip-fluting scars**: 8/13 **Grinding**: Absent **Serration**: Absent **Cross-section**: thick and plano-convex
S.D.5.1	3.7	1.0	0.7	0.1	0.1	
Range	25.8-37.6	12.5-15.9	3.2-5.8	0.4-0.6	0.2-0.4	

Table 28. Swan Island Typical Endblade Metric Attributes.

flaked, resembles those at Port au Choix (Photo 21e). The last three endblades (Photo 21f-g), small in size, do not compare well with any type known.

Endscrapers (n=102; Photos 22 to 24)
One hundred and two endscrapers from the Swan Island collection were examined and classified within seven categories (Table 29)

Triangular (n=1; Photo 22c)
One endscraper has an asymmetric triangular outline. Dorsal flaking is generalized; ventral surface is intact except for light thinning near the bulb of percussion. The working edge is asymmetric and convex, relatively thick and steep. The specimen could easily be at home in the Phillip's Garden (PAC) endscraper sample.

face is generalized, whereas, on the ventral face it is limited to the lateral edges.

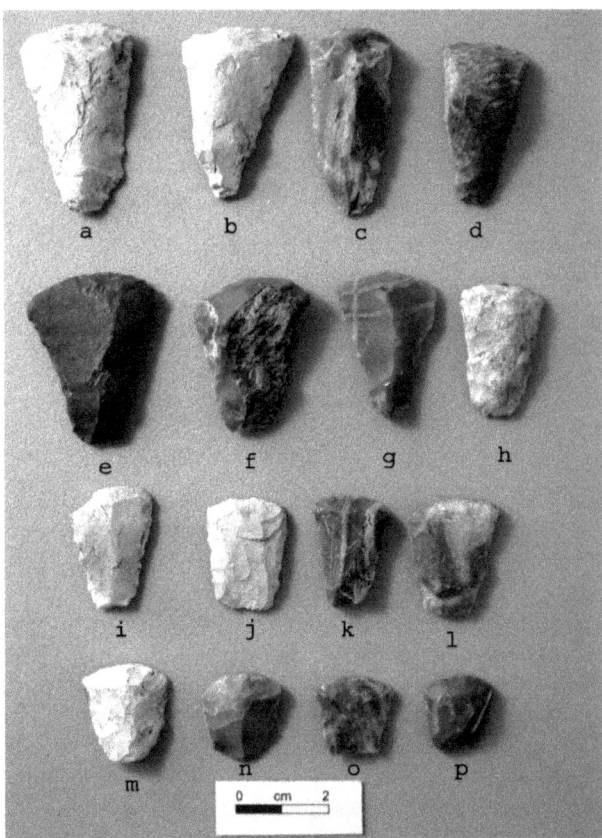

Photo 23. Swan Island selected endscraper sample: elongated (a-d); contracting stem (e-h); thumbnail (i-p).

Elongated (n=14; Photo 23 a-d)
Fourteen endscrapers have an elongated form. They are produced on large flakes that in most cases retain the striking platform and percussion bulb at the proximal end. The working edges are considerably wider than the proximal ends; they can either be convex or straight with an angle ranging from semi-abrupt to abrupt. Lateral sides are generally straight, or slightly convex in a few cases, gradually tapering down to the proximal end. Dorsal flaking varies from crude to generalize and systematic bilateral edge retouch appears to argue in favour of hafting preparation. On the ventral surface, 10 specimens show retouches along a unique edge; three others show thin pressure flaking in the vicinity of the percussion bulb; the last three specimens are untouched.

Contracting stem (n=18; Photo 23 e-h)
Eighteen endscapers constitute this group. Morphologically, this type resembles closely the previous one with the difference that the lateral margins show evidence of contraction (beginning slightly under the working edge), which gives the appearance of a distinct stem element. Like the elongated specimens, all but one are manufactured on large flake blanks. The working edges of most specimen are convex and, in a few cases, asymmetrical. Here again working edges are considerably wider than the proximal ends. Scraping angle ranges from

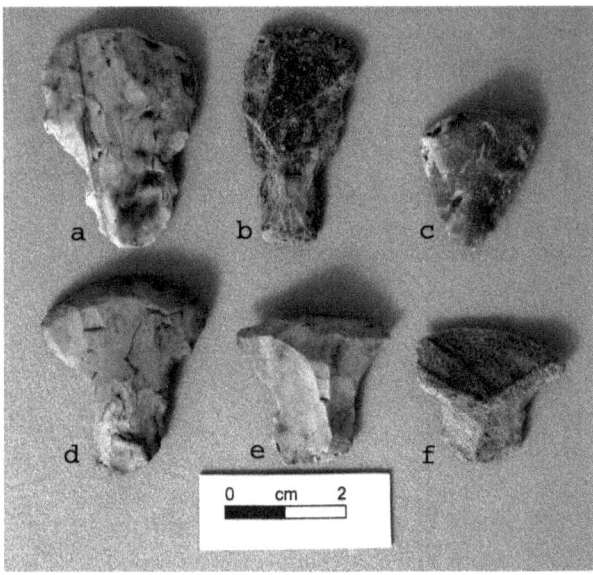

Photo 22. Swan Island selected endscraper sample: notched stem (a-b); triangular (c); flared-end (d-g).

Thumbnail (n=50; Photo 23i-p)
Fifty specimens constitute this group. Essentially, they correspond to the definition provided earlier in this chapter for this type.

Flared-end (n= 4; Photo 22d-g)
Four specimens clearly exhibit flared distal ends. Three of them resemble closely Groswater-type endscrapers with their pronounced distal spurs and hafting stems. The specimens are produced on expanding flakes showing striking platforms and bulb of percussion at the proximal end. The working edge is convex on all and scraping angle varies from steep to semi-abrupt to low. Lateral sides have been narrowed to a stem. Dorsal flaking is either irregular, rudimentary or absent. Ventral face is mostly intact except for unilateral retouch on two specimens. The fourth specimen also exhibits, but to a lesser extent, flared corners. It appears to have been produced on an elongated flake. The working edge is convex and relatively steep. Lateral edges have been retouched so as to produce a stem. Flaking on the dorsal

		Length				Width			Thickness		
Type	N	%	Mean	S.D.	Range	Mean	S.D.	Range	Mean	S.D.	Range
Thumbnail	50	49.0	19.5	3.2	12.3-25.3	16.4	1.9	13.1-20.2	4.9	1.0	3.0-7.2
Triangular	1	1.0	23.0	–	–	19.7	–	–	5.6	–	–
Flared-end	4	3.9	24.6	5.2	20.3-32.0	24.0	4.1	18.0-27.3	6.4	1.1	5.2-7.9
Elongated	14	13.7	32.2	3.7	27.6-39.2	19.0	2.8	15.0-23.9	5.0	0.9	3.5-6.4
Contracting stem	18	17.7	27.3	5.3	17.6-40.0	20.9	3.8	13.7-27.7	5.1	1.2	13.7-27.7
Notched	2	2.0	35.3	0.1	35.3-35.4	21.5	4.4	18.4-24.5	4.4	0.5	4.0-4.7
Blade, flake and microblade	13	12.7	21.2	6.3	15.3-37.5	14.9	2.2	10.9-18.8	3.9	1.2	2.4-6.9
Total	102	100.0									

Table 29. Swan Island Endscraper Metric Attributes by Types.

steep to semi-abrupt to acute. In most cases, dorsal flaking is rudimentary and marginal retouche is bilateral. Ventral surfaces are retouched unilaterally on eight roximal end on two specimens; one shows irregular flaking in the lower two-thirds of the object and four others have an intact ventral surface.

Notched stem (n= 2; Photo 22a-b)
Two endscrapers display notched stems. The first one is produced on a thin elongated flake, and shows rudimentary bifacial flaking. Two crudely-made notches are positioned on the lateral edges near the basal third of the artifact. Working edge is thin, convex with a weak angle. The second specimen is manufactured from a tongue-shaped flake and retains the striking platform and the bulb of percussion at the proximal end. The working edge is wide and well-rounded. Dorsal flaking is generalized but crude; ventral surface is intact except for the scar left by the removal of a thin pressure flake near the bulb of percussion. Bilateral notches are again located in the basal third portion of the object.

Microblade, blade and flake endscrapers (n=13)
This category includes 13 specimens. Four are fashioned at one end of a microblade. They are unifacial; working edge is relatively thin, slightly convex or straight with a semi-abrupt edge angle. Lateral edges are parallel and slightly convergent in one case. Dorsal faces are minimally retouched, showing either a central ridge or a microblade removal scar; one retains evidence of thin longitudinal flaking. All specimens are snapped transversally somewhere along their mid-sections. Three endscrapers are produced on blade-like flakes. Two of them are long and large presenting in one case, an extremely thick and steep working edge and in the other a lower angle. On both specimens, aside from the working edge, flaking is restricted to unilateral marginal retouch. The third specimen is thinner, presents a convex and semi-abrupt working edge. Retouch is strictly dorsal and includes both lateral margins. Five other endscrapers are expediently fashioned from random flakes. Their morphology varies and follows the original flake shape they were made from. Working edge convexity varies

Photo 24. Swan Island endscraper reduction sequence.

from well-rounded to slightly convex and edge angle is semi-abrupt to acute. Dorsal retouch affects three of them. All of them present unilateral edge retouch, either on their ventral or dorsal face. Ventral face is in most case intact except for two specimens bearing unilateral edge retouch. Another endscraper is produced at the distal end of a biface thinning flake. It is small in size and retains all the characteristics of the original biface thinning flake with the striking platform and bulb of percussion. The working edge is convex, thin and steep. The dorsal surface retains only flake detachment scars; the ventral face is untouched. Fine retouches affects one side of the object.

Chapter 4. The Stylistic Evidence

Pittman Site – White Bay
Endblades (n=29; Photos 25 and 26)
At the Pittman site, 29 complete specimens were examined. The typical endblade (n=20) is quite distinctive: it is short, broad and thin and presents a quasi-equilateral triangular outline (Photo 25). Length/width/thickness ratios (Table 30; Figure 8h) of this tiny endblade clearly set it apart from any other endblade types examined in this study. Lateral edges are clearly curvilinear; the base shows a rather deep concavity. Cross-section is plano-convex and extremely thin. The dorsal face exhibits fine parallel opposed flaking; this pattern is, in most cases, replicated on the

Photo 26. Pittman miscellaneous endblades (c-e); Cape Ray style (a); South coast style (b).

ventral face, although a few specimens show an irregular flaking pattern. Basal treatment consists of longitudinal flakes thinning. No evidence of tip-fluting can be observed. Without seeing the endblade preforms, one might have easily concluded that the endblades were made on thin flakes; the preforms however indicate that they were bifacially fashioned and that tip-fluting occurred. Grinding was not observed on any of the specimens.

Of the nine remaining specimens, four small endblades display a well-defined basal concavity. A short specimen (Photo 26d) could easily resemble the Pittman type if it was not for its narrowness and the absence of a basal concavity. Another longer endblade appears to have been expediently fashioned on a microblade. Of the three remaining endblades, one could be at home in a South Coast assemblage (Photo 26a); a second one, in Cape Ray (Photo 26b); the third one, in white quartzite (Photo 26c), cannot be associated with any known type.

Photo 25. Pittman typical endblades.

Typical Pittman endblades; n=20 (69%)

Metric attributes (mm)	Length	Width	Thickness	Ratio W/L	Ratio T/W	
Mean	20.4	15.1	3.0	0.7	0.2	**Base shape**: Deeply to slightly concave
S.D.	2.3	1.3	0.5	0.1	0.0	**Tip-fluting scars**: 1/20 **Grinding**: Absent **Serration**: Absent
Range	16.7-25.7	13.0-16.7	1.7-3.7	0.6-0.9	0.1-0.3	**Cross-section**: extremely thin and

Table 30. Pittman Typical Endblade Metric Attributes.

Endscrapers (n=78; Photos 27 and 28)

The 78 endscrapers examined at the Pittman site are classified in seven groups (Table 31).

Triangular (n=16; Photo 27a-d)

Sixteen endscrapers have a triangular outline and are conformable with the definition proposed earlier for the same type at the Phillip's Garden site in Port au Choix. Thus, to avoid repetition the collection will not be discussed in details.

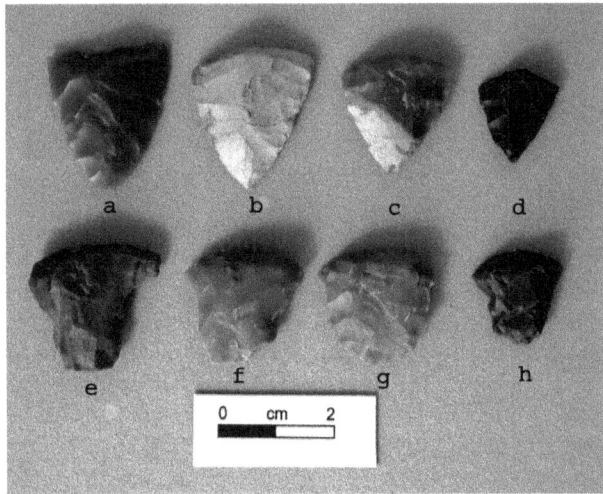

Photo 27. Pittman selected endscraper sample: triangular (a-d); flared-end (e-h).

Thumbnail (n=31; Photo 28a-h)

Thirty-one endscrapers constitute this group. Here again detailed description is not provided as they meet the criteria previously assigned to this type. However, it is noteworthy that seven of the smaller specimens have an asymmetrical working edge (Photo 27 g, h).

Flared-end (n=7; Photo 27e-h)

Seven endscrapers bear flaring distal ends: two of them are single-spured, the remaining five, double-spured. The single-spur specimens are produced on relatively thick flake, one of which still retains its original striking platform and bulb of percussion. Working edges are mostly straight with a steep angle. Both exhibit dorsal retouch and lateral edges appear to have been narrowed for hafting purposes. Ventral retouch is confined to the proximal end and marginal edges. The double-spur specimens have moderate to slightly convex working edges; four of them have a thick edge with a steep angle; the fifth one shows a thinner and lower edge angle. Dorsal retouch is generalized on four specimens and minimal on one. Here again, bilateral retouch appears to aim at the production of a hafting element. Ventral surfaces are all affected by proximal thinning; three specimens show fine retouches at the point where lateral margins intersect the working edge.

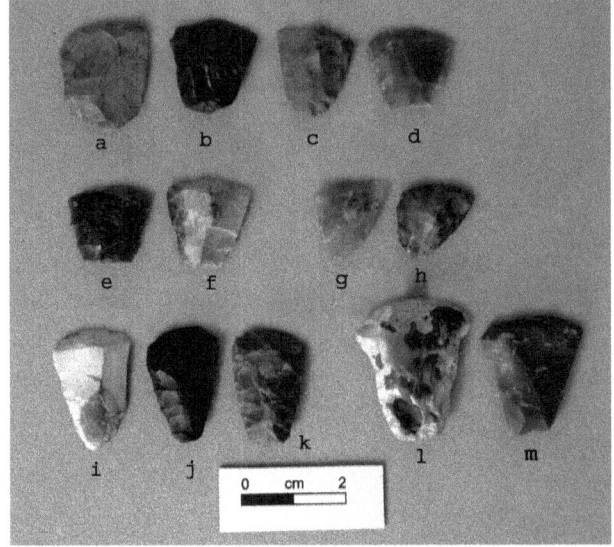

Photo 28. Pittman selected endscraper sample: thumbnail (a-h); elongated (i-k); contracting stem (l-m).

Elongated (n=3; Photo 28g-i)

Three endscrapers have an elongated/triangular shape. The working edges range from well-rounded to slightly convex; they are moderately thick with bevel angles varying from semi-abrupt to abrupt. Lateral edges are straight, tapering off to the proximal end which retains the striking platform and bulb of percussion. Dorsal flaking is generalized in two specimens; the third specimen only displays unilateral marginal retouch. The ventral surface is intact on one specimen; it consists of

			Length			Width			Thickness		
Type	N	%	Mean	S.D.	Range	Mean	S.D.	Range	Mean	S.D.	Range
Thumbnail	31	39.7	17.5	3.4	11.7-27.3	16.2	2.0	13.6-21.5	4.7	0.7	3.6-6.2
Triangular	16	20.5	19.1	3.6	14.1-24.1	18.2	3.8	11.3-26.6	4.4	0.9	2.8-5.8
Flared-end	7	9.0	17.7	2.2	15.2-20.7	18.5	2.9	14.9-22.6	5.8	0.8	4.7-7.2
Elongated	3	3.8	21.9	0.7	21.1-22.4	14.4	0.7	14.0-15.2	4.9	0.5	4.4-5.3
Contracting stem	2	2.6	24.5	3.3	22.2-26.8	21.6	1.5	20.5-22.6	5.2	0.8	4.6-5.7
Disk and ovoid	3	3.8	27.3	2.8	25.0-30.4	19.4	3.1	17.3-22.9	6.5	1.3	5.0-7.5
Blade, flake and microblade	16	20.5	18.7	4.8	13.5-28.3	13.2	3.2	9.8-21.2	3.7	0.9	2.4-5.7
Total	78	100.0									

Table 31. Pittman Endscraper Metric Attributes by Types.

longitudinal flaking on a second and of transversal flaking in the last one. The three specimens resemble closely those described (elongated ones) at Port au Choix and more likely constitute earlier versions of the thumbnail type.

Contracting stem (n=2; Photo 28j-k)
Two specimens display contracting stems. They have a triangular or tapered outlined morphology. The working edge is slightly convex, moderately thick with a steep angle. Constriction of the stem begins slightly under the working edge. Dorsal flaking is irregular and partial grinding is visible on one specimen. On the ventral face, fine pressure flaking covers the bulb of percussion of one specimen; the other specimen bears continuous fine lateral retouch on one edge and evidence of longitudinal flake removal from the base on the opposite edge.

Ovate (n=3)
Three endscrapers are produced on ovate-shaped (tear-drop) flakes. They present well-rounded (convex) working edges which can either be thick or thin with a semi-abrupt or steep bevel edge. Flaking is bifacial on two specimens made of white quartzite. The third specimen, made of black chert, displays generalized dorsal flaking, while its ventral face is minimally retouched at the proximal end. Edges are bilaterally retouched on the dorsal face.

Microblade, blade and flake endscrapers (n=16)
Two endscrapers are fashioned on microblade fragments and are transversally snapped in their mid-section. Four other specimens are produced at the distal end of blade-like flakes. Another four are produced on random flakes; they exhibit a great variety of morphology, resembling the original flakes from which they were made. The last six specimens are produced at the distal end of small biface thinning flakes.

SUMMARY

The purpose of this chapter has been to provide an empirical description based on qualitative and quantitative data of the artifact collections of eight Middle Dorset sites with the specific intent to identify regional stylistic trends. Of the two artifact categories examined, endblades certainly take on an emblematic role as each region produced a distinct and recognizable endblade type. Those from the Dildo Island and Pittman sites appear to be the most distinctive (Table 32). This distinctiveness is not only observed qualitatively, quantitative data expressing length/width/thickness ratios also indicates a range of variation (Figure 8). Identifying endscraper regional stylistic patterns is a difficult exercise as most of the collections examined share more-or-less the same types and it is clearly established that the thumbnail type prevails in most regions, with the exception of Trinity Bay. However, the notion of style cannot be totally abandoned and the study highlighted regional differences in the proportions of specific endscraper types at each of the sites (Table 33). For instance, tiny quartz crystal endscrapers clearly dominate on Dildo Island, expedient endscrapers made on a blade, flake or microblade support are frequent at Phillip's Garden and triangular endscrapers are more prevalent at the west coast sites Phillip's Garden and Cape Ray as well as at Pittman on the east side of the Northern Peninsula. These differences will be examined in more detail in the following chapter. The next step in this case study is to combine raw material and stylistic data for each of the eight sites in order to provide a definition of the different regional expressions.

Middle Dorset Variability and Regional Cultural Traditions

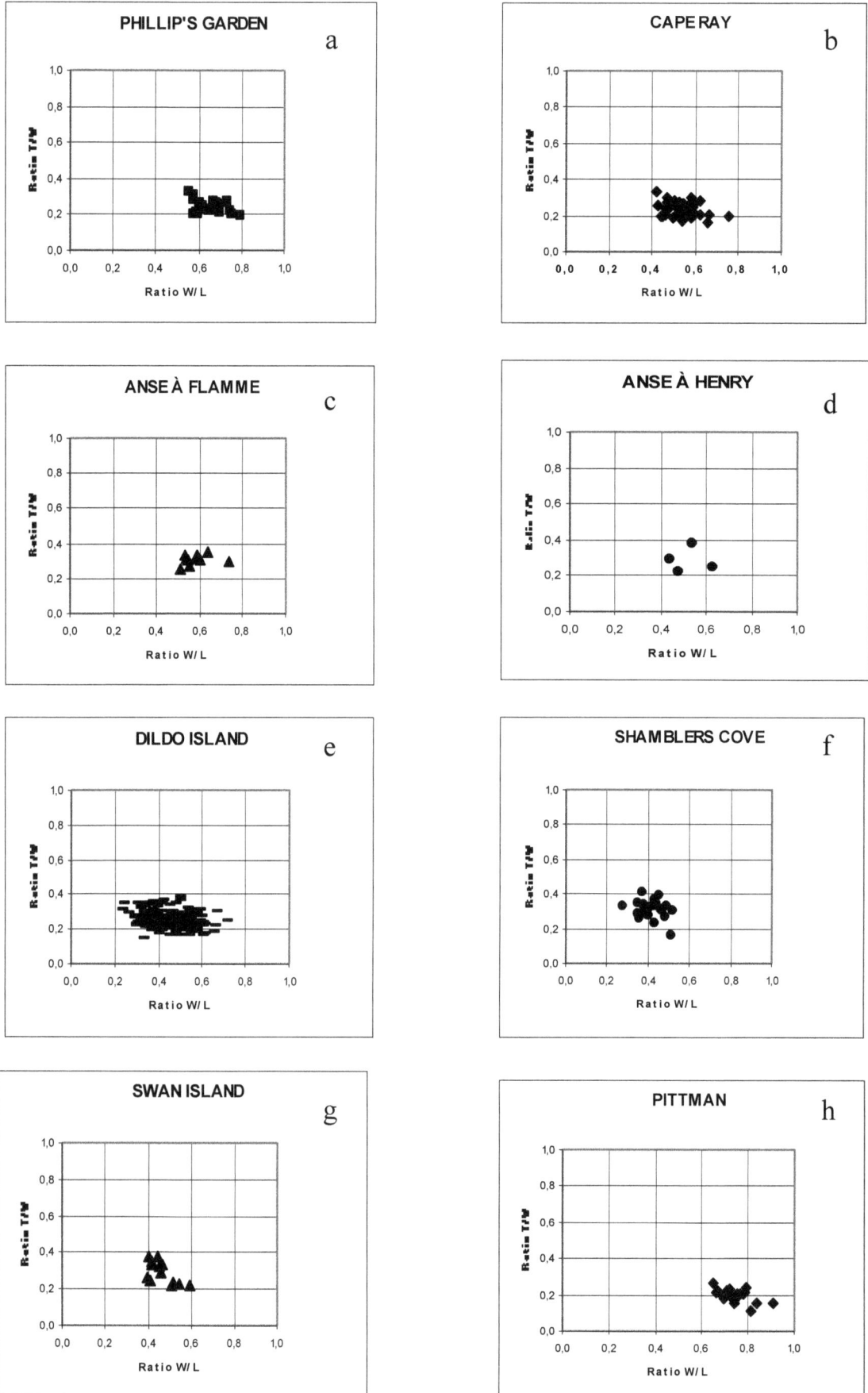

Figure 8. Endblade Length/Width/Thickness Ratios.

Endblade Attributes	Basal concavity	Tip-fluting scars	Grinding	Serration	Cross-section
Phillip's Garden	Deeply concave	frequent	rare	absent	plano-convex
Cape Ray	Deeply concave	frequent	rare	absent	plano-convex
Anse à Flamme	Slightly concave	frequent	absent	absent	plano-convex
Anse à Henry	Deeply to slightly concave	frequent	absent	absent	plano-convex
Dildo Island	Straight to slightly concave	frequent but often obliterate by the grinding process	extremely frequent	extremely frequent	triangular or diamond-shaped
Shamblers Cove	Slightly concave	almost always	absent	absent	thick and plano-convex
Swan Island	Slightly concave to straight	frequent	absent	absent	thick and plano-convex
Pittman	Deeply to slightly concave	rare	absent	absent	extremely thin and plano-convex

Table 32. Summary Endblade Attributes by Sites.

	Phillip's Garden		Cape Ray		Dildo Island		Swan Island		Pittman	
Endscraper types	N	%	N	%	N	%	N	%	N	%
Thumbnail	26	**40.0**	54	**36.7**	13	8.1	50	**49.0**	31	**39.7**
Triangular	8	12.3	10	6.8	1	0.6	1	1.0	16	**20.5**
Flared-end	2	3.1	9	6.1	2	1.2	4	3.9	7	9.0
Elongated	6	9.2	17	11.6	-	-	14	**13.7**	3	3.8
Contracting stem	-	-	15	10.2	3	1.9	18	**17.7**	2	2.6
Notched	-	-	-	-	-	-	2	2.0	-	-
Tongue-shaped	-	-	7	4.8	4	2.5	-	-	-	-
Disk and ovoid	-	-	4	2.7	-	-	-	-	3	3.8
Quadrangular	-	-	1	0.7	2	1.2	-	-	-	-
Trapezoidal	-	-	-	-	3	1.9	-	-	-	-
Shallow Bay	-	-	-	-	2	1.2	-	-	-	-
Quartz crystal	-	-	-	-	118	**73.3**	-	-	-	-
Blade, flake and microblade	23	35.4	30	20.4	13	8.1	13	12.7	16	20.5
Total	65	100.0	147	100.0	161	100.0	102	100.0	78	100.0

Table 33. Endscraper Type Frequencies by Sites.

CHAPTER 5. SUMMARY: TOWARDS A DEFINITION OF REGIONAL TRADITIONS

The previous two chapters identified regional technological patterns in eight Middle Dorset assemblages. In Chapter 3, raw material use-patterns were examined and I concluded that for most regions there was a strong reliance on regionally available raw materials. In Chapter 4, I provided an assemblage-by-assemblage empirical stylistic description and again concluded that each region produced significant distinctive artifact styles. The material presented demonstrates that there is regional variability in the Middle Dorset record in Newfoundland and on the island of Saint-Pierre. In this chapter, I combine and synthesize the information from those two chapters and propose a definition for each of the regional expressions or traditions (Figure 9).

NEWFOUNDLAND NORTHWEST COAST

At Phillip's Garden (Port au Choix), on the Newfoundland northwest coast, harpoon endblades are finely flaked and relatively short and broad. They exhibit a basal concavity, which in some specimens can be quite pronounced. The ventral face shows evidence of tip-fluting; lateral edges are slightly convex. Endscrapers come in a variety of forms and, in conformity with most of the sites examined in this study, the thumbnail type prevails. However, noticeable at Port au Choix is the relative abundance of expedient endscrapers produced from Carbonate Sequence chert pebbles and the presence of well-crafted triangular endscrapers, the latter type being also present at Cape Ray and Pittman sites. Regional raw materials such as radiolarian Cow Head and Carbonate Sequence cherts were used extensively. In combination they constitute 71%, 90% and 55% of the endblade, endscraper and microblade assemblages respectively (Table 17). The use of quartz crystal is important (32%) in microblade production; this trend is also observed at most of the other sites. It should be noted that most of the Cow Head cherts used at Port au Choix exhibit poor fossil preservation and radiolarians could only be observed from thin sections using high power microscopes.

NEWFOUNDLAND SOUTHWEST COAST

Apart from the fact that they are slightly longer and narrower, the typical Cape Ray endblades bear some resemblances in their outline with the Port au Choix specimens. All present a basal concavity and most of them exhibit, on the ventral side, the central ridge characteristic of the tip-fluting technique. Contrasting with Port au Choix, some specimens display evidence of basal grinding. Once again, the thumbnail endscraper type prevails, but a wide array of types is also represented including elongated, contracting stem, flared-end and triangular endscrapers. Stepping aside from the stylistic argument, this certainly calls to mind a progressive reduction sequence. Cow Head chert clearly dominates in all categories: endblades (98%); endscrapers (83%); microblades (61%). Carbonate Sequence cherts are used more parsimoniously: endscrapers (4%) and microblades (2%). Quartz crystal constitutes 32% of the microblade assemblage. Albeit incontestably of western origin, Cow Head chert does not outcrop in the direct vicinity of the Cape Ray site and the closest acquisition area is located about 130 km to the north, in the back country between the modern towns of Stephenville and Corner Brook (Figure 4). Therefore, the occupants of Cape Ray would have had to engage in some procurement practices involving quarries farther up the west coast. Unlike the Cow Head chert used at Phillip's Garden (Port au Choix), the Cow Head chert used at Cape Ray shows exquisite radiolarian preservation often visible to the naked eye or using a hand lens. Although using cherts from the same generic Cow Head Group, the Middle Dorset people from Cape Ray and Port au Choix had different procurement patterns and were obviously obtaining their raw materials from distinct and specific outcrops.

NEWFOUNDLAND SOUTH COAST AND SAINT-PIERRE

On the Newfoundland south coast, the l'Anse à Flamme and l'Anse à Henry (Saint-Pierre) sites could reasonably be grouped together as being part of the same stylistic region as both sites appear to share a number of features. From the limited samples we have from the area, and keeping in mind that at both sites only the endblades were analysed, the first impression one gains is that of stylistic diversity: endblades come in a variety of styles, some of which are not particularly well-crafted, others bearing no resemblance with any known type. It is obvious, however, that some of the specimens hint at links with neighbouring areas, namely Trinity Bay and Cape Ray (Figure 2).

At both sites, raw material use-patterns are quite similar and include three major rock groups: Marystown Group rhyolites (equivalent to Grand Colombier and Cap Rouge rhyolites in Saint-Pierre), Cow Head Group and Conception Group cherts. The use of Conception Group chert is also a common occurrence at other south coast sites (Penney 1984; Rast 1999; Robbins 1985).

With respect to endblade style and the common use of Conception Group chert, one cannot escape seeing an obvious link with the Trinity Bay area and it is perhaps possible to conceive, and here I concur with Robbins (1985), that Trinity Bay and the Newfoundland south coast, including the island of Saint-Pierre, might have been part of the same "territory" used by the same Dorset groups. This is not unreasonable considering that the travel distance between the two regions is significantly reduced if one were to cross the narrow Avalon Isthmus from Trinity Bay to Placentia Bay (see Figure 5).

Chapter 5. Summary: Towards A Definition of Regional Traditions.

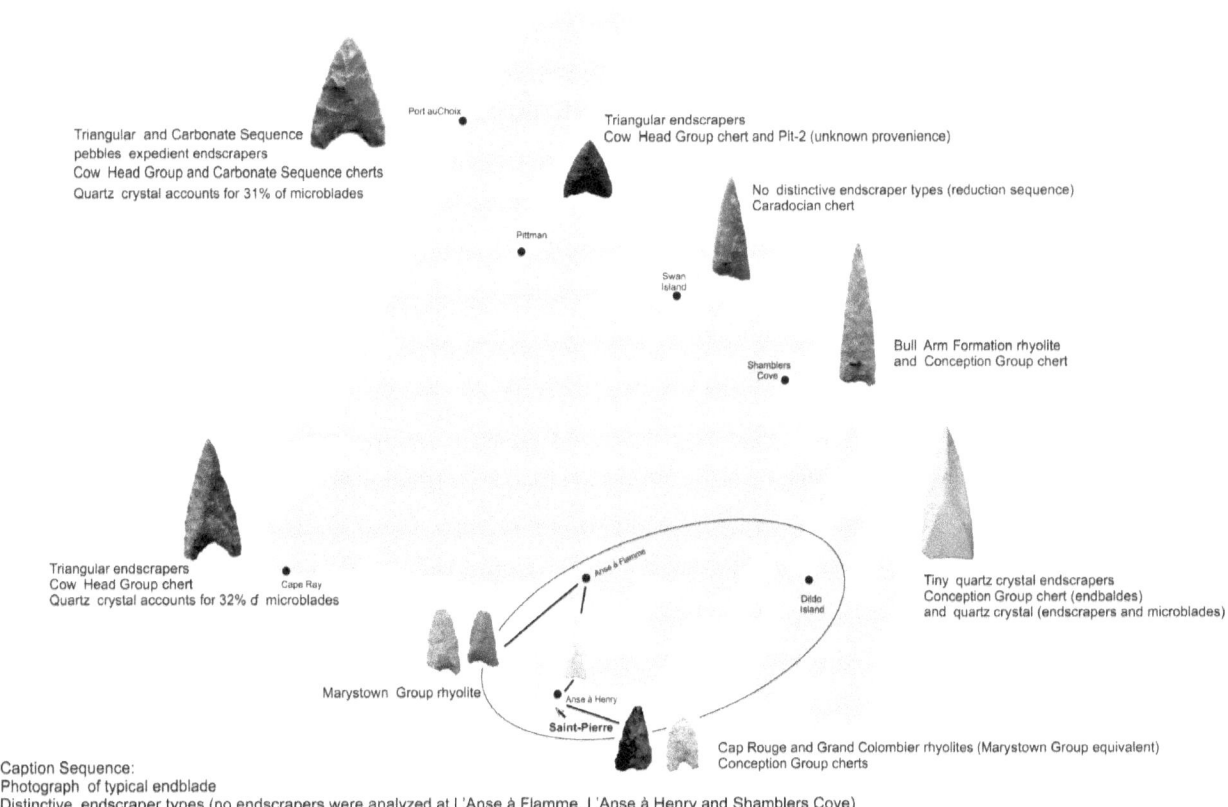

Figure 9. Summary of Regional Traditions

At present, a firm technological tradition is difficult to identify on the south coast, including Saint-Pierre. This situation could be attributed to the small artifact sample size examined at both sites. On the other hand, the ephemeral nature of the occupation at these sites could point to an "en route" type of site between regions; in this case the south coast/Saint-Pierre and Trinity Bay.

TRINITY BAY

The Trinity Bay Dorset (Evans 1982, Robbins 1985; LeBlanc 1997a) is probably one of the most distinctive (and spectacular) regional expressions of the Middle Dorset culture in Newfoundland. The typical endblade exhibits three triangular polished facets on one or both if its faces and is adorned by extremely fine bilateral serrations. Tiny quartz crystal endscrapers are unequivocally the main type represented. Raw material use-patterns are extremely straightforward and present a clear dichotomy: on the one hand, a battleship blue-grey chert (turning to a whitish-beige when weathered) from the Conception Group constitutes 98% of the endblade assemblage. On the other hand, quartz crystal dominates the endscraper (88%) and microblade (96%) sample. Non-local materials are but a trace in the Dildo Island assemblage. Both in Trinity Bay, the Stock Cove (Robbins 1985) and Frenchman's Island (Evans 1982) sites share similar technological characteristics.

BONAVISTA BAY

At the Shamblers Cove site in Bonavista Bay, only endblades were examined. The assemblage is homogeneous consisting of specimens that are rather long and finely flaked, exhibiting straight or slightly concave bases and thick cross-sections (speed-bump-like). On most specimens, the proximal end on the dorsal face, displays a well-defined scar left by the removal of basal thinning flakes. The ventral face shows evidence of tip-fluting. Rhyolites from the Bull Arm Formation constitute 53% of the assemblage and Conception Group chert 13%. This is not surprising as both of these rock formations co-occur in Bonavista Bay. Unidentified raw materials account for 33.3% of the assemblage.

NOTRE-DAME BAY

On Swan Island in Notre-Dame Bay, typical endblades are generally long and slender and appear to be less carefully flaked than those at Shamblers Cove. The ventral face shows evidence of tip-fluting. Basal concavities are either absent or not that pronounced. Cross-section is plano-convex and rather thick resembling somewhat the one observed at Shamblers Cove.

The thumbnail type predominates but the array of styles exhibited in the endscraper sample appears to be the perfect example of endscraper types belonging to a reduction sequence where one type might have led into the next: elongated type → contracting stem → thumbnail (see Photo 24). Caradocian chert is used extensively in all tool categories: endblades (78%); endscrapers (77%); and microblades (73%). Exogenous raw materials are of minute occurrence at the site.

For the Newfoundland east coast, Robbins (1985: 140) makes the observation that endblades tend to be longer and narrower that those from the west coast. From my own examination at the Shamblers Cove and Swan Island sites, I concur with Robbins statement and I would also add that tip-fluting scars (or tip-fluting ridges) remain mostly intact indicating that no subsequent work was done to modify those ridges. Tip-fluting is a technological feature observed at all sites; however, in many cases the tip-fluting scars have been obliterated by further retouching or grinding.

WHITE BAY

At the Pittman site in White Bay, the typical endblade is short, thin and broad presenting a quasi-equilateral triangular outline. It is finely flaked on both faces and lacks the ventral tip-fluting generally characteristic of Dorset endblades. In light of the stylistic data presented here, I would have to disagree with the statements of Robbins (1985: 142) and Erwin (2001: 156), that the Pittman endblade assemblage contains specimens sharing attributes with both Newfoundland west coast (Port au Choix) and the northeast coast (Bonavista Bay). My research demonstrates, on the contrary, the unique character of the Pittman endblade style. As with most sites, the thumbnail endscraper is the prevalent type at the Pittman site. The triangular and blade/flake/microblade types are also significant constituents of the endscraper assemblage; this is also observed at Port au Choix and Cape Ray. Worth noting also for Pittman is the relatively high representation of flared-end endscrapers.

Together, Cow Head and Carbonate Sequence cherts are used in moderate proportions. A black fine-grained chert of uncertain origin (Pit-2) is used in similar percentages. Further research is needed to determine the precise origin of the latter. Exogenous raw materials are of parsimonious occurrence, consisting mainly of Caradocian cherts.

CHAPTER 6. CONCLUSION

This study has explored the issue of variability within the Middle Dorset culture on the island of Newfoundland and the island of Saint-Pierre in the French Archipelago of Saint-Pierre and Miquelon. Practice theory provided the conceptual framework to interpret variability and it is argued that the variability expressed in the Middle Dorset material record reflects distinct regional traditions. Using a case study, the main objective was to demonstrate the existence of Middle Dorset regional groups in Newfoundland and in Saint-Pierre.

Newfoundland and Saint-Pierre was a fertile ground to test this hypothesis. The comparative study of specific aspects of the lithic technology at eight Middle Dorset sites identified a strong degree of regional specialization in the technological practices of these Palaeoeskimo people. This specialization is expressed in terms of raw material utilization-patterns and artifact style. In fact, in most assemblages the regional traits (or characteristics) are so distinctive that one would have little difficulty distinguishing artifact style from one region from those of another if they were to be hand-picked from a sample of unknown provenience. This is particularly true in the case of endblades. At most sites, there is also a clear reliance on regionally available raw materials. Regional cherts and rhyolites are predominantly used in the production of endblades and endscrapers. The sole exception is the Dildo Island assemblage where over 88% of endscrapers are made from quartz crystal. There is also a recurrent reliance on quartz crystal for the manufacture of microblades (Phillip's Garden, Cape Ray, Dildo Island and Pittman). As noted earlier, quartz crystal is ubiquitous on the island and has no heuristic value for assessing regional provenience; however, its relative importance in some of these assemblages suggests that it could have been available and/or easily accessible in the vicinity of some of these sites. This type of lithic procurement pattern, involving the use of regionally available rocks and quartz crystal, is not unique to Newfoundland. In Nunavik (Desrosiers and Rahmani in press) and Baffin Island (Odess 1998:430-431), for example, Dorset assemblages also exhibit regional raw material utilization-patterns as well as a "quasi-normalized" (Desrosiers and Rahmani in press) use of quartz crystal in the production of microblades.

The data presented in this research also focus attention on a number of observations concerning interaction, or its absence, between regions. Based on artifact style and the use of raw materials, it appears as if each of the regions was operating like a closed system as little evidence of contact between regions was observed. Except for the south coast sites l'Anse à Flamme and l'Anse à Henry where a link with the Trinity Bay area is clearly documented,[12] only in rare occasions did specimens from one region appear in assemblages from other regions. Where this has occurred raw materials always travelled with style; *i.e.* raw material use did not vary independently of style. For instance, whenever Dildo Island ground and serrated endblades were found in assemblages external to Trinity Bay they were invariably made from Conception Group chert (see Anse à Flamme, Anse à Henry and Shamblers Cove). Similarly, Shamblers Cove typical endblades made of local Bull Arm Formation rhyolite were found in the extra-regional Swan Island collection. This implies that the artifacts (at least those considered in this study) were more than likely introduced in some fashion as finished objects and their rare occurrence does not reveal any evidence of regular and sustained inter-regional contact or exchange. An examination of the debitage collections from each of the sites could further confirm or invalidate this statement. Taking endblade style as an example, it also appears that style in itself was not a component that migrated or was borrowed between regions; indeed, a given regional endblade type was always produced from regionally available lithologies.

Returning to the south coast sites (Anse à Flamme and Anse à Henry) where Trinity Bay polished endblade types were of common occurrence, it is worth mentioning that the specimens were moving in only one direction: from Trinity Bay to the south coast sites. In the Dildo Island sample, I never found artifacts resembling specimens from the south coast sites.

Broadening the scope, the evidence indicates only the faintest contact with Dorset groups in Labrador. Thus, I would have to disagree with the statement that the Middle Dorset period was a time of considerable communication and interaction between resident Newfoundland and Labrador groups (Jordan 1986; Nagle 1986: 101; Tuck and Fitzhugh 1986: 166). Among the Newfoundland/Saint-Pierre collections examined, only three endblades (Phillip's Garden, Pittman and Dildo Island), one endscraper (Dildo Island), and four microblade fragments (Pittman) were made of Ramah quartzite. This constitutes only 0.16% of the total number of artifacts analysed (n= 4870). Based on the evidence presented here interaction was tenuous at best, at least with reference to contact from Labrador to Newfoundland.

For the reverse direction, from Newfoundland to Labrador, Nagle notes that:

> […] cherts from western Newfoundland comprise a modest, but consistent, percentage

---

[12] At these sites, endblades of the Dildo Island – Trinity Bay type are frequent and it is hypothesized that those Newfoundland south coast sites and the Trinity Bay area could be part of one same exploitation region used by the same Dorset group (see also Robbins 1985).

of all flakes stone in Middle Dorset sites located in central Labrador, and are even found in trace amounts as far as Avayalik [...]. Furthermore, nearly three-quarters of a small surface collection of Middle Dorset artifacts from Battle Harbour in southern Labrador are made of several varieties of chert from Newfoundland (Nagle 1986: 101) (See also footnote [13]).

Nagle contrasts this situation with the Early and Late Dorset periods where Newfoundland cherts were nearly absent from Labrador collections. This is not surprising since neither Early nor Late Dorset people were ever present on the island of Newfoundland.

I see the trace occurrence of northern Labrador Ramah quartzite in the Newfoundland collections, not as evidence of contact but rather as artifacts that may have been brought to the island during initial colonization by Dorset people. The presence of so-called "Newfoundland cherts" in some Labrador collections is, on the other hand, more difficult to interpret. Given that Middle Dorset groups appear to have been well established throughout the different regions on the island of Newfoundland and in Saint-Pierre, and that Middle Dorset presence in Labrador was extremely limited, I would be more inclined to consider the eventuality of sporadic visits of Newfoundland groups to Labrador; formalized and regular contacts are unlikely.

The evidence presented in this study does not support strong links with Labrador nor does it support sustained inter-regional contacts among Newfoundland/Saint-Pierre Middle Dorset groups. On the contrary, my research demonstrated the highly localized nature of Middle Dorset technological practices. Within each region Middle Dorset groups developed a conformity in their technological practices, a sameness, which in turn reveals specific and distinct social entities. Echoing McGhee (1976), Plumet (1986) and Sutherland (1996) I suggest that, much like the historical –*miut* groups in the Arctic, these technological practices reflect traditions of discrete territorially-defined social groups. The picture I am proposing for the Newfoundland and Saint-Pierre region is a world in which there were contemporaneous Middle Dorset groups, each living in discrete territories, with their own technological practices and specific developmental histories.

To stress the importance of the relationship between identity and region and/or territory in Arctic cultures, I believe Collignon's study of the Inuinnait (Central Arctic) relations with their territory is germane to my study. She clearly establishes that Inuit identity is constructed with reference to their land and that group names are constructed using an important place in their territory, to which the suffix –*miut* is added (2006: 43). To my knowledge, Burch (1976) was the first scholar to draw attention to the significance of –*miut* in his paper on the "Nunamiut" concept. In essence, it is the territory that gives the Inuit their identity. From this perspective, the notion of distinct territorially-defined Middle Dorset social groups is extremely meaningful.

To draw analogies to the Paleoindian and the Archaic periods, I see similarities in terms of the Middle Dorset period being Archaic-like. In contrast to the Paleoindian period, characterized by a high degree of mobility (rapid population spread; long-distance lithic raw material procurement patterns), the Archaic period is one of relative stability. Groups settled down in discrete regions and developed a wide diversity of ideologies, arts, crafts, and technologies. Indeed, the Newfoundland/Saint-Pierre example provides the first compelling evidence for the observation – technologically, culturally, geographically – of the emergence of distinct regional groups or bands in the Palaeoeskimo record anywhere.

Were those regional groups aware of the presence of each other? Was their technological specificity identifiable by outsiders as ethnic markers? Undoubtedly, this specificity contributed to a sort of engagement, an awareness of and a discourse about others. Perhaps not to achieve any political goal, but it may have had a resonance at the regional or pan-regional scale (Pauketat 2001b: 9).

This research has dealt with a select set of data to reveal insights about the social aspects embedded in material culture. At a phenomenological level, the study has essentially been concerned with the spatial distribution of Middle Dorset cultural traits. There is nothing extraordinary about the empirical observations made in each of the regions; they simply indicate that specific techniques were practiced. We need not concern ourselves so much with the presence or absence of particular traits. More important is the recognition that individual artifacts, and ultimately the observed regional-scale patterns, are cultural constructs resulting from day-to-day technological practices that were developed, conditioned and reproduced within a singular social setting, the *habitus*. It is only then that variation becomes significant. In the context of this study, practice theory generates a richer account of the technological variability encountered in the archaeological record and could serve as a model in examining variability in the Arctic record.

---

[13] Nagle appears to lump as Newfoundland chert, all cherts originating from the Newfoundland west coast. If my understanding is correct, he defines Newfoundland chert as: Ordovician radiolarian-bearing Cow Head chert which, he states, extends from the tip of the Northern Peninsula to Port au Port. The present study has shown that at least two distinctive chert types are largely available on the Newfoundland west coast: Cow Head Group cherts and Carbonate Sequence cherts. Those are quite distinctive on the basis of their lithology and geographical distribution.

APPENDIX 1 – SITE DESCRIPTIONS

This appendix contains a brief summary of the archaeological activities conducted at the sites examined in this study.

Phillip's Garden site (EeBi-1)
Long: 57° 22'W
Lat: 50° 43'N
The Phillip's Garden is located on the north shore of the Pointe Riche Peninsula in the community of Port au Choix. To this day, the site is probably the largest Dorset site reported in Newfoundland and in eastern Arctic with its estimated 70 Middle Dorset dwellings. The site has been the object of archaeological attention for at least 75 years. William John Wintemberg and Diamond Jenness were the first to visit in 1927 and again in 1929. At that time, both agreed that the remains from Phillip's Garden belonged to the newly Dorset culture identified in Cape Dorset, Baffin Island (Jenness 1925). As part of an intensive archaeological survey on the Newfoundland northwest coast, Elmer Harp returned to the site in 1949 and 1950 for further testing and the excavation of two Dorset houses. Harp resumed his investigation at Phillip's Garden between 1961 and 1964; his work resulted in the partial and complete excavation of 20 houses. On the behalf of Parks Canada, M.A.P. Renouf subsequently conducted a multi-year research project (1984-2006), during which several additional house depressions were located. A magnetometer survey conducted in 2001 (Easthaugh 2002) brought the estimated total of houses at the site to at least 67. Over the years, Renouf with the help of her graduate students undertook an extensive and focused research program addressing a number of important issues in contemporaneous Palaeoskimo research such as: settlement-subsistence studies and faunal analysis; dwelling contemporaneity; house architecture; geophysical (magnetometer) survey; paleo-environmental studies.

C14 dates: 1970 ± 60 (Beta 23977); 1920 ± 110 (Beta 15638); 1900 ± 110 (Beta 23978); 1890 ± 90 (Beta 42967); 1850 ± 110 (Beta 15379); 1770 ± 120 (Beta 42968); 1736 ± 48 (P 692); 1712 ± 40 (P 695); 1683 ± 49 (P 736); 1659 ± 48 (P 693); 1640 ± 70 (Beta 160975); 1632 ± 47 (P 679); 1602 ± 49 (P 694); 1593 ± 49 (P 683); 1580 ± 54 (P 727); 1570 ± 70 (Beta 15381); 1565 ± 53 (P 733); 1538 ± 55 (P 729); 1520 ± 90 (Beta 19084); 1509 ± 47 (P 696); 1502 ± 49 (P 676); 1480 ± 40 (Beta 160976); 1465 ± 51 (P 734); 1410 ± 100 (Beta 66435); 1370 ± 90 (Beta 66436); 1360 ± 80 (Beta 160977); 1321 ± 49 (P 737); 1250 ± 60 (Beta 15639). Dates taken from Renouf 2006.

References:

Bell, Trevor, J. Macpherson and M.A.P. Renouf.
2005   Late Prehistoric Human Impact on Bass Pond, Pond, Port au Choix. *Newfoundland and Labrador Studies* 20 (1):107-129. Special Issue, Humans on the Landscape: Interdisciplinary Studies at Port Choix. St. John's.

Eastaugh, Edward, J. H.
2002   On the 2001 Field Season at Point Riche, Port au Choix, National Historic Site. Unpublished report for the Archaeology Division, Parks Canada, Atlantic Region. Halifax.

Erwin, John, C.
1995   An Intra-site Analysis of Phillip's Garden: A Middle Dorset Palaeo-Eskimo Site at Port au Choix, Newfoundland. Unpublished M.A. thesis. Department of Anthropology, Memorial University of Newfoundland. St. John's.

Jenness, Diamond
1933   The Problem of the Eskimo. In *The American Aborigine: Their origin and Antiquity*, edited by D. Jenness. Russell and Russell, New York.

1925   A New Eskimo Culture in Hudson Bay. *The Geographical Review* 15: 428-437.

Harp, Elmer Jr.
1976   Dorset Settlement Patterns in Newfoundland and Southeastern Hudson Bay. In *Eastern Arctic Prehistory: Palaeoeskimo Problems*, edited by M.S. Moreau, pp. 119-138. Memoirs of the Society for American Archaeology, No. 31.

1964   *The Cultural Affinities of the Newfoundland Dorset Eskimo*. National Museums of Canada, Bulletin 200. Ottawa.

1951   An archaeological survey in the Strait of Belle Isle area. *American Antiquity* 3: 203-220.

n.d.   Elmer Harp's Field Notes for 1961-1964. Unpublished report on file, Department of Tourism and Culture, Historic Resources Division, Government of Newfoundland and Labrador. St. John's.

Hodgetts, L. M., M. A. P. Renouf, M. S. Murray; D. McCuaig-Balkwill and L. Howse.
2003   Changing subsistence practices at the Dorset Palaeoeskimo site of Phillip's Garden, Newfoundland. *Arctic Anthropology* 40 (1): 106-120.

Hodgetts, Lisa, M.
2001   Using bone measurements to determine the season of Harp seal hunting at the Dorset Palaeoeskimo site of Phillip's Garden. *Newfoundland and Labrador Studies* 20 (1): 91-106. Special Issue, Humans on the Choix. St. John's.

Murray, Maribeth, S.
1992   Beyond the laundry list: the analysis of faunal remains from a Dorset dwelling at Phillip's Garden (EeBi-1), Port au Choix, Newfoundland. Unpublished M.A. thesis. Department of Anthropology, Memorial University of Newfoundland. St. John's.

Renouf, M.A.P
2006   Re-investigating a Middle Phase Dorset dwelling at Phillip's Garden, Port au Choix, Newfoundland, In *Dynamics of Northern Societies: Proceedings of the SILA/NABO Conference on Arctic and North Atlantic Archaeology, Copenhagen, May 10th-14th 2004*, edited by J. Arneborg and B. Grønnow, pp. 119-128.

National Museum, Studies in Archaeology and History, Vol. 10. Copenhagen.

2002   Archaeology at Port au Choix, 1990 to 1992 Excavations. *Occasional Papers in Northeastern Archaeology, No. 12*. Copetown Press, St. John's.

2000   Symbolism and Subsistence: Seals and Caribou at Port au Choix, Northwestern Newfoundland. In *Animals, Bones and Human Societies*, edited by P. Rowley-Conwey, pp. 65-72. Oxbow Press, Oxford.

1993   Palaeo-Eskimo Seal Hunters at Port au Choix, Northwestern Newfoundland. *Newfoundland Studies* 9 (2): 185-212.

1992   The 1991 Field Season, Port au Choix, National Historic Park: Report of Archaeological Excavations. Unpublished report for the Archaeology Division, Parks Canada, Atlantic Region. Halifax.

1991   Archaeological Investigations at the Port au Choix National Historic Park: Report of the 1990 Field Activities. Unpublished report for the Archaeology Division, Parks Canada, Atlantic Region. Halifax.

1987   Archaeological Investigations at the Port au Choix National Historic Park: Report of the 1986 Field Activities. Unpublished report for the Archaeology Division, Parks Canada, Atlantic Region. Halifax.

1986   Report of 1985 Excavations at the Point Riche and Phillip's Garden Sites, Port au Choix National Historic Park. Unpublished report for the Archaeological Division, Parks Canada, Atlantic Region. Halifax.

1985   Report of 1984 Excavations at the Point Riche and Phillip's Garden Sites, Port au Choix National Historic Park. Unpublished report for the Archaeology Division, Parks Canada, Atlantic Region. Halifax.

Renouf, M.A. P. and Maribeth S. Murray
1999   Two winter dwellings at Phillip's Garden. A Dorset site in northwestern Newfoundland. *Artic Anthropology* 36: 118-131.

Wintemberg, William, J.
1929   Preliminary Report of Fieldwork in 1927. *Annual Report to the National Museum of Canada for 1927*. National Museum of Canada Bulletin 56: 40-41. Ottawa.

1939   Eskimo Sites of the Dorset Culture in Newfoundland. *American Antiquity* 2: 83-103.

1940   Eskimo Sites of the Dorset Culture in Newfoundland: Part II. *American Antiquity* 4: 309-333.

Cape Ray Light site (CjBt-1)
Long: 59° 18'W
Lat: 47° 37'N
The site is situated on the southwestern corner of Newfoundland, two miles southwest of the community of Cape Ray along the coastline in front of the Cape Ray lighthouse. Initial investigation at the site was carried out by Helen Devereux in 1964; it produced a large Middle Dorset sample. Subsequent excavations were undertaken by Urve Linnamae (1975) in the summers of 1967 and 1968; she identified a series of features which she described as living and activity areas. Linnamaes' work at Cape Ray was highly significant as she provided the first definition of the Dorset culture in Newfoundland. In 1996 and 1997, Lisa Mae Fogt (1998) returned to the site to uncover the remains of a Middle Dorset dwelling, an external hearth and associated midden.

C14 dates:
2370 ± 85 (Gx-1199); 1810 ± 100 (Gak-1906); 1565 ± 95 (Gx-1198); 1360 ± 90 (Gak 1970). Dates taken from Linnamae 1975.

References:
Brown, Stuart
2001   The Cape Ray Site (CjBt-1) Site Assessment, August 1995. Unpublished report on file at Historic Resources Division, Department of Tourism, Culture and Recreation, Government of Newfoundland and Labrador. St. John's.

Devereux, Helen
1966   The Cape Ray Light Site. Unpublished report on file at the Archaeological Survey of Canada, Canadian Museum of Civilization. Ottawa.

Fogt, Lisa Mae
1998   The Excavation and Analysis of a Dorset Palaeoeskimo Dwelling at Cape Ray, Newfoundland. Unpublished M.A. thesis. Department of Anthropology, Memorial University of Newfoundland. St. John's.

Linnamae, Urve
1975   *The Dorset Culture. A Comparative Study in Newfoundland and the Arctic*. Technical Papers of the Newfoundland Museum No.1. Historic Resources Division, Department of Tourism, Culture and Recreation, Government of Newfoundland and Labrador. St. John's.

Anse à Henry
Long: 56° 10'N
Lat: 46° 48' W
The l'Anse à Henry site is located at the northern tip of the island of Saint-Pierre on the French Archipelago of Saint-Pierre and Miquelon. Rumors of prehistoric findings in the 1970s have been reported; the remains, however, appear to have left the archipelago. A formal archaeological reconnaissance conducted in 1979 by J. Chapelot (CNRS) did not produce any results. The first concrete evidence of an aboriginal presence was revealed in 1984 during the course of a geological investigation at the site; an exploratory trench yielded a few flakes and artifacts. Funded by the Conne River Micmac Band, the first systematic survey conducted in 1997 by Sylvie LeBlanc and Dr. J.A. Tuck revealed evidence of Maritime Archaic, Recent Indian, Groswater and Middle Dorset occupation at the site. Subsequently, a five year survey and excavation project (1999-2004) was launched. Survey and excavations yielded well over a thousand lithic artifacts and located two well-structured Recent Indian camp sites.

C14 dates:
Recent Indian camp site 2002: 1025 ± 50 BP (BGS 2404); 1175 ± 45 (BGS 2405); 1210 ± 45 (BGS 2401); 1230 ± 50

(BGS 2400); 1290 ± 45 (BGS 2402); 1300 ± 50 (BGS 2248); 1310 ± 45 (BGS 2403).

Recent Indian camp site 2003-2004: 370 ± 40 BP (BGS 2610); 370 ± 45 (BGS 2609); 380 ± 45 (BGS 2608); 510 ± 50 (BGS 2616); 520 ± 50 (BGS 2613); 530 ± 55 (BGS 2510); 540 ± 80 (BGS 2493); 540 ± 40 (BGS 2611); 1280 ± 70 (BGS 2615); 1410 ± 70 (BGS 2612). The next two dates were obtained in the same excavation area but without being associated with a fire-place; they could probably be associated with the Groswater culture as many Groswater artifacts were found within this same area; 2140 ± 65 (BGS 2614); 2575 ± 45 (BGS 2492). All dates taken from LeBlanc 2003 and 2005.

References:
LeBlanc, Sylvie
2005   Anse à Henry. Aire de fouille 2003-2004. Rapport Final. Rapport d'activités Mission d'archéologie 2004. Rapport déposé à la Direction de l'Architecture et du Patrimoine, Sous-Direction de l'Archéologie, Ministère de la Culture et de la Communication, Paris, 78p. ms.

2004   L'Anse à Henry Campagne 2003. Rapport Préliminaire. Rapport d'activités. Mission d'archéologie 2003. Rapport déposé à la Direction de l'Architecture et du Patrimoine, Sous-Direction de l'Archéologie, Ministère de la Culture et de la Communication, Paris, 59p. ms.

2003   Campement Indien Récent à l'Anse à Henry. Rapport d'activités. Mission d'archéologie 2002. Rapport déposé à la Direction de l'Architecture et du Patrimoine, Sous-Direction de l'Archéologie, Ministère de la Culture et de la Communication, Paris, 71p. ms.

2001   Cinq Mille Ans d'Occupation à l'Anse à Henry. Rapport d'étape. Phase 2. Mission de Reconnaissance. Rapport déposé à la Direction de l'Architecture et du Patrimoine, Sous-Direction de l'Archéologie, Ministère de la Culture et de la Communication, Paris, 27p. ms.

2000a   Cinq Mille Ans d'Occupation à l'Anse à Henry. Rapport d'étape. Phase 1. Mission de Reconnaissance. Rapport déposé à la Direction de l'Architecture et du Patrimoine, Sous-Direction de l'Archéologie, Ministère de la Culture et de la Communication, Paris, 33p. ms.

2000b   Middle Dorset (1900 to 1100 B.P.) Regional Variablity on the Island of Newfoundland and in Saint-Pierre et Miquelon, In *Identities and Cultural Contacts in the Arctic*, edited by M. Appelt, J. Berglund and H.C. Gullov, pp. 97-105. The Danish National Museum & Danish Polar Centre, Copenhagen.

1997a   Reconnaissance Archéologique des Îles de l'Archipel de Saint-Pierre et Miquelon. Rapport déposé à la Direction de l'Architecture et du Patrimoine, Sous-Direction de l'Archéologie, Ministère de la Culture et de la Communication, Paris, 22p. ms.

1997b   Report on an Initial Archaeological Reconnaissance of Oentjoi Gtjigan and Miquelem. Unpublished report submitted to Miawpukek Band, Conne River, Newfoundland.

Anse à Flamme (CjAx-1)
Long: 55° 53'W
Lat: 47° 37'N
The l'Anse à Flamme site is located at the eastern end of Long Island in Hermitage Bay. Excavation at the site was undertaken by Gerald Penney (1984) during the course of a three year archaeological reconnaissance (1979-1981) project on the Newfoundland southwest coast. The site yielded Maritime Archaic, Groswater, Middle Dorset and Recent Indian (Little Passage) lithic assemblages. The site was instrumental in defining the previously unrecognized Little Passage Complex of the Recent Indian culture.

C14 dates:
Maritime Archaic 3590 ± 110 BP (S-1976); unspecified Palaeoeskimo 2000 ± 105 BP (S-1975); Middle Dorset 1335 ± 115 BP (S-1977); Recent Indian 1130 ± 80 BP (I-11077). Uncalibrated dates. Dates taken from Penney 1984.

References:
Penney, Gerald
1984   The Prehistory of the Southwest Coast of Newfoundland. Unpublished M.A. thesis. Department of Anthropology, Memorial University of Newfoundland, St. John's.

1981   A Point Peninsula Rim Sherd from l'Anse à Flamme, Newfoundland. *Canadian Journal of Archaeology* 5: 171-173.

1980   A Preliminary Report on the Excavation of the l'Anse à Flamme site (CjAx-1). In Archaeology *in Newfoundland and Labrador, 1980*, edited by J. Sproul-Thomson and B. Ransom pp. 95-110. Historic Resources Division, Department of Tourism, Culture and Recreation, Government of Newfoundland and Labrador. St. John's.

Dildo Island (CjAj-2)
Long: 53° 35'W
Lat: 47° 33'N
Dildo Island is a small island located at the bottom of Trinity Bay, on the east coast of Newfoundland. The island is about 20 minutes by boat from the community of Dildo. Initial archaeological investigations by Don Locke (1970s), Ingeborg Marshall (1990) and William Gilbert in 1995 (1996) indicated an aboriginal occupation of the island by Recent Indian and Middle Dorset people. Further excavations also confirmed a Groswater Eskimo presence on the island. In the historic period the island was visited by Henry Crout in 1613 who reported seeing a Beothuk camp. Documentary evidence indicates the presence of an English civilian fort in the early 18th century. The island was also was utilized in the late 18th century by fishermen from Trinity on the north side of Trinity Bay. In the 1880s it was the site of the first cod hatchery in North America. Large scale archaeological survey and excavation begun in 1995 under the Baccalieu Trail Heritage Corporation are still ongoing. The excavation program focused on the recovery of Recent Indian camp sites and two Middle Dorset dwellings.

C14 dates:
Recent Indian: 720 to 960 AD (Beta 168485); 600 to 960 AD (Beta 168486); 790 to 1000 AD (Beta 195095); 710 to 910 AD

Middle Dorset Variability and Regional Cultural Traditions

(Beta 195096); 660 to 810 AD (Beta 195097). Calibrated dates. Recent Indian dates obtained from W. Gilbert, pers. comm. 2006.

Middle Dorset: **House 1:** 1230 ± 60 BP (Beta 116905) unpublished date; **House 2:** 1880 ± 40 BP (BGS 2235); 1850 ± 60 (BGS 2130); 1820 ± 45 (BGS 2132); 1720 ± 40 (BGS 2133); 1660 ± 90 (BGS 2127); 1660 ± 60 (Beta 116907); 1660 ± 40 (BGS 2131); 1660 ± 40 (BGS 2238); 1610 ± 45 (BGS 2146); 1540 ± 65 (BGS 2129); 1530 ± 70 (Beta 116908); 1525 ± 45 (BGS 2236); 1520 ± 40 (Beta 116910); 1410 ± 40 (BGS 2234); 1350 ± 40 (Beta 151064); 1320 ± 55 (BGS 2233); 1310 ± 50 (Beta 116909); 1300 ± 70 (Beta 116906). Corrected and calibrated dates. Dates taken from LeBlanc 2003.

Groswater: 2210 ± 90 BP (Beta 116904). Corrected and calibrated date. Unpublished date.

References:
Gilbert, William
2006   A Report on the Archaeological Excavations conducted at the Recent Indian Site on Dildo Island during 2004. Unpublished report on file at Historic Resources Division, Department of Tourism, Culture and Recreation, Government of Newfoundland and Labrador. St. John's.

2003   A Report on the Archaeological Excavations conducted at the Recent Indian Site on Dildo Island during 2001 and 2002. Unpublished report on file at Historic Resources Division, Department of Tourism, Culture and Recreation, Government of Newfoundland and Labrador. St. John's.

1996   Baccalieu Trail Archaeological Project, 1995, Phase Three: Dildo Island. Unpublished report on file at Historic Resources Division, Department of Tourism, Culture and Recreation, Government of Newfoundland and Labrador. St. John's.

LeBlanc, Sylvie
2003   A Middle Dorset Dwelling in Trinity Bay, Newfoundland. *Etudes/Inuit/ Studies* 27 (1-2): 493-513

2000   Middle Dorset (1900 to 1100 B.P.) Regional Variability on the Island of Newfoundland and in Saint-Pierre et Miquelon, In *Identities and Cultural Contacts in the Arctic*, edited by M. Appelt, J. Berglund and H.C. Gullov, pp. 97-105. The Danish National Museum & Danish Polar Centre, Copenhagen.

1998   Dildo Island 1998: Summary of Field Activities. Unpublished report in file at Historic Resources Division, Department of Tourism, Culture and Recreation, Government of Newfoundland and Labrador. St. John's.

1998   Dildo Island 1997 Field Season: Interim Report. Unpublished report on file at Historic Resources Division. Department of Tourism, Culture and Recreation, Government of Newfoundland and Labrador. St. John's.

1997   Dildo Island Archaeological Project. The Dorset Occupation of Dildo Island. Preliminary Field Report - 1996. Unpublished report on file at Historic Resources Division, Department of Tourism, Culture and Recreation, Government of Newfoundland and Labrador. St. John's.

Shamblers Cove (DgAj-01)
Long: 53°36'W
Lat: 49° 04'N
The Shamblers Cove site lies on the west side of Bonavista Bay between Cape Freels and Terra Nova Park. Excavation at the site was conducted by Dr. J.A. Tuck in 1982 as part of a salvage archaeological project (construction of the Shamblers Cove-Greenspond causeway). The archaeological material uncovered indicates an intense Middle Dorset occupation and evidence of sporadic occupations by Groswater Palaeoeskimo and Recent Indian (Beaches and Little Passage). European evidence from the 19th and 20th centuries is also reported. Three Areas (1, 5 and 7) produced most of the artifacts, which were by large of Middle Dorset origin. Hearth features and a tent ring were uncovered in these Areas. Areas 8, 9 and test pit 6 also yielded small Middle Dorset artifact samples. In all, the excavation at Shamblers Cove encompassed more than 130 square meters and produced over 500 artifacts.

C14 dates:
Middle Dorset: 1890 ± 100 B.P (Beta 5369); 3080 ± 140 B.P (Beta 5371); 2340 ± 60 B.P (Beta 5372); Recent Indian 720 ± 70 BP (Beta 5370). Dates taken from Tuck 1983.

References:
Auger, Reginald
1982   Salvage Excavation at Shamblers Cove, Bonavista Bay. Unpublished report prepared for Planning and Research Division, Department of Transportation. Report on file at Historic Resources Division, Government of Newfoundland. St. John's.

Tuck, J.A.
1983   Excavations at Shamblers Cove 1982: A Stage 3 Impact Report. Unpublished report on file at Historic Resources Division, Department of Tourism, Culture and Recreation, Government of Newfoundland and Labrador. St. John's.

Swan Island site (DiAs-10)
Long: 55° 02'W
Lat: 49° 27'N
Swan Island is located north-west of Long Island in Bay of Exploits, Eastern Notre-Dame Bay. The site lies on a gravel beach in Swan Island Harbour on the south side of the Island, approximately one meter above the high tide mark. The site was discovered in 1981 by Dr. Ralph Pastore during the course of the Beothuk Archaeology Project, an archaeological reconnaissance set to assess Beothuk presence in the Bay of Exploits. The survey yielded surface flake scatters and two Middle Dorset endblades, two bifaces, a microblade and 111 flakes were recovered from test units. Dr. Pastore returned in 1984; unfortunately, he did not produce any report on that second visit. Most of the Swan Island collection held at the Newfoundland museum was obtained from private collections by Don Locke. The artifact count for the site reaches well over

1200 artifacts, consisting mostly of Middle Dorset material and a handful of Little Passage artifacts.

C14: no dates

References:

Pastore, Ralph
1981   Swan Island Survey – 1981. Unpublished report on file at Historic Resources Division, Department of Tourism, Culture and Recreation, Government of Newfoundland and Labrador. St. John's.

1982   A Preliminary Report of a Survey of Eastern Notre Dame Bay. In Archaeology *in Newfoundland and Labrador, 1981, Annual Report No. 2,* edited by Jane Sproull Thomson and Callum Thomson, pp. 152-173. Historic Resources Division, Government of Newfoundland. St. John's.

Pittman Site (DkBe-1)
Long: 56°36'W
Lat: 49° 48'N
Located along the western shore of Sop's Arm at the bottom of White Bay, the Pittman site lies in a sheltered cove on the eastern shore at the northern tip of Sop's Island. The first archaeological findings at the Pittman site were made in 1873 by Lloyd. The site was later visited by Jenness and by A.H. Mallery. Systematic excavation was undertaken in 1967-1968 by Helen Devereux and carefully reported by Linnamae. The site yielded a large Middle Dorset component and a few diagnostic Maritime Archaic and Groswater artifacts.

C14 dates:
2780 ± 100 BP (GAK-1903); Middle Dorset 1340 ± 100 BP (Gak- 1904). Dates not calibrated. Dates taken from Linnmae 1975.

References

Devereux, Helen
1969   Five Archaeological Sites in Newfoundland - A Description. Unpublished report on file at Historic Resources Division, Government of Newfoundland. St. John's.

Jenness, Diamond
1929   *Notes on the Beothuk Indians of Newfoundland.* National Museum of Canada, Bulletin 56: 36-39

Linnamae, Urve
1975   *The Dorset Culture. A Comparative Study in Newfoundland and the Arctic.* Technical Papers of the Newfoundland Museum No.1. Historic Resources Division, Department of Tourism Government of Newfoundland and Labrador. St. John's.

Linnamae, Urve
1967   The Pittman Site - DkBe-1: A Report of Preliminary Archaeological Investigations carried out at Sops Island, White Bay, Newfoundland. Unpublished report on file at Historic Resources Division, Department of Tourism, Culture and Recreation, Government of Newfoundland and Labrador. St. John's.

Lloyd, T. G. B
1975   On the stone implements of Newfoundland. *Journal of the Royal Anthropological Institution.* Vol. 5: 233-248

Mallery, A.D.
1951   *Lost America.* The Overlook Company, Columbus, Ohio.

Wintemberg, W.J.
1939   Eskimo Sites of the Dorset Culture in Newfoundland. *American Antiquity* 2: 83-103.

APPENDIX 2 – RADIOCARBON DATES

Phillip's Garden	Cape Ray	Anse à Flamme	Dildo Island House 2	Shamblers Cove	Pittman
1970 ± 60					
1920 ± 110					
1900 ± 110					
1890 ± 90				*1890 ± 100	
			1880 ± 40		
1850 ± 100			1850 ± 60		
			1820 ± 45		
	*1810 ± 100				
1770 ± 120					
1736 ± 48					
			1720 ± 40		
1712 ± 40					
1683 ± 49					
			1660 ± 90		
			1660 ± 60		
			1660 ± 40		
			1660 ± 40		
1659 ± 48					
1640 ± 70					
1632 ± 47					
			1610 ± 45		
1602 ± 49					
1593 ± 49					
1580 ± 54					
1570 ± 70					
1565 ± 53	*1565 ± 90				
			1540 ± 65		
1538 ± 55					
			1530 ± 70		
			1525 ± 45		
1520 ± 90			1520 ± 40		
1509 ± 47					
1502 ± 49					
1480 ± 40					
1465 ± 51					
1410 ± 100			1410 ± 40		
1370 ± 90					
1360 ± 80	*1360 ± 90				
			1350 ± 40		*1340 ± 100
		*1335 ± 115			
1321 ± 49					
			1320 ± 55		
			1310 ± 50		
			1300 ± 70		
1250 ± 60					
Source: Renouf 2006	**Source:** Linnamae 1975	**Source:** Penney 1984	**Source:** LeBlanc 2003	**Source:** Tuck 1983	**Source:** Linnamae 1975

Dates are calibrated except those indicated with an asterisk. Dates are reported as in original source. Laboratory numbers are available in Appendix 1. No Middle Dorset C14 dates were obtained from the Swan Island and Anse à Henry sites.

APPENDIX 3 – THIN SECTION DESCRIPTIONS

This appendix provides the detailed petrographic information obtained from the thin sectioning of individual raw material sample. Petrographic description was carried out by Sherif A. Awadallah at the Department of Earth Sciences, Memorial University of Newfoundland. Thin section descriptions are provided by sites and by sample number. Description is strictly qualitative, based on visual attributes and microscopic data. Data establishing geological provenience includes the age and the name of the group and formation in which the material is found.

PORT AU CHOIX (8 samples)

PG-1: Cow Head chert

Visual: Grain size is aphanitic. Fracture is conchoidal showing rare linear fractures. Luster is glossy; translucency is opaque except along the edges. Structure is massive. Colour is brownish black (5YR 2/1) to olive black (5Y2/1).
Microscope: Angular fragments 1-2 mm in size. The sample is rich in sponge spicules and shows numerous circular patches of coarse microcrystalline quartz up to 0.1 mm in size. Some of the patches hint at a wall structure. Those are radiolarians or rather ghosts of radiolarians heavily recrystallized. The matrix is rich in clay. Round and cubic opaque minerals (pyrite) up to 0.05 mm in size are common.
Origin: Cambro-Ordovician Cow Head Group, western Newfoundland.

PG-2: Replacement chert from the Carbonate Sequence

Visual: Grain size is aphanitic. Fracture is conchoidal. Luster is glossy to dull; translucency is opaque. Structure is massive. Colour is greyish black (N2) to black (N1).
Microscope: Cryptocrystalline quartz groundmass; rare fractures filled with microcrystalline quartz. Dolomite rhombs 0.02 mm in size present up to 5%. Cross-polar light shows a strong orientational pattern where the long axis of the quartz crystals is aligned (J. Waldron, pers. comm. 2002).
Origin: Cambro-Ordovician carbonate-shelf sequence, western Newfoundland.

PG-3: Cow Head chert

Visual: The grain size is aphanitic. Fracture is conchoidal. Luster is glossy; translucency is opaque. Structure is well laminated. Most of the sample is dusky green (5G3/2) to dusky yellowish green (10GY 3/2). Some laminae are greenish black (5GY2/1).
Microscope: Fine and well defined laminae. Laminae are defined by colour variation; the variation is due to the percentage of clay in the matrix. Opaque mineral percentage is high in some parts of the sample; some are round and 0.05 mm in size. Pyrite is one of the mineral present; this is indicative of an anaerobic environment (I. Knight, pers. comm. 2001). Most of the thin section is composed of a cryptocrystalline groundmass showing some sponge spicules and oval particles, identified as ghost of radiolarians. 5% of radiolarians are made of microcrystalline to cryptocrystalline quartz; their oval shape results from being flattened. Some clay rich laminae are 1.5 mm thick; one side of these laminae is rich in crystalline quartz suggesting preferential accumulation on that side. Some layers show an increase in the amount of sponge spicules (0.5-0.01 mm in size) forming up to 30% in some part of the thin section. Sponge spicules are parallel to each other suggesting that they fell through the water column (I. Knight, pers. comm. 2001). Clusters of varicoloured thread - like- objects are present in one part of the sample. Carbonates are rare < 1%.
Origin: Cambro-Ordovician Cow Head Group, western Newfoundland.

PG-4: Replacement chert from the Carbonate Sequence

Visual: Grain size is aphanitic. Fracture is conchoidal. Luster is glossy; the thin portion of sample is translucent, the thicker portion is opaque and translucent solely along the edges. Structure is massive except for fractures. The outside rind of the sample has not recrystallized into quartz; this is a characteristic feature of nodular chert in limestone (J. Waldron, pers. comm. 2002). Colour is medium dark grey (N4) to olive grey (5Y4/1).
Microscope: Cryptocrystalline groundmass. Faint lamination. Groundmass is rich in carbonate 20-40%. Well-developed and common dolomite rhombs up to 0.03 mm in size.
Origin: Cambro-Ordovician carbonate-shelf-sequence, western Newfoundland.
Picture: Appendix 3 – Photo 1.

PG-5 Cow Head chert

Visual: Grain size is aphanitic. Fracture is conchoidal. Luster is glossy to dull. Translucency is opaque. Structure is strongly laminated. Laminae are less than 1mm thick, some are deformed. Colour is dark grey (N3) to black (N1). Rare thick laminae (1 to 2 mm) at the edges that are medium grey (N5) in colour.
Microscope: Microfossil rich sample. Common to abundant well preserved radiolarians (up to 0.25 mm in size) forming up to 10% of the thin section and sponge spicules (0.01-0.5 mm in size) in a groundmass made of micro-cryptocrystalline quartz rich in carbonate and dolomite rhombs (<0.01 mm in size). Carbonate and dolomite material may reach 5% in some parts. Some other macrofossil (brachiopod?) has been partly been replaced by chalcedony. Some irregular laminae (0.1 mm thick) are composed of microcrystalline quartz with common dolomite rhombs (up to 0.05 mm in size). Some of these laminae contain up to 30% dolomite rhombs.
Origin: Cambro-Ordovician Cow Head Group, western Newfoundland.

PG-6: Cow Head chert

Visual: Grain size is aphanitic. Fracture is conchoidal to irregular. Luster is glossy to dull; sample is mainly opaque but is translucent along the edges of the grey laminae only. Structure is well laminated; laminae are planar-wavy with sharp contacts. Colour is greyish black (N2) for most of the sample with laminae 1-4 mm thick (thick laminae are internally laminated) that are medium dark grey (N4).
Microscope: Well defined laminae alternating between microcrystalline and cryptocrystalline quartz. Laminae are more deformed and not as well defined as in sample PG-5. PG-6 is richer in clay than PG-5. Well preserved radiolarians and sponge spicules (10-20%). Spicules are mostly present in the clay-rich layers. Within the radiolarians, chalcedony particles 0.2-0.3 mm in size are present; some of them are spectacular. Carbonates are rare.
Origin: Cambro-Ordovician Cow Head Group, western Newfoundland.
Picture: Appendix 3 – Photo 2.

PG-7 Cow Head chert

Visual: Grain size is aphanitic. Fracture is conchoidal. Luster is

glossy to dull; sample is mainly opaque but is translucent along the edges of the grey laminae only. Structure is laminated with irregular to wavy laminae 1-2 mm thick; contacts between laminae are sharp. Colour varies within samples from dark grey (N3) to black (N1). Some samples are greenish black (5GY2/1) with black laminae (N1) and olive grey (5Y4/1) laminae. Some samples have thick black (N1) laminae (0.5 cm) with irregular laminae of medium grey (N5) to medium dark grey (N4). Some samples are fractured.
Microscope: Microcrystalline to cryptocrystalline groundmass rich in sponge spicules and well preserved radiolarians (~0.2mm in size), some of which maybe replaced by chalcedony. The laminae are defined by the proportion of microcrystalline quartz that varies from 10-15% up to 90%. Carbonate rhombs are rare, less than 5%, but are present in the microcrystalline layers. Some lenses of cryptocrystalline quartz.
Origin: Cambro-Ordovician Cow Head Group, western Newfoundland.

PG-8: Cow Head chert
Visual: Grain size is aphanitic. Fracture is conchoidal. Luster is glossy to dull; translucency is opaque. Structure is well laminated; laminae have wavy contacts. Most of the sample is greenish black (5GY2/1). The thin laminae < 1 mm are greyish black (N2). On the edge of the thin section there is a 1-2 mm dark greenish grey (5GY4/1) rim with sharp upper and lower contacts.
Microscope: Laminae are defined by the increase in the percentage of clay in the matrix. Alternating of hydrocarbon, organic rich clay layers and clean laminae. Laminae show ill-defined contacts. Most of the thin section is made of a groundmass of microcrystalline quartz with round to oval shaped particles (ghost of radiolarians) 0.2-0.3 mm in size forming 10-25% of the thin section. Some of these particles are replaced by chalcedony. Carbonate and dolomite rhombs are rare, less than 5%. Spicules are less common than in other samples.
Origin: Cambro-Ordovician Cow Head Group, western Newfoundland.
Picture: Appendix 3 – Photo 3.

CAPE RAY (7 samples)

RAY- 1: Cow Head chert
Visual: Grain size is aphanitic. Fracture is conchoidal. Luster is glossy to dull on the weathered surface. Translucency is mostly opaque but slightly translucent along the edges. Structure is mainly massive except for fractures and small cavities (pin-tip holes). Radiolarians are visible with hand lens. The colour of the inner/middle part of the sample is greyish olive green 5GY3/2. The outer rim varies from dusky yellow green 5GY5/2 to pale yellowish brown 10YR6/2 or yellow brown 5YR5/2.
Microscope: Groundmass of cryptocrystalline quartz with scattered microcrystalline grains forming up to 5-10% of the sample. Some of these coarser grains are concentrated in certain parts of the thin section in layers that have diffuse upper and lower contacts. Common radiolarians 0.1 -0.25 mm in size forming 10-20% of the sample. Foram test ~1%, 0.1 mm in size. The radiolarians are mostly visible in cross-polar. Some are filled with clay mineral rather than silica, others are surrounded by pyrite. Some sponge spicules. Rare carbonate rhombs 0.05-0.1 mm in size. Some elongated grains 0.25-0.01mm in size are replaced by quartz. Hexagonal particles 0.1 mm in size have a fibrous internal structure? The smaller and clearer hexagonal particles look like quartz prisms.
Origin: Cambro-Ordovician Cow Head Group, western Newfoundland.

RAY- 2: Cow Head chert
Visual: Grain size is aphanitic. Fracture is sub-conchoidal. Luster is dull; translucency is opaque. Structure shows fractures and layers > 1cm. Radiolarians are visible with hand lens. Colour is a pale yellowish brown 10YR6/2.
Microscope: Groundmass of cryptocrystalline quarts that may contain percentage of lime mud. Rare and scattered microcrystalline quartz grains (0.01-0.02 mm in size) forming a discontinuous layer. Well preserved radiolarians most common in fractures.
Origin: Cambro-Ordovician Cow Head Group, western Newfoundland.

RAY- 3: Cow Head chert
Visual: Grain size is aphanitic. Fracture is sub-conchoidal (round) to conchoidal. Luster is dull; translucency is opaque. Structure is massive except for fractures. The colour varies from a pale red 10R6/2 to pale yellowish brown 10YR6/2. Radiolarians are visible with hand lens.
Microscope: Cryptocrystalline matrix that appears muddy. Common fractures. Common carbonate grains (up to 10%) some have a rhomb shape but most are round and ~0.05 mm in size. Common well preserved radiolarians (0.1-0.2 mm in size) forming up to 30% of the sample. Scattered opaques (0.02-0.03 mm in size) some are cubic. Some of these opaques are confined to certain parts of the thin section.
Origin: Cambro-Ordovician Cow Head Group, western Newfoundland.
Picture: Appendix 3 – Photo 4.

RAY- 4: Cow Head chert
Visual: Grain size is aphanitic. Fracture is sub-conchoidal (round) to conchoidal. Luster is dull to slightly glossy; translucency is opaque. Structure is massive. Colour ranges from greyish brown 5YR3/2 to greyish red 5R4/2.
Microscope: Thick thin section. Structure is a massive reddish brown (hematite-rich) matrix showing parallel lamination. Well preserved radiolarians ~0.05 mm in size forming up to 10-15% of the sample. Some oval shaped grains (0.1-0.2 mm in size) composed of minute quartz grains. In parts of the thin section, there are concentrations of quartz grains (up to 80%) that show some kind of structure; these may be a fossil replacement. These concentrations look like parallel bedding.
Origin: Cambro-Ordovician Cow Head Group, western Newfoundland.

RAY- 5: Cow head Chert
Visual: Grain size is aphanitic. Fracture is conchoidal. Luster is glossy to dull; translucency is opaque. Structure is massive and shows rounded fractures (pin-tip holes). Colour of the inner/core part varies from dusky yellow green 5GY5/2 to greyish green 10GY5/2 with spots of greyish olive green 5GY3/2. The rim is mostly greyish orange pink 5YR7/2 to yellowish grey 5Y7/2.
Microscope: Cryptocrystalline-microcrystalline groundmass that may contain some carbonate. Common radiolarians 20-30% that are up to 0.5 mm in size. Common fractures filled with coarse quartz grains 0.05mm in size. Some fractures are filled with spectacular chalcedony. Sponge spicules are rare < 5%; they are visible under plane light. Under plane light there are particles that are up to 0.1 mm in size, they are light brown in colour but are dark or opaque under polarized light. These may be made of cryptocrystalline carbonate.

Origin: Cambro-Ordovician Cow Head Group, western Newfoundland.
Pictures: Appendix 3 – Photos 5 and 6.

RAY-6: Cow Head chert

Visual: Grain size is aphanitic. Fracture is conchoidal. Luster is glossy to dull; translucency is opaque. The structure shows abundant fractures and round grains but is otherwise massive. Radiolarians visible with hand lens in the beige part of the sample. The colour varies from greenish grey 5GY6/1 in the fresh cut inner/core part to a yellowish grey 5Y7/2 to light brownish grey 5Y6/1 on the outer/weathered surface.
Microscope: Groundmass of cryptocrystalline quartz and carbonate. < 5% microcrystalline quartz (<0.01 mm in size). Carbonate rhombs 0.05 mm in size are present in some parts of the thin section where they form up to 10%. Oval shaped particles 0.2-0.1 mm in size forming up to 5-10% and are composed of microcrystalline quartz. Few radiolarians, not so well preserved. Spicules (~5%) are 0.01 to 0.05 mm in size.
Origin: Cambro-Ordovician Cow Head Group, western Newfoundland.

RAY-7: Cow Head chert

Visual: Grain size is aphanitic. Fracture is conchoidal. Luster is glossy to dull and translucency is opaque. Structure is massive. Radiolarians visible with hand lens. Colour on fresh part is dark greenish grey 5GY4/1 but other part is olive grey 5Y4/1. Spots or mottles of brownish grey 5YR4/1 to greyish red 5R4/2; weathered surface is pale yellowish brown 10YR6/2 to light brown 5YR 6/4.
Microscope: Groundmass of cryptocrystalline - microcrystalline quartz. Groundmass is rich in carbonate (up to 50%). Rounded grains and carbonate rhombs 0.03 mm in size are common. Abundant well preserved radiolarians (40-50%) 0.2-0.5 mm in size. Radiolarians are more coarsely recrystallized compared to other samples. Rare carbonate angular fragment 0.1 mm in size which may be a fossil's fragment.
Origin: Cambro-Ordovician Cow Head Group, western Newfoundland.
Picture: Appendix 3 – Photo 7.

ANSE À FLAMME (6 samples)

AF-1a: Marystown Group specular hematite rhyolite

Visual: Grain size is aphanitic. Fracture is conchoidal. Luster is dull; translucency is opaque. Structure is laminated (<0.1mm thick); shows fractures, some of which are filled with metallic silvery mineral. Colour is light brownish grey 5YR6/1 to pale yellowish brown 10YR6/2; some parts are dusky brown 5YR2/2 to black N1 probably along fractures.
Microscope: Matrix of microcrystalline quartz with patches or diffuse layers of cryptocrystalline quartz. Angular quartz grains 0.05-0.1 mm in size form about 5% of the sample. Common fractures filled with polycrystalline quartz 0.01-0.1 mm. The metallic silvery mineral is identified as specular hematite, a recrystalized red earthy hematite, also known as Alaska Diamond.
Origin: Upper Precambrian Marystown Group on the Burin Peninsula (S. O'Brien, pers. comm. 2001). Saint-Pierre equivalent: Trépied Formation on Grand Colombier Island (Aubert De La Rue 1951: 53; J-L. Rabottin, pers. comm. 1999).

AF-1b: Marystown Group specular hematite rhyolite

Visual: Grain size is aphanitic. Fracture is conchoidal to sub-conchoidal. Luster is dull; translucency is opaque. Structure is internally laminated 0.1-0.2 mm. Some metallic silvery minerals found in spots and along fractures and in some layers. Colour is yellowish grey 5Y7/2 to greyish orange 10YR7/2; black (N1) metallic mottles along fractures and in some layers.
Microscope: Graded layers each 0.5 - 4mm thick. Contacts of the layers vary from sharp to irregular and diffuse. Within each layers, the change from the coarse (lower) to the fine (upper) part of the layer is more or less abrupt. The thinner layers are almost half coarse and half fine while the thicker layers have a thicker coarse part (4/5) compared to the thinner part (1/5). Some layers are only defined by the increase in the percentage of the coarse angular grains (0.1 mm). Some fractures are filled with dark minerals (specular hematite). Those minerals are also found along some of the layers. Some layers are made of cryptocrystalline quartz with sharp upper and lower contacts. Faults and fractures cut the laminae. Some of these cracks are filled by coarser quartz. Accessory minerals are rare. Under plane light, irregular angular particles 0.1 mm in size are seen. These are isotropic. Opaques are common forming 10-30% of the thin section; they are ~0.03mm in size some them of are cubic.
Origin: Same than AF-1a.

AF-2: Cow Head chert

Visual: Grain size is aphanitic. Fracture is conchoidal. Luster is glossy; translucency is opaque. Structure is massive except for fractures and pin-tip holes. Colour of the inner/core is greyish olive green 5GY3/2 with brownish grey 5YR4/1 mottles or spots. Colour of the outer/rim is pinkish grey 5YR8/1 to yellowish grey.
Microscope: Microcrystalline / cryptocrystalline groundmass that may have some clay material or carbonate. The sample has diffuse laminae defined by the increase in the percentage of the microcrystalline quartz. Common radiolarians 0.2-0.5 mm in size forming 20-30% of the sample. Rare forams (only 1 or 2 tests). Rare to common sponge spicules <0.01-0.2 mm in size. Under plane light, there are elongated ~2 mm long, less than 0.2 mm wide light brown particles; some of these are lying parallel to the layering observed in the thin section. These particles are dark under cross-polar and may be conodonts?
Origin: Cambro-ordovician Cow Head Group, western Newfoundland.
Picture: Appendix 3 – Photo 8.

AF-3: Marystown Group Tuff

Visual: Grain size is aphanitic. Fracture is conchoidal. Luster is dull to glossy; translucency is opaque. Structure is massive, except for minor fractures. Colour varies from light olive grey 5Y6/1 to brownish grey 5YR4/1 to olive grey 5Y4/1.
Microscope: Microcrystalline to cryptocrystalline groundmass. Faint to diffuse laminae defined by the increase in the percentage of the microcrystalline quartz. Fractures filled with coarse quartz. Opaque minerals (~0.03 mm in size) form about 10% of the sample; some of them are cubic. Under plane light, these are the elongated or wedge shaped particles that are light brown in colour but dark under cross-polar.
Origin: Upper Precambrian Marystown Group on the Burin Peninsula (S. O'Brien, pers. comm. 2001).

AF-4a: Marystown Group Hare Hills Formation rhyolite (Felsic volcanic)

Visual: Grain size is aphanitic. Fracture is irregular to sub-conchoidal. Luster is dull; translucency is opaque. Structure is massive with fractures. Colour on the fresh cut surface is moderate red 5R4/6 to dusky red 5R3/4. Colour of the outer rim is pale red 10R6/2 to medium pink 4R7/2.

Microscope: Microcrystalline to cryptocrystalline groundmass of quartz. Structure is massive with fractures. Fractures are filled or stained by deep red very fine minerals (epidote manganese: piedmontite). Some fractures are filled by microcrystalline quartz that are angular and 0.05 mm in size.
Origin: Upper Precambrian Marystown Group, Hare Hills Tuff Formation on the Burin Peninsula (O'Brien, Strong and Evans 1977: 3) and equivalent Cap Rouge Formation on the island of Saint-Pierre (Rabu and Chauvel 1983: 49).

AF-4b: Marystown Group Hare Hills Formation rhyolite (Felsic volcanic)

Visual: Grain size is aphanitic. Fracture is sub-conchoidal. Luster is dull; translucency is opaque. Structure is massive except for fractures. Colour of the fresh cut surface when wet is dusky red 5R3/4 to very dark red 5R2/6. Colour of the outer rim part is pale red 10R6/2.
Microscope: Microcrystalline groundmass of quartz <0.01mm in size. The sample is laminated; layering is defined by the increase in the percentage of the finer (matrix) material. These finer/matrix rich intervals are fractures filled with angular elongated quartz that are 0.1-03 mm in size. Piedmontite is visible in fractures. Under plane light, there is an abundance of elongated particles 0.05-0.01 mm in size; opaques are showing under cross-polar light. Opaques count for 5-10% of the sample and are 0.03 mm in size; some of them are cubic.
Origin: Same as AF-4a.

ANSE À HENRY - SAINT-PIERRE (4 samples)

A-H-1: Trépied Formation rhyolite (Grand Colombier Island)

Visual: Sample is aphanitic with common black spots or grains. The sample is internally fractured. Fracture is irregular. Luster is glossy to dull; translucency is opaque. Structure is laminated but mostly massive. Most of the sample is light brownish grey 5YR6/1 to light olive grey 5Y6/1. The laminae are darker, brownish grey 5YR4/1. These laminae have sharp upper and lower contacts; they are 1-4 mm thick and are internally laminated.
Microscope: Laminated. Laminae are defined by the percentage of microcrystalline quartz. The laminae vary in thickness from 2-3 mm to less than 0.2 mm. Contacts are sharp to faint. Some laminae have an irregular to lens shape. The percentage of quartz crystals may increase or decrease from one side of the laminae to the other (grading impression). Fractures are rare. Some fractures are filled with microcrystalline angular quartz that are up to 0.1 mm in size.
Origin: Upper Precambrian Formation du Trépied on Grand Colombier Island. Newfoundland equivalent: Marystown Group.

AH-2: Cap Rouge Formation rhyolite

Visual: Grain size is aphanitic. Fracture is irregular to conchoidal. Luster is dull; translucency is opaque. Structure is massive but shows some fractures. Colour on wet and fresh cut surface: moderate red 5R 5/4 to dusky red 5R 3/4. Colour on weathered and dry surface is pale red 5R 6/2 to 10 R 6/2.
Microscope: Microcrystalline quartz, angular and 0.05-0.1 mm in size. Rare angular feldspar grains (up to 0.5 mm in size). Some fractures filled with angular coarse quartz ~ 0.5 mm. Rare mica flakes (0.5 mm in size).
Origin: Upper Precambrian Cap Rouge Formation in Saint-Pierre. Newfoundland equivalent: Hare Hills Tuffs Formation, Marystown Group.
Picture: Appendix 3 – Photo 9.

AH-3: Cap Rouge Formation rhyolite

Visual: Grain size is aphanitic. Fracture is irregular. Luster is dull; translucency is opaque. Internal structure is massive except for rare fractures. Colour on a fresh and wet surface is dusky red 5R 3/4 to very dusky red 10R 2/2; dry and fresh surface is blackish red 5R 2/2; weathered and dry surface is greyish orange pink 10R 8/2 to pale red 10R 6/2.
Microscope: Microcrystalline quartz groundmass, with 50% of scattered angular-subangular quartz grains (~0.1 mm in size). Some parts of the thin section appear laminated with a decrease in the percentage of the coarse grains 30-40%. Less than 5% angular opaques (0.05-0.1 mm in size).
Origin: Same as AH-2.

AH-4: Cap Rouge Formation rhyolite

Visual: Grain size is aphanitic. Fracture is conchoidal to irregular. Luster is dull; translucency is opaque. Internal structure is massive except for fractures filled with quartz grains 0.1-0.3 mm in size. Colour on wet and fresh surface is dusky red 5R 3/4; on weathered and dry greyish red 5R 4/2.
Microscope: Matrix of microcrystalline quartz with up to 70% of scattered angular grains of quartz. Many of the grains are 0.05-0.2 mm in size, some of them are aligned in one direction. Some fractures are up to 2 mm wide and filled with angular quartz 0.1-0.2 mm in size.
Origin: Same as AH-2 and 3.

DILDO ISLAND (12 samples)

DIL-01: Conception Group chert

Visual: Grain size is aphanitic. Fracture is irregular but conchoidal. Luster is dull; translucency is opaque. Structure is massive with some fractures along which weathering (colour change) is more pronounced. Colour on wet and fresh cut surface is dark greenish grey 5GY 4/1; along fractures greenish grey 5GY 6/1. Colour on weathered and dry portion is yellowish grey 5Y 8/1 with areas of pale yellowish brown 10YR 6/2 to pale brown 5YR 5/2.
Microscope: Microcrystalline groundmass (< 0.01 mm). Layering (?) may be due to the increase in the fine-grained/muddy material. Fractures filled with angular chert fragments and coarser (up to 0.07 mm), angular quartz grains. Most of the fractures are irregular.
Origin: Late Proterozoic. Conception Group (King 1990).

DIL-02: Conception Group chert

Visual: Grain size is aphanitic to very fine-grained. Fracture is irregular but conchoidal. Luster is dull; translucency is opaque. Structure is massive and layered; some layers may be 1-2mm thick. Colour on wet and fresh cut is greyish olive green 5GY 3/2 to dusky yellowish green 10GY 3/2. Colour on weathered and dry surface is very pale orange 10YR 8/1, some parts are medium brown 5YR 3/2 to greyish brown 5YR 3/2.
Microscope: Microcrystalline quartz groundmass, massive. Angular grains (0.02-0.04 mm in size) forming 40-60% of the sample. Some elongated needle-like grains 0.05 - 0.01 mm in size. Presence of 1-2% angular opaque minerals 0.01 - 0.02 mm in size.
Origin: Late Proterozoic. Conception Group (King 1990).

DIL–03: Conception Group chert

Visual: Grain size is aphanitic-very fine grained. Some scattered grains or fragments (0.1-0.3 mm in size). Fracture is irregular but conchoidal. Luster is dull; translucency is opaque. Structure parts are layered (0.1-0.3mm thick). Other parts show

no layering but fragments/grains of various sizes between 0.1-0.3 mm. Colour on wet and fresh cut varies from greyish olive green 5GY 3/2 to greyish green 10GY 5/2; some parts are dusky yellowish green 10GY 3/2. Colour on weathered and dry surface is greyish yellow 5Y 8/4 to pale yellowish grey 5Y 7/2 and greyish orange 10YR 7/4.
Microscope: Matrix of microcrystalline quarts with scattered angular grains of quartz up to 0.5 mm in size but mostly 0.2-0.3 mm forming 5-10% of the sample. Some fractures are filled with angular quartz, feldspar (some of which may have been altered into clay minerals). Rare mica flakes up to 1mm long varying in size. Under plane light, the sample consists of 20-30% grains of chert that are 0.5-1mm in size.
Origin: Late Proterozoic. Conception Group (King 1990).

DIL-4: Conception Group chert
Visual: Grain size is aphanitic to very fine grained. Fracture is conchoidal. Luster is dull; translucency is opaque. Structure is massive. Colour on wet and fresh cut is greyish olive green 5 GY 3/2. Colour on weathered and dry surface dark greenish grey 5GY 4/1 to dusky yellow green 5GY 5/2.
Microscope: Massive, matrix of microcrystalline (< 0.01mm) quartz. Fractures are rare if not absent. Angular quartz grains of 0.01 mm in size form 10-20% of the sample.
Origin: Late Proterozoic. Conception Group (King 1990).
Picture: Appendix 3 – Photo 10.

DIL-05: Conception Group chert
Visual: Grain size is aphanitic. Fracture is conchoidal. Luster is dull; translucency is opaque. Structure shows some faint layering without real visible change in grain size. Dark areas are surrounded by lighter coloured rims (more weathering). Colour on wet and fresh cut is dark yellow green 5GY 5/2 to greyish olive green 5GY 3/2; fractures are greyish yellow green 10GY 5/2; dark spots are dusky green 5GY 3/2. Colour on weathered and dry surface is dusky yellow green 5GY 5/2 to greyish green 10GY 5/2 with 1-2 mm areas (spots) of greyish red 10R 4/2.
Microscope: Microcrystalline groundmass with common fractures, which are either straight or irregular. Fractures are filled with angular quartz 0.01-0.02mm in size.
Origin: Late Proterozoic. Conception Group (King 1990).

DIL-06: Conception Group chert
Visual: Grain size is aphanitic. Fracture is conchoidal. Luster is dull; translucency is opaque. Structure is massive except for internal lines that may be weathering along fractures. Colour on wet and fresh cut is greyish green 10GY 5/2 to greyish olive green 5GY. Colour on weathered and dry is greyish orange 10YR 7/4 to pale yellowish brown 10YR 6/2; some areas are greyish brown 5YR 3.
Microscope: Groundmass of microcrystalline quartz with rare fractures.
Origin: Late Proterozoic. Conception Group (King 1990).

DIL-07: Conception Group chert
Visual: Grain size is aphanitic. Fracture is irregular but conchoidal. Luster: dull; translucency is opaque. Structure is massive except for small black spots. Colour on wet and fresh cut is dusky yellowish green 5GY 5/2 to greyish olive green 5GY 3/2. Colour on weathered and dry surface is greyish orange 10YR 7/4 to pale yellowish brown 10YR 6/2; some areas are greyish yellow green 5GY 7/2.
Microscope: Massive, microcrystalline groundmass. Rare to common needle-like objects (0.25 -0.05 mm in size).
Origin: Late Proterozoic. Conception Group (King 1990).

DIL-08: Conception Group chert
Visual: Grain size is aphanitic. Fracture is irregular but conchoidal. Luster is dull; translucency is opaque. Structure is massive, except for some rare fractures. Colour on wet and fresh cut is dusky yellow green 5GY 5/2 to greyish olive green 5GY 3/2. Colour on weathered and dry surface is greyish green 10GY 5/2 to yellowish grey 5Y 7/2 to pale olive 10Y 6/2; scattered spots (0.1- 0.2 mm) of pale yellowish brown 10YR 6/2.
Microscope: Microcrystalline quartz groundmass of quartz with some spots (~0.5 mm) brighter in colour, more angular and maybe coarser. Some fractures are filled with angular grains 0.05-0.15mm in size.
Origin: Late Proterozoic. Conception Group (King 1990).

DIL-09: Conception Group chert
Visual: Grain size is aphanitic but some layers appear medium grained. Fracture is irregular but conchoidal. Luster is dull; translucency is opaque. Structure is layered with layers 1-3 cm thick; layering is defined by variation in colour or grain size. Colour on wet and fresh cut is greyish olive green 5GY 3/2 to dark greenish grey 5GY 4/1; colour on weathered and dry surface is greenish grey 5GY 6/1 to greyish yellow green 5GY 7/2; scattered areas are light olive grey 5Y 6/1; 2 or 3 spots of dark yellowish brown 10YR 4/2 to light olive grey 5Y 5/2.
Microscope: Microcrystalline groundmass of quartz showing 5-10% of angular grains 0.02-0.06 mm in size. Common needle-like grains (spicules?) 0.01-0.05 mm in size.
Origin: Late Proterozoic. Conception Group (King 1990).

DIL-10: Conception Group chert
Visual: Grain size is aphanitic. Fracture is conchoidal. Luster is dull; translucency is opaque. Structure is massive. Colour on wet and fresh cut is greyish olive green 5GY 3/2; colour on weathered and dry surface is greenish grey 5GY 6/1 to greyish green 10GY 5/2; some weathered parts are pale orange 10YR 8/2.
Microscope: Microcrystalline (<0.01mm) groundmass. Fractures are irregular and filled with angular 0.01-0.03 mm quartz grains. Some larger fractures are filled with angular to round grains of chert made of cryptocrystalline material. Fractures are 1-2 mm long and 0.1 mm wide.
Origin: Late Proterozoic. Conception Group (King 1990).

DIL-11: Conception Group chert
Visual: Grain size is aphanitic. Fracture is irregular but conchoidal. Luster is dull; translucency is opaque. Structure is massive, rare fractures where weathering is more intense (colour change). Colour on wet and fresh cut is greyish olive green 5GY 3/2. Colour on weathered and dry surface is very pale orange 10YR 8/2 to greyish orange pink 5 YR 7/2; some areas are pale brown 5YR 5/2 to dark yellowish brown 10YR 4/2.
Microscope: Massive microcrystalline-cryptocrystalline groundmass. Fractures filled with angular quartz grains 0.05-0.1 mm in size. Some spicules (?) seen in plane light.
Origin: Late Proterozoic. Conception Group (King 1990).
Picture: Appendix 3 – Photo 11.

DIL-12: Conception Group chert
Visual: Grain size is aphanitic. Fracture is irregular but conchoidal. Luster is dull; translucency is opaque. Structure is massive, except for minor fractures. Colour on wet and fresh cut is greyish olive green 5GY 3/2 to dusky yellowish green 10GY 3/2. Colour on weathered and dry surface is very pale orange 10YR 8/2 to light brown 5YR 6/4.
Microscope: Microcrystalline groundmass. Rare irregular

fractures filled with angular quartz grains 0.01 0.05 mm in size. Sample shows 10-20% of opaques (organics?) that are 0.01-0.03 mm in size.
Origin: Late Proterozoic. Conception Group (King 1990).

SHAMBLERS COVE (6 samples from the Beaches site)

SH-1: Bull Arm Formation rhyolite (rhyolithic ash-flow)
Visual: Grain size is aphanitic. Fracture is irregular but conchoidal. Luster is dull, translucency is opaque. Structure is massive showing crude lamination and fractures. Colour: Dark grey N3; weathered or fractured part medium grey N4.
Microscope: Cryptocrystalline groundmass. Opaques reach up to 30% of the sample, some are cubic, subangular to subrounded (~0.1 mm in size). Some of these opaques appear parallel to each other or bedded. Microcrystalline quartz angular grains constitute 10-20% of the sample, they are ~0.1 mm in size. Rare angular carbonate grains 0.5-1.5 mm in size. Minerals include sericite and riebecktite.
Origin: Upper Precambrian Musgravetown Group, Bull Arm Formation (O'Brien and Knight 1988).

SH-2: Bull Arm Formation rhyolite (rhyolithic ash-flow)
Visual: Grain size is aphanitic. Fracture is irregular and subconchoidal. Luster is dull to slightly glossy; translucency is opaque. Structure is massive to faintly laminated. Outer surface of the sample is weathered. Colour is brownish grey 5YR4/1 and blackish red 5R2/2 along fractures.
Microscope: Cryptocrystalline groundmass with scattered angular quartz grains that form up to 20%. These angular grains are 0.25-0.5 mm in size. In some parts of the thin section, the percentage of these angular grains increases. Rare fractures filled with quartz. Opaques up to 5% some are angular and cubic ~0.05 mm in size. Some angular grains 0.02-0.1 mm in size. Minerals include sericite and riebecktite.
Origin: Upper Precambrian Musgravetown Group, Bull Arm Formation (O'Brien and Knight 1988).

SH-3: Bull Arm Formation rhyolite (rhyolithic ash-flow)
Visual: Grain size is aphanitic to granular. Fracture is irregular and subconchoidal. Luster is dull; translucency is opaque. Structure is massive. Outer surface of the sample is weathered. Colour varies from light bluish grey 5B7/1 to medium light grey N6. Wet fresh part is medium dark grey N4.
Microscope: Microcrystalline groundmass with scattered angular grains forming up to 30% of the sample. These grains are angular to subangular (~0.1 mm in size). Common in some parts of the thin section are angular yellow grains (0.05-0.2 mm in size) that have an oval shape. Common grey angular grains 10-20% (0.04 - 0.05 mm in size) are dark under cross-polar. These could be some sort of fossils (?). Opaques form ~5%, some are angular and ~0.05 mm in size. Minerals include sericite and riebecktite.
Origin: Upper Precambrian Musgravetown Group, Bull Arm Formation (O'Brien and Knight 1988).
Picture: Appendix 3 – Photo 12.

SH-4: Bull Arm rhyolite Formation (rhyolithic ash-flow)
Visual: Grain size is slightly granular (silt size). Fracture is irregular but conchoidal. Luster is dull; translucency is opaque. Structure is massive to faintly laminated and fractured (rare). Outer surface of the sample is weathered. Colour is greenish grey 5GY6/1 to light olive grey 5Y6/1. Wet fresh cut surface is dusky yellowish green 10GY3/2.
Microscope: Microcrystalline to cryptocrystalline groundmass with common (10-20%) angular quartz grains that are 0.1 mm in size. Faint layering or laminae in some parts of the thin section; the laminae are defined by the increase in the percentage of the matrix or clay. Rare carbonate material replaced by quartz. Rare accessory minerals. Opaques form up to 5% of the sample, some are angular and ~0.05 mm in size. Scattered grey angular grains form up to 20% of the sample. These are 0.04-0.1 mm in size and are dark under cross-polar light. Minerals include riebecktite.
Origin: Upper Precambrian Musgravetown Group, Bull Arm Formation (O'Brien and Knight 1988).

SH-5: Bull Arm Formation rhyolite (rhyolithic ash-flow)
Visual: Grain size is slightly granular (silt size). Fracture is irregular but conchoidal. Luster is dull; translucency is opaque. Structure is massive with faint lamination and fractures. Outer surface of the sample is weathered. Colour is pale green 10G6/2 to light bluish grey 5B7/1. Fresh wet cut surface is dusky yellowish green 5GY5/2.
Microscope: Microcrystalline groundmass with 20-30% angular quartz that are 0.1-0.2 mm in size. Presence of elongated objects, up to 1cm in length, made of very fine indistinguishable particles. Some of these particles are internally laminated with an alignment of coarser scattered grains. Grey angular grains (up to 20%) some of which are up to 1 mm in size and are being replaced by quartz. Minerals include sericite and riebecktite.
Origin: Upper Precambrian Musgravetown Group, Bull Arm Formation (O'Brien and Knight 1988).

SH-6: Bull Arm Formation rhyolite (rhyolithic ash-flow)
Visual: Grain size is aphanitic. Fracture is irregular but conchoidal. Luster is dull; translucency is opaque. Structure is massive except faint laminations and fractures. Outer surface weathered. Colour is greenish grey 10GY5/2 to greyish yellow green 5GY7/2 (weathers). Fresh wet cut surface is dark grey N3 to black N1.
Microscope: Microcrystalline to cryptocrystalline groundmass with 10-20% angular quartz grains that are 0.05-0.1 mm in size. Less than 5% opaques; some of the opaques are restricted within fractures, some are cubic and ~0.05 mm in size. Up to 20% of grey angular grains some of which are up to 0.05 -0.02 mm in size; the latter are dark under cross-polar light. Minerals include riebecktite.
Origin: Upper Precambrian Musgravetown Group, Bull Arm Formation (O'Brien and Knight 1988).

SWAN ISLAND (8 samples)

SW-1: Conception Group chert
Visual: Grain size is aphanitic. Fracture is irregular to conchoidal. Luster is dull to glossy; translucency is opaque. Fracture is massive to faintly laminated; joints or fissures are linear < 0.3 mm. Core/fresh cut surface is greyish olive green (5GY 3/2) while the weathered surface is yellowish grey (5Y 8/1).
Microscope: Structure is massive to faintly laminated. Some of the laminae are defined by the increase in the concentration of coarse grains. Most of the thin section is made up of groundmass of crystalline quartz. Most of the grains are < 0.01 mm. Coarse angular grains (0.1 mm) are present throughout the thin section forming about 10% of the thin section. Opaque grains are small (~0.01 mm), angular and form up to 10%. Some of the opaques are concentrated or clustered into round particles about 1 mm in size.
Origin: Late Proterozoic. Conception Group (King 1990).This sample is identical to sample Dil-2 and shares its origin.

SW-2: Caradocian chert

Visual: Grain size is aphanitic to granular. Fracture is curved. Luster is dull to glossy; translucency is opaque. Structure is highly fractured. Colour is dusky yellowish green (5GY 5/2) to greyish olive green (5GY 3/2). Weathered surface is very pale orange (10YR 8/2).

Microscope: 80 % of the thin section consists of groundmass of yellowish brown microcrystalline to cryptocrystalline grains. The colouration may be due to clay minerals that are present in the groundmass. Set in this groundmass are rounded clusters or halo (0.5 -1mm in size) of microcrystalline quartz (0.01 mm - bigger than the groundmass) showing a core of one or two needle-like isotropic particles (spicules).This rounded halo of microcrystalline may result from the alteration or recrystalization of spicule opaline silica. 20% of the thin section consists of cryptocrystalline quartz that is massive with no rounded patches. The only structure in this part consists of fractures filled with microcrystalline quartz.

Origin: Mid-Ordovician. Bay of Exploits, Caradocian cherts (Dean 1978).

SW-3: Caradocian chert

Visual: Grain size is aphanitic to granular. Fracture is curved to conchoidal. Luster is dull to glossy; translucency is opaque. Structure is massive except for minor fractures (< 0.1 mm). Colour varies from dusky yellowish green (5GY 5/2) to greyish green (10GY 5/2).

Microscope: Very well crystallized quartz. Most of the thin section consists of angular interlocking grains of quartz that are 0.05 mm in size. Larger angular quartz grains (0.1 mm) are also present and form ~20% of the sample. This rock is almost 100% spicules (0.03-0.2 mm); it might also include spiky elements (broken ornaments) from radiolarians. The spicules are mostly isotropic but some have been converted into quartz.

Origin: Mid-Ordovician. Bay of Exploits, Caradocian cherts (Dean 1978).

SW- 4: Conception Group chert

Visual: Grain size is aphanitic. Fracture is curved to conchoidal. Luster is dull to glossy; translucency is opaque. Structure is massive; rare fractures filled with opaque material. Colour ranges from dusky yellowish green (5GY 5/2) to greyish olive green (5GY 3/2).

Microscope: Groundmass of microcrystalline to crypotocrystalline quartz. Less than 10% sub-angular quartz grains (~ 0.0 5mm in size). Opaques form up to 10% they are ~0.05mm in size. Some of them are angular.

Origin: Late Proterozoic. Conception Group (King 1990).This sample is identical to sample Dil-4 and shares its origin.

SW-5: Caradocian chert

Visual: Grain size is aphanitic to granular. Fracture is curved to conchoidal. Luster is dull to glossy; translucency is opaque. Structure is massive; common fractures filled with white material (no carbonate) some small cavities are also present. Colour ranges from dusky yellowish green (5GY 5/2) to greyish olive green (5GY 3/2).

Microscope: Microcrystalline quartz, angular, interlocking (< 0.1 mm in size) forming 80-100% of the sample. One elongated fracture is filled with polycrystalline quartz that increase in size from ~0.01mm at the margins to ~0.1 mm in the middle of the fracture. Opaques are up to 5%; they are < 0.1mm in size and sub-angular. Like SW-3, this sample is almost 100% spicules, most of which are isotropic although some have been recrystalized and cemented by quartz. These are possibly some kind of a fossil replacement. Under polarized light, the particles appear as parallel lines or as a slightly radial pattern.

Origin: Mid-Ordovician. Bay of Exploits, Caradocian cherts (Dean 1978).

SW-6: Caradocian chert

Visual: Grain size is aphanitic to granular. Fracture is curved to conchoidal. Luster is dull to glossy; translucency is opaque. Colour fresh surface is dusky yellowish green (5GY) while the weathered surface is yellowish grey (5Y 8/1).

Microscope: Structure is faintly laminated. Laminae are defined by the slight variation in grain size. Most of the thin section is made of crystalline quartz that is angular and 0.1 mm in size. As for samples SW-3 and SW-5, this sample is almost 100% spicules. The latter are only visible in plane light. Some are 0.01-0.2 mm and are isotropic. Calcite (up to 0.3-1 mm) constitutes fracture fill. Pyrite cubic particles are < 5%. Accessory minerals are < 1%.

Origin: Mid-Ordovician. Bay of Exploits, Caradocian cherts (Dean 1978).

SW-7: Caradocian chert

Visual: Grain size is aphanitic to granular. Fracture is curved to conchoidal. Luster is dull to glossy; translucency is opaque. Structure is massive; small cavities are filled by black particles. Colour is dusky yellowish green (5GY 5/2) to greyish olive green (5GY 3/2).

Microscope: Groundmass of microcrystalline to cryptocrystalline quartz. Scattered clusters of coarse crystalline quartz 0.01-0.02 mm in size; these clusters form up to 20% of the grains in some parts of the thin section. In plane light, the clusters show up as a combination of numerous radiolarians and thin elongated grains, which could be sponge spicules or broken ornament from radiolarians.

Origin: Mid-Ordovician. Bay of Exploits, Caradocian cherts (Dean 1978).

Picture: Appendix 3 Photo 13.

SW-8: Caradocian chert

Visual: Grain size is aphanitic to granular. Fracture is curved to conchoidal. Luster is glossy; translucency is opaque. The structure is massive; linear joints (<0.01 mm) cut across the sample. Colour is dusky yellowish green (5GY 5/2) to greyish olive green (5GY 3/2).

Microscope: Groundmass of microcrystalline quartz grains (< 0.01 mm in size). No lamination or structure. Massive. 5-10% of larger quartz angular grains (0.1mm in size). No clear spheres or radiolarians observed but vague tiny small elongated grains (0.01-0.1 mm) which could be scattered sponge spicules or broken ornaments from radiolarians. Opaques are < 5%; they are ~0.01 mm in size and sub-angular to sub-rounded.

Origin: Mid-Ordovician. Bay of Exploits, Caradocian cherts (Dean 1978).

PITTMAN SAMPLES (7 samples)

PIT-1: Cow Head chert

Visual: The grain size is aphanitic. Fracture is conchoidal. Luster is glossy; translucency is opaque. Structure is massive except for some fractures. Colour is black (N1) to greyish black (N2).

Microscope: Structure is laminated; laminae between 1.5 to 2.5 mm thick. Layers appear graded.
Layers are composed of microcrystalline quartz. The percentage of carbonate ranges from 20 to 30% in the darker finer grain layers. Some layers are rich in coarse (0.05-0.1 mm) angular quartz grains; they contain 10-20% of carbonate grains, some of which are 0.1-0.1 mm in size and show dolomite rhombs. In

plane light, ghosts of radiolarians are also apparent in these same layers. Other layers have of very fine-crypotocrystalline grains (0.05-0.1 mm) some of which have carbonate inclusions suggesting that the quartz replaced some of the carbonates in this sample. Some cavities and fractures are filled with calcite. Some microfaults cut across laminae. Laminae appear to be internally laminated. Some layers appear graded with a concentration of the coarser grains at the base of the laminae.
Origin: Cambro-Ordovician Cow Head Group, western Newfoundland (same as PG-1).

PIT 2a and b: Possibly Carbonate Sequence
Visual: Grain size is aphanitic to granular. Fracture is conchoidal to irregular. Luster is dull to glossy; some of the light coloured samples are translucent along the edges. Samples are mostly massive and structureless although some of the light coloured samples are faintly laminated. Some of the samples have scattered dark-black grains (pyrite?) concentrating in cavities on the weathered surface. Samples vary in colour from medium grey (N5) and medium light grey (N6) to dark grey (N3) or greyish black (N2).
Microscope: PIT- 2a: Microcrystalline groundmass with quartz forming up to 100% of the sample. Carbonate grains (calcite or dolomite) are common (10-30%) but are not uniformly distributed throughout the samples. Carbonate rhombs present but partly replaced by chert. Some cavities are filled with carbonate that is partially replaced by chalcedony.
Microscope: PIT- 2b: Microcrystalline quartz groundmass but up to 10% of sub-angular to sub-rounded quartz grains are clustered in some parts of the thin section. Carbonate up to 20% with well developed rhombs. Some fractures are filled with carbonate.
Origin: Unknown but possibly carbonate sequence due to the presence of carbonate.

PIT-3: Caradocian chert
Visual: Grain size is aphanitic to granular. Fracture is conchoidal. Luster is dull to glossy; translucency is opaque. Structure appears massive except for fractures, some of the fractures are planar others are irregular. Colour is greyish olive green (5GY3/2) to dusky yellowish green (10GY 3/2). Weathered surface is greyish yellowish green (5GY 7/2).
Microscope: Microcrystalline groundmass with quartz forming 80 to 90%. Coarse angular quartz (0.05-0.1 mm in size) form about 5-10%. Elongated fracture filled with polycrystalline quartz. Opaque minerals are present < 5%; they are very fine < 0.05 mm in size. Accessory minerals < 1%. Radiolarian fragments and sponge spicules are common.
Origin: This sample is identical to sample SW-3 and shares its origin: Caradocian chert.

PIT- 4: Caradocian chert
Visual: Grain size is aphanitic. Fracture is curved to conchoidal. Luster is dull to glossy; translucency is opaque. Structure is massive except for fractures, some of which are planar others are irregular (stylolites?). Some fractures are filled with black material (pyrite?). Colour is dusky yellow green (5GY5/2) to greyish olive green (5GY 3/2). Weathered surface is yellowish grey (5Y 7/2).
Microscope: Microcrystalline quartz up to 100%. Carbonate shades suggest replacement. Rare (< 5%) elongated quartz grains (<0.05 mm in size). Some joints or fractures are filled with carbonate. In plane light, spicules and many microcrystalline spheres (radiolarians) are visible.
Origin: This sample is identical to sample SW-2 and shares its origin: Caradocian chert.

PIT-5: Conception Group
Visual: Grain size is granular. Fractures are irregular but some are curved to conchoidal. Luster is dull to earthy; translucency is opaque. Structure is mostly massive but the sample shows few laminae <1-2 mm thick. The sample is heavily weathered and presents a thick weathering rind. Weathered surface varies from pale yellowish brown (10YR 6/2) to dark yellowish brown (10YR 4/2). Fresh cut shows colour varying from very light grey (N8) to pinkish grey (5YR 8/1) to yellowish grey (5Y 8/1). Irregular fractures filled with different coloured material pale yellowish brown (10YR 6/1). Surrounded by the thick rind, the core portion of the sample has a green-blue battleship colour.
Microscope: The inner part (or core) of the thin-section consists of microcrystalline quartz with about 10% of elongated angular grains (0.05 - 0.1 mm in size) and about 10% of carbonate grains of similar size. Some of the carbonate and quartz grains have a needle-like shape. The outer/weathered part of the thin section has less coarse grains and a greater percentage of clays. Opaques are about 5%. Carbonate percentage is less, some of it forming part of the matrix. Contact between the core and weathering rind is sharp.
Origin: This sample is identical to the Dildo Island samples and shares their origin. Late Proterozoic. Conception Group (King 1990).

PIT- 6: Caradocian chert
Visual: Grain size is aphanitic (except for clasts) to granular. Fracture is conchoidal to irregular (some fractures are visible). Luster is dull to glossy; translucency is opaque. Colours vary within the sample; sharp contacts between the different colours. One sample is dusky yellowish green (10GY 3/2) in its middle part and surrounded by light olive grey (5Y 6/1) to greenish grey (5GY 6/1) material.The contact is sharp but is circular around the middle green part. The light coloured part of the sample has angular clasts (1-2 mm in size) of light coloured material. Looks like solution carrying fragments and clasts in fissures or joints. Other sample has gradational to sharp contacts between the dusky yellowish green (10GY 3/3) part of the sample and greyish yellowish green (5GY 7/2) part of the sample.
Microscope: Microcrystalline quartz form 90 to 100%. Most of the grains are < 0.01 mm in size. Layers are 0.2 to 0.3 mm thick). Opaques form about 5%. Fractures are elongated, filled mostly with quartz but some carbonate grains are also present. Radiolarians (0.1 mm in size) are rare <1 % but visible.
Origin: This sample is identical to sample SW-2 and shares its origin: Caradocian chert.
Picture: Appendix 3 Photo 14.

Appendix 3

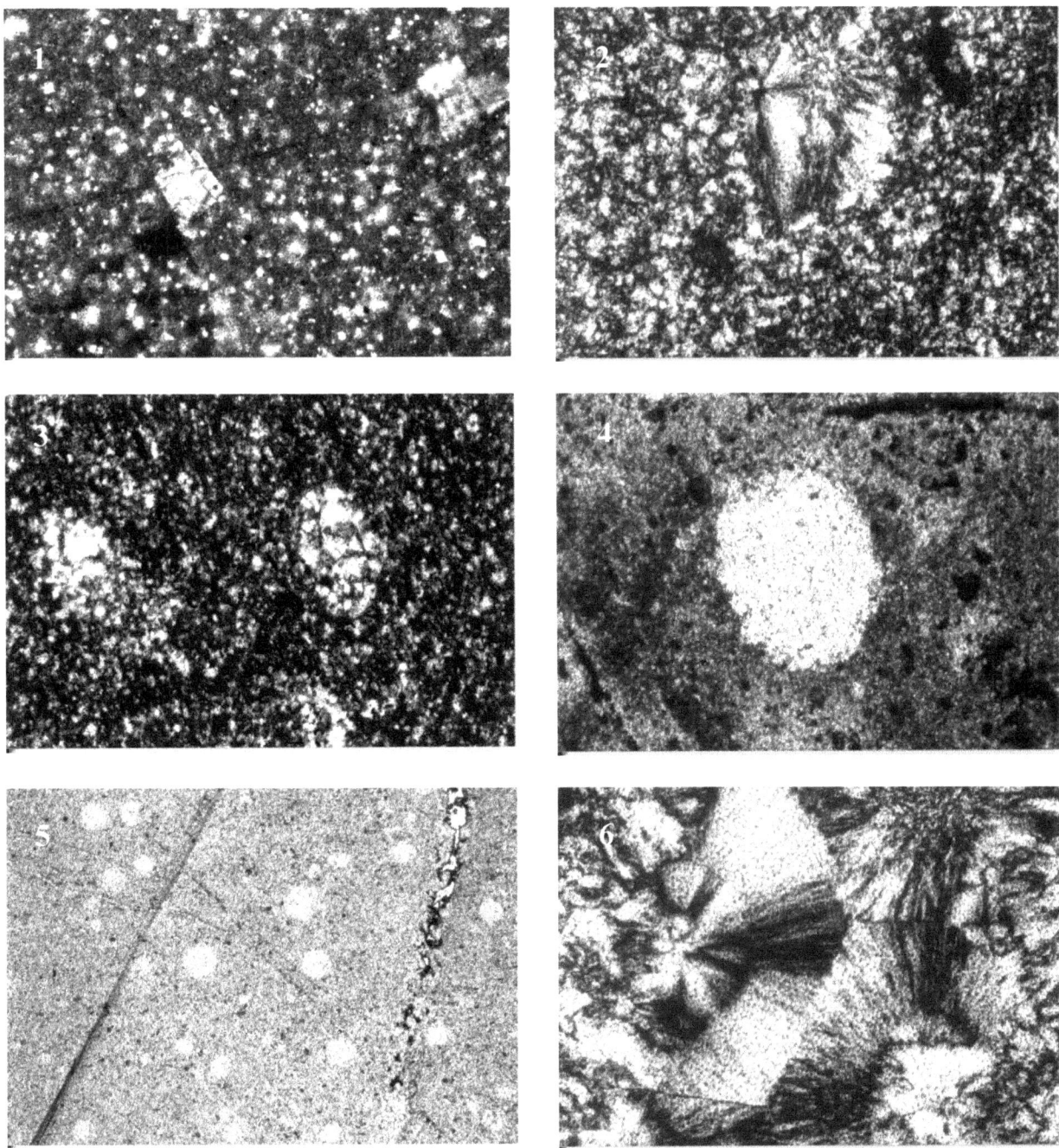

Appendix 3 -. Microphotographs of thin sections.

1. Sample PG-4: Carbonate Sequence chert showing well developed dolomite rhombs.
2. Sample PG-6: Cow Head Group chert showing chalcedony within a radiolarian.
3. Sample PG-8: Cow Head Group chert showing radiolarians.
4. Sample Ray-3: Cow Head Group chert showing a radiolarian.
5. Sample Ray-5: Cow Head Group chert showing multiple radiolarians and a fracture.
6. Sample Ray-5: Cow Head Group chert showing chalcedony.

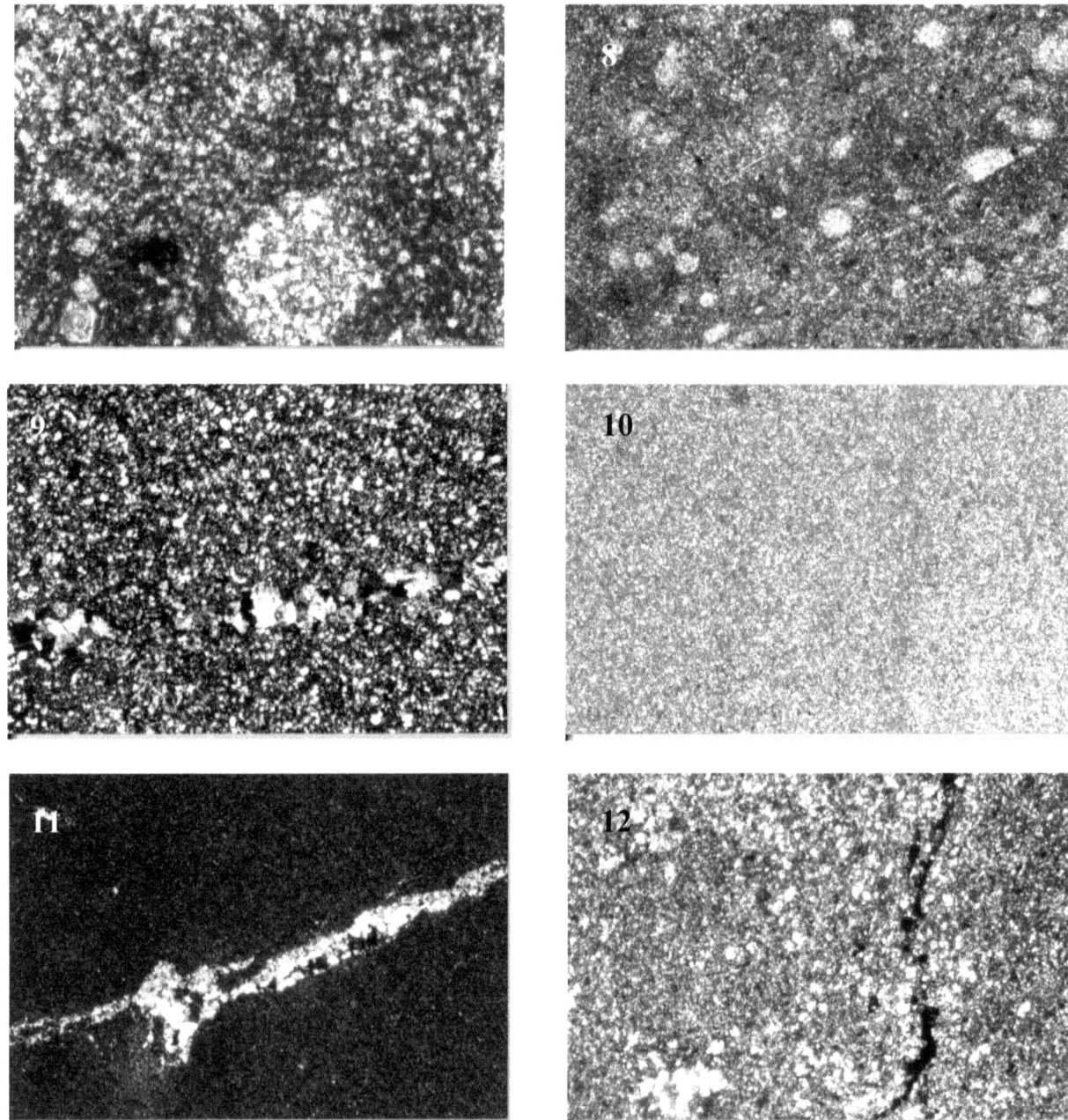

Appendix 3 - Microphotographs of thin sections (cont'd).

7. Sample Ray-7: Cow Head Group chert showing radiolarian and carbonate rhombs.
8. Sample AF-2: Cow Head Group chert showing multiple radiolarians.
9. Sample AH-2: Cap Rouge rhyolite showing fracture filled with angular coarse quartz.
10. Sample Dil-4: Conception Group chert showing massive structure.
11. Sample Dil-11: Conception Group chert showing massive structure and fracture filled with angular quartz grains.
12. Sample SH-3: Bull Arm Formation rhyolite showing massive structure and angular quartz grains.

Appendix 3

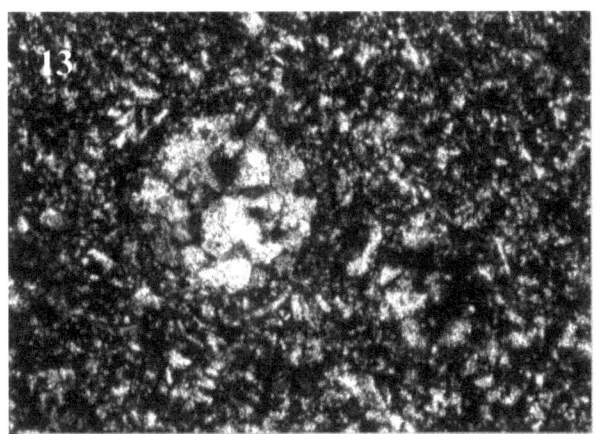 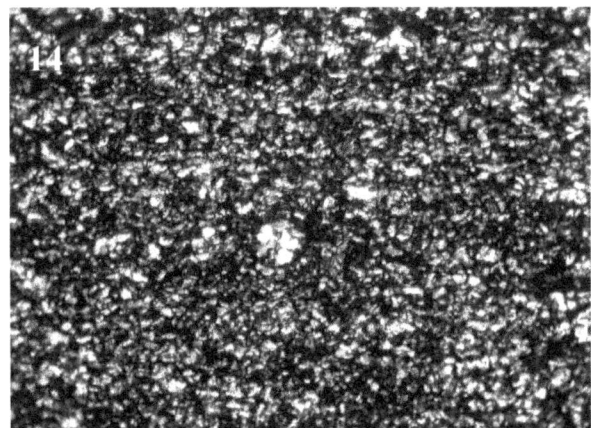

Appendix 3 - Plate 1. Microphotographs of thin sections (cont'd).

13. Sample SW-7: Caradocian chert showing a radiolarian.
14. Sample Pit-6: Caradocian chert showing a radiolarian.

REFERENCES CITED

Aitchison, Jonathan C., P.G. Flood and J. Malpas
1998 Lowermost Ordovician (basal Tremadoc) radiolarians from the Little Port Complex, western Newfoundland. *Geological Magazine* 135 (4): 413-419.

Arnold, C. D.
1980 A Palaeoeskimo occupation on southern Banks Island, N.W.T. *Arctic* 33 (3):400-426.

Atlantic Geoscience Society
2001 *The Last Billion Years. A Geological History of the Maritime Provinces of Canada*. Nimbus Publishing Ltd., Halifax.

Aubert de La Rue, E.
1951 *Recherches Géologiques et Minières aux Îles Saint-Pierre et Miquelon*. Office de la Recherche Scientifique Outre-Mer, Ministère de la France Outre-Mer. Paris.

Auger, Réginald
1984 Factory Cove: Recognition and Definition of the Early Palaeo-Eskimo Period in Newfoundland. Unpublished M. A. thesis. Department of Anthropology, Memorial University of Newfoundland. St. John's.

Barth, F.
1969 *Ethnic Groups and Boundaries. The Social Organization of Culture Difference*. Little Brown and Company, Boston.

Bielawski, E.
1988 Palaeoeskimo variability: the Early Arctic Small Tool Tradition in the Central Canadian Arctic. *American Antiquity* 53(1): 52-74.

Binford, Lewis R.
1983 *Working at Archaeology*. Studies in Archaeology. Academic press, New York.

Bishop, Paul
n.d. Final Report: 1973 Excavations at Norris Point, Gros Morne National Park. Unpublished report on file at the Archaeology Division, Parks Canada, Atlantic Region. Halifax.

Blackman, M.J., and C. Nagle
1983 Characterization of Dorset Paleoeskimo Nephritic Jade Artifacts from Central Labrador. In *Proceedings of the 22nd Symposium on Archaeometry (1982)*, edited by A. Aspinall and S.E. Warren, pp. 411-419. University of Bradford.

Blackwood, R. F.
1989 The Gander Zone in Central Newfoundland. In *Geology of Newfoundland and Labrador*, edited by J.P. Hodych and A.F. King, pp. 33-40. The Newfoundland Journal of Geological Education Vol. 10. St. John's.

Blades, Brooke S.
2003 End Scraper Reduction and Hunter-Gatherer Mobility. *American Antiquity* 68 (1): 141-156.

Bourdieu, Pierre
1990 *The Logic of Practice*. Standford University Press, Standford.

1980 *Le Sens Pratique*. Éditions de Minuit, Paris.

1977 *Outline of a Theory of Practice*. Cambridge University Press, Cambridge.

1972 *Esquisse d'une Théorie de la Pratique, précédée de trois études d'ethnologie kabyle*. Édition Droz, Genève.

Burch, Ernest S.
1976 The "Nunamiut" Concept and the Standardization of Error. In *Contributions to Anthropology: the Interior Peoples of Northern Alaska*, edited by Edwin S. Hall Jr., pp. 52-97. National Museums of Man, Mercury Series, Archaeological Survey of Canada, Paper No. 49. Ottawa.

Burzynski, Michael
1999 *Gros Morne National Park*. Breakwater Books/Gros Morne Co-operating Association and Parks Canada. St. John's.

Burzynski, M. and A. Marceau
1995 *Rocks Adrift. The Geology of Gros Morne National Park*. Gros Morne Co-operating Association. Rocky Harbour, Newfoundland.

Carignan, Paul
1975 *The Beaches: a multi-component habitation site in Bonavista Bay*. National Museums of Man, Mercury Series, Archaeological Survey of Canada, Paper No. 39. Ottawa.

Collignon, Béatrice
2006 *Knowing Places: The Inuinnait, Landscapes, and the Environment*. Circumpolar Research Series No. 10. Canadian Circumpolar Institute (CCI) Press, Edmonton.

Collins, Henry B.
1956 The T-1 Site at Native Point, Southampton Island, N.W.T. *Anthropological Papers of the University of Alaska* 4 (2): 63-89.

Colman-Sadd, Stephen and Susan A. Scott
1994 *Newfoundland and Labrador: Traveller's Guide to Geology and Guidebook to Stops of Interest*. Newfoundland Department of Mines and Energy, Geological Survey Branch. St. John's.

Coniglio, Mario
1987 Biogenic chert in the Cow Head Group (Cambro-Ordovician), western Newfoundland. *Sedimentology* 34: 813-823.

Cox, Steven L.
1978 Palaeo-Eskimo Occupations of the North Labrador Coast. *Arctic Anthropology* 15 (2): 96-118.

Dean, Paul L.
1978 *The Volcanic Stratigraphy and Metallogeny of Notre-Dame Bay, Newfoundland*. Geology Report 7, Memorial University of Newfoundland. St. John's.

Dean, Paul L., and J.R. Meyer
1982 Metallogenic study of Mid-Ordovician cherts and shales of central Newfoundland. In *Current Research*. Newfoundland Department of Mines and Energy, Geological Survey, Report 82-1, pp. 175-187. St. John's.

Desrosiers, Pierre M., and N. Rahmani
In press Essai sur l'exploitation des matières lithiques au Nunavik durant le Paléoesquimau. In *Des Tunit aux Inuit*, edited by D. Gendron and D. Arseneault. Nunavik Monograph Series No. 2. Avatak Cultural Institute, CELAT, Montréal.

Dibble, Harold L.
1995 Paleolithic Scraper Reduction: Background, Clarification, and Review of the Evidence to Date. *Journal of Archaeological Method and Theory* 2 (4): 299-368.

Dietler, Michael and Ingrid Herbich
1998 Habitus, techniques, style: an integrated approach to the social understanding of material culture and boundaries. In *The Archaeology of Social Boundaries*, edited by M.T. Stark, pp. 232-263. Smithsonian Institution Press, Washington.

Dobres, Marcia-Anne
2000 *Technology and Social Agency: Outlining a Practice Framework for Archaeology*. Blackwell Publishers Inc, Oxford.

Dobres, Marcia-Anne and J. Robb (eds)
2000 *Agency in Archaeology*. Routledge, London.

Dobres, Marcia-Anne and Christopher R. Hoffman (eds)
1999 *The Social Dynamics of Technology. Practice, Politics and World View*. Smithsonian Institution Press, Washington.

1994 Social Agency and the Dynamics of Prehistoric Technology. *Journal of Archaeological Method and Theory* 1 (3): 211-258.

Dornan, Jennifer L.
2002 Agency and Archaeology: Past, Present and Future Directions. *Journal of Archaeology Methods and Theory* 9 (4): 303-329.

Dumond, Don E.
1987 A Reexamination of Eskimo-Aleut Prehistory. *American Anthropologist* 89: 32-53.

Elling, H.
1996 The Independence I and the Old Nuulliit cultures in relation to the Saqqaq culture. In *The Paleo-Eskimo Cultures of Greenland. New Perspectives in Greenlandic Archaeology. Papers from a Symposium at the Institute of Archaeology and Ethnology, University of Copenhagen, May 21-24, 1992*, edited by B. Grønnow, pp. 191-198. Danish Polar Centre, Copenhagen.

Emerson, Thomas E. and Dale L. McElrath
2001 Interpreting Discontinuity and Historical Process in Midcontinental Late Archaic and Early Woodland Societies, In *The Archaeology of Traditions*, edited by T. R. Pauketat, pp. 195-217. University Press of Florida, Gainsville, Florida.

Erwin, John C.
2005 Revisiting the Dorset Soapstone Quarry in Fleur de Lys, Newfoundland. In *Contributions to the Study of the Dorset Palaeo-Eskimos*, edited by Patricia D. Sutherland, pp. 121-131. Mercury Series, Archaeology Paper 167. Canadian Museum of Civilization, Gatineau.

2001 A Prehistoric Soapstone Quarry in Fleur de Lys, Newfoundland. Unpublished Ph. D. thesis. Department of Archaeology, University of Calgary. Calgary.

Evans, C.O.
1982 Frenchman's Island Site (ClAl-1). Preliminary field report. In *Archaeology in Newfoundland and Labrador 1981, Annual Report 2*, edited by J.S. and C. Thomson, pp. 210-225. Historic Resources Division, Department of Tourism. Government of Newfoundland and Labrador. St. John's.

Fitzhugh, William W.
1997 Biogeographical archaeology in the Eastern North American Arctic. *Human Ecology* 25: 385-418.

1976 Paleoeskimo Occupations of the Labrador Coast. In *Eastern Arctic Prehistory: Paleoeskimo Problems*, edited by M.S. Maxwell, pp. 103-118. Memoirs of the Society for American Archaeology, No. 31. National Museums of Canada and the School of American Research.

1972 *Environmental Archaeology and Cultural Systems in Hamilton Inlet, Labrador*. Smithsonian Contributions to Anthropology No. 16. Smithsonian Institution Press, Washington.

Fogt, Lisa Mae
1998 The Excavation and Analysis of a Dorset Palaeoeskimo Dwelling at Cape Ray, Newfoundland. Unpublished M.A. thesis. Department of Anthropology, Memorial University of Newfoundland. St. John's.

Friesen, Max T.
2000 The Role of Social Factors in Dorset-Thule Interaction. In *Identities and Cultural Contacts in the Arctic*, edited by M. Appelt, J. Berglund and H.C. Gulløv, pp. 206-220. The Danish National Museum & Danish Polar Centre, Copenhagen.

Gramly, R. M.
1978 Lithic Source Areas in Northern Labrador. *Arctic Anthropology* 15 (2): 36-47.

Harp, Elmer Jr.
1969/70 Late Dorset Art from Newfoundland. *Folk* 11-12: 109-124.

1964 *The Cultural Affinities of the Newfoundland Dorset Eskimo*. National Museums of Canada, Bulletin 200. Ottawa.

Hayes, Geoffrey M., Joan Brenner Coltrain, and Dennis H. O'Rourke
2005 Molecular Archaeology of the Dorset, Thule, and Sadlermiut: Ancestor-Descendant Relationships in Eastern North American Arctic. In *Contributions to the Study of the Dorset Palaeo-Eskimos*, edited by Patricia D. Sutherland, pp. 11-32. Canadian Museum of Civilization, Mercury Series, Archaeology Paper 167. Gatineau.

Helmer, J. W.
1996 A Tale of Three Villages: Assessing the Archaeological Potential of Three Late Dorset Settlements on Little Cornwallis Island, N.W.T. In *The Paleo-Eskimo Cultures of Greenland – New Perspectives in Greenlandic Archaeology*, edited by B. Grønnow, pp. 295-308. Publication No.1. Danish Polar Center, Copenhagen.

1991 The Palaeo-Eskimo Prehistory of the North Devon Lowlands. *Arctic* 44(4):301-317.

Hodder, Ian
2000 Agency and Individuals in long-term processes. In *Agency in Archaeology*, edited by M-A. Dobres and J. Robb, pp. 21-33. Routledge, London.

Hodgetts Lisa M., M.A.P. Renouf, Maribeth S. Murray, Darlene McCuaig-Balkwill and Lesley Howse
2003 Changing subsistence practices at the Dorset Paleoeskimo site of Phillip's Garden, Newfoundland. *Arctic Anthropology* 40 (1): 106-120.

Hodych, J.P., A.F. King and E.R.W. Neale
1989 Rocks and Time. Geology Overview of the Island of Newfoundland. In *Geology of Newfoundland and Labrador*, edited by J.P. Hodych and A.F. King, pp. 1-16. The Newfoundland Journal of Geological Education Vol. 10. St. John's.

Howley, James P.
2000 *The Beothuks or Red Indians. The Aboriginal Inhabitants of Newfoundland*. Prospero, Canadian Collection, Toronto.

Irving, W.N.
1957 An Archaeological survey of the Susitna valley. *Anthropological Papers of the University of Alaska* 6 (1): 37-52.

James, Noel P. and R.K. Stevens
1986 *Stratigraphy and Correlation of the Cambro-Ordovician Cow Head Group, Western Newfoundland*. Geological Survey of Canada, Bulletin 366. Ottawa.

Jenness, Diamond
1929 Notes on the Beothuk Indians of Newfoundland. *National Museums of Canada, Annual Report for 1927*, Bulletin 56, pp. 36-39. Ottawa.

1928 The National Museum of Man. *American Anthropologist* 1(30): 178-180.

1925 A New Eskimo Culture in Hudson Bay. *The Geographical Review* 15: 428-437.

Jensen, Jens Fog
2005 Palaeo-Eskimo Continuity and Discontinuity in West Greenland. In *Contributions to the Study of the Dorset Palaeo-Eskimos*, edited by P. Sutherland, pp. 93-103. Mercury Series, Archaeology Paper 167. Canadian Museum of Civilization, Gatineau.

Jordan, Richard H.
1986   Palaeo-Eskimos in Atlantic Canada: A Regional Comparison of Newfoundland and Labrador Middle Dorset. In *Palaeo-Eskimo Cultures in Newfoundland, Labrador and Ungava*, edited by J.A Tuck and W. W. Fitzhugh, pp. 135-150. Memorial University of Newfoundland, Reports in Archaeology 1. St. John's.

1980   Preliminary results from archaeological investigations on Avayalik Island, extreme northern Labrador. *Arctic* 33(3): 607-627.

Kean, Baxter F.
1989   Mountain building in the Dunnage zone of Central Newfoundland. In *Geology of Newfoundland and Labrador*, edited by Hodych and A.F. King, pp. 41-46, Special Issue of The Newfoundland Journal of Geological Education Vol. 10. St. John's.

King, Arthur F.
1990   *Geology of the St. John's area*. Department of Mines and Energy, Government of Newfoundland and Labrador, Report 90-2. St. John's.

1989   Geological evolution of the Avalon Peninsula, Newfoundland, In *Geology of Newfoundland and Labrador*, edited by Hodych and A.F. King, pp. 17-32, Special Issue of The Newfoundland Journal of Geological Education Vol. 10. St. John's.

Knight, Ian
1989   The ancient tropical continental shelf of western Newfoundland. In *Geology of Newfoundland and Labrador*, edited by Hodych and A.F. King, pp. 63-76, Special Issue of The Newfoundland Journal of Geological Education Vol.10. St. John's.

Knight, Ian, N.P. James and H.W. Williams
1995   Cambrian-Ordovician carbonate sequence. In *Geology of the Appalachian-Caledonian Orogen in Canada and Greenland*, edited by H.W. Williams, pp. 67-86, Geological Survey of Canada, No. 6.

Knuth, E.
1984   *Reports from the Mux-Ox Way. A compilation of previously published articles with insertion of some new illustrations and with a slightly altered radiocarbon dating list*. Copenhagen, May 1984.

Lazenby, M.E.C.
1980   Prehistoric Sources of Chert in Northern Labrador: Fieldwork and Preliminary Analyses. *Arctic* 33 (3): 628-645.

Le Blanc, Raymond J.
1994   *The Crane Site and the Palaeoeskimo Period in the Western Canadian Arctic*. Archaeological Survey of Canada, Mercury Series Paper 148. Canadian Museum of Civilization, Gatineau.

LeBlanc, Sylvie
2005   Anse à Henry. Aire de Fouille 2003-2004. Rapport Final. Rapport d'Activités Mission d'Archéologie 2004. Rapport déposé à la Direction de l'Architecture et du Patrimoine, Sous-direction de l'Archéologie, Ministère de la Culture et de la Communication, Paris, 78p. ms.

2004   L'Anse à Henry Campagne 2003. Rapport Préliminaire. Rapport d'Activités. Mission d'Archéologie 2003. Rapport déposé à la Direction de l'Architecture et du Patrimoine, Sous-direction de l'Archéologie, Ministère de la Culture et de la Communication, Paris, 59p. ms.

2003a Un Campement Indien Récent à l'Anse à Henry. Rapport d'activités. Mission d'Archéologie 2002. Rapport déposé à la Direction de l'Architecture et du Patrimoine, Sous-direction de l'Archéologie, Ministère de la Culture et de la Communication, Paris, 71p. ms.

2003b A Middle Dorset Dwelling in Trinity Bay, Newfoundland. *Études/Inuit/Studies* 27 (1-2): 493-513.

2001   Cinq Mille Ans d'Occupation à l'Anse à Henry. Rapport d'Étape. Phase 2. Mission de Reconnaissance. Rapport déposé à la Direction de l'Architecture et du Patrimoine, Sous-direction de l'Archéologie, Ministère de la Culture et de la Communication, Paris, 27p. ms.

2000a Cinq Mille Ans d'Occupation à l'Anse à Henry. Rapport d'Étape. Phase 1. Mission de Reconnaissance. Rapport déposé à la Direction de l'Architecture et du Patrimoine, Sous-direction de l'Archéologie, Ministère de la Culture et de la Communication, Paris, 33p. ms.

2000b Middle Dorset (1900 to 1100 B.P.) Regional Variability on the Island of Newfoundland and in Saint-Pierre et Miquelon, In *Identities and Cultural Contacts in the Arctic*, edited by M. Appelt, J. Berglund and H.C. Gulløv, pp. 97-105. The Danish National Museum & Danish Polar Centre. Copenhagen.

1999   Dildo Island Dorset Archaeological Project: 1999 Field Season. Unpublished report on file, Government of Newfoundland and Labrador, Historic Resources Division, Department of Tourism and Culture. St. John's.

1998   Dildo Island 1997 Field Season: Interim Report. Unpublished report on file, Government of Newfoundland and Labrador, Historic Resources Division, Department of Tourism and Culture. St. John's.

1997a   Dildo Island Archaeological Project. The Dorset Occupation of Dildo Island. Preliminary Field Report - 1996. Unpublished report on file, Government of Newfoundland and Labrador, Historic Resources Division, Department of Tourism and Culture. St. John's.

1997b   Report on an Initial Archaeological Reconnaissance of Oentjoi Gtjigan and Miquelem. Unpublished report submitted to Miawpukek Band, Conne River, Newfoundland.

Lemonnier, Pierre
1993   Introduction, In *Technological Choices. Transformation in Material Cultures since the Neolithic*, edited by Pierre Lemonnier, pp. 1-35. Routledge, London.

1992   Elements for an Anthropology of Technology. *Anthropological Papers* No 88, Museum of Anthropology, University of Michigan, Ann Arbor.

1983   L'étude des systèmes techniques, une urgence en technologie culturelle. *Techniques et Cultures* 1: 11-26.

Leroi-Gourhan, André
1973   Évolutions et techniques. *Milieu et techniques*. Albin Michel, Paris.

1964   Le geste et la parole, Tome 1, *Technique et langage*. Albin Michel, Paris.

Linnamae, Urve
1975   *The Dorset Culture. A Comparative Study in Newfoundland and the Arctic*. Technical Papers of the Newfoundland Museum, No 1. St. John's.

Loring, Stephen
2002   And They Took Away the Stones from Ramah : Lithic Raw Material Sourcing and Eastern Arctic Archaeology. In *Honoring our Elders. A History of Eastern Arctic Archaeology*, edited by W.W. Fitzhugh, S. Loring and D. Odess, pp. 163-185. Arctic Studies Center, Contributions to Circumpolar Anthropology 2. National Museum of Natural History, Smithsonian Institution Press, Washington.

Mauss, Marcel
1979   The Notion of Body Techniques, In *Sociology and Psychology, Essays*: pp. 97-119.

1947   *Manuel d'ethnographie*. Payot, Paris.

1935   Les Techniques du Corps. In *Sociologie et Psychologie*, Parts 11-V1.

Maxwell, Moreau S.
1985   *Prehistory of the Eastern Arctic*. Academic Press, New York.

1980   Dorset site variation on the Southeast Coast of Baffin Island. *Arctic* 33(3): 505-516.

Maxwell, Moreau S. (editor)
1976a   *Eastern Arctic Prehistory: Paleoeskimo Problems*. Memoirs of the Society for American Archaeology, No. 31. National Museums of Canada and the School of American Research.

1976b   Introduction In *Eastern Arctic Prehistory: Paleoeskimo Problems*, edited by M.S. Moreau, pp. 1-5. Memoirs of the Society for American Archaeology, No. 31. National Museums of Canada and the School of American Research.

McCaffrey, M.T.
1989   L'acquisition et l'échange de matières lithiques durant la Préhistoire récente: un regard vers la fosse du Labrador. *Recherches Amérindiennes au Québec* 19 (2-3): 95-107.

McGhee, Robert
2004   *The Last Imaginary Place: a Human History of the Arctic World*. Key Porter, Toronto.

2000   Radiocarbon Dating and the Time of the Thule Migration. In *Identities and Cultural Contacts in the Arctic*, edited by M. Appelt, J. Berglund and H.C. Gulløv, pp. 181-191. The Danish National Museum & Danish Polar Centre, Copenhagen.

1996   *Ancient People of the Arctic*. University of British Columbia Press, Vancouver.

1976   Paleoeskimo Occupations of Central and High Arctic Canada. In *Eastern Arctic Prehistory: Paleoeskimo Problems*, edited by M.S. Moreau, pp. 15-39. Memoirs of the Society for American Archaeology, No. 31. National Museums of Canada and the School of American Research.

Morrow, Juliet E.
1997   End scraper morphology and use-life: an approach for studying Paleoindian lithic technology and mobility. *Lithic Technology* 22 (1): 70-85.

Nagle, Christopher L.
1986   Flake Stone Procurement and Distribution in Dorset Culture Sites along the Labrador Coast.

In *Palaeo-Eskimo Cultures in Newfoundland, Labrador and Ungava*, edited by J.A.Tuck and W.W. Fitzghuh, pp. 95-110. Memorial University of Newfoundland, Reports in Archaeology 1. St. John's.

1985   Lithic Raw Materials Resource Studies in Newfoundland and Labrador: a Progress Report. In *Archaeology in Newfoundland and Labrador 1984*, edited by J. S. Thompson and C. Thomson, pp. 86-121. Historic Division, Government of Newfoundland and Labrador. St. John's.

1984   Lithic Raw Material Procurement and Exchange in Dorset Culture along the Labrador Coast. Unpublished Ph.D. dissertation, Department of Anthropology, Brandeis University, Waltham, Massachusetts.

1982   1981 Field Investigations at the Fleur de Lys Soapstone Quarry, Baie Verte, Newfoundland. In *Archaeology in Newfoundland and Labrador 1981, Annual Report No 2*, edited by J.S. Thomson and C. Thomson, pp. 102-120. Historic Division, Government of Newfoundland and Labrador. St. John's.

Nagy, Murielle
1994   A critical review of the Pre-Dorset/Dorset transition. In *Threads of Arctic Prehistory: Papers in honour of William E. Taylor, Jr.*, edited by D. Morrison and J.P. Pilon, pp. 1-14. Mercury Series, Archaeological Survey of Canada, Paper 149. Canadian Museum of Civilization, Hull.

O'Brien, Sean J. and A.F. King
2005   Late Neoproterozoic (Ediacaran) Stratigraphy of Avalon Zone Sedimentary Rocks, Bonavista Peninsula, Newfoundland. In *Current Research*, Newfoundland and Labrador Department of Natural Resources, Geological Survey, Report 05-1, pp. 101-113. St. John's.

O'Brien, Sean J. and I. Knight
1988   The Avalon Geology of Southwest Bonavista Bay: Portions of the St. Brendan's (2C/13) and Eastport (2C/12) map areas. In *Current Research*, Newfoundland Department of Mines and Energy, Geological Survey, Report 88-1, pp. 93-205. St. John's.

O'Brien, Sean J., P.G. Strong and J.L. Evans
1977   *The Geology of the Grand Bank (1M/4) and Lamaline (1L/13) Map Areas, Burin Peninsula, Newfoundland*. Mineral Development Division. Department of Mines and Energy, Government of Newfoundland and Labrador, Report 77-7. St. John's.

Odess, Daniel
2005   One of These Things is Not Like the Other: Typology, Chronology, and the Concept of Middle Dorset, In *Contributions to the Study of the Dorset Palaeo-Eskimos* edited by Patricia, D. Sutherland, pp. 81-91. Mercury Series, Archaeological Paper 167. Canadian Museum of Civilization, Gatineau.

1998   The Archaeology of Interaction: Views from Artifact Style and Material Exchange in Dorset Society. *American Antiquity* 63 (3): 417-435.

Odess, Daniel, Stephen Loring and William W. Fitzhugh
2000   Skraeling: First Peoples of Helluland, Markland, and Vinland. In *Vikings. The North Atlantic Saga* edited by W.W. Fitzhugh, pp. 193-205. Smithsonian Institution, Washington.

Park, Robert W.
2008   Contact between the Norse Vikings and the Dorset Culture in Arctic Canada. *Antiquity* 82: 189-198

2000   The Dorset-Thule Succession Revisited. In *Identities and Cultural Contacts in the Arctic*, edited by M. Appelt, J. Berglund and H.C. Gulløv, pp. 192-205. The Danish National Museum & Danish Polar Centre, Copenhagen.

1993   The Dorset-Thule Succession in Arctic North America: Assessing Claims for Culture Contact. *American Antiquity* 58: 203-234.

Parker, S. P. (editor)
1994   *Dictionary of Geology and Mineralogy*. McGraw Hill, New York.

Pastore, Ralph
1981   Swan Island Survey – 1981. Unpublished report on file, Government of Newfoundland and Labrador, Historic Resources Division, Department of Tourism and Culture. St. John's.

Pauketat, Timothy R. (ed)
2001a   *The Archaeology of Traditions. Agency and History Before and After Columbus*, University Press of Florida. Gainsville, Florida.

2001b   A New Tradition in Archaeology, In *The Archaeology of Traditions. Agency and History Before and After Columbus*, edited by Timothy, R. Pauketat, pp. 1-16. University Press of Florida. Gainsville, Florida.

Penney, Gerald
1984   The Prehistory of the Southwest Coast of Newfoundland. Unpublished M.A. thesis. Department of Anthropology, Memorial University of Newfoundland. St. John's.

Pintal, Jean-Yves
1998 *Aux Frontières de la Mer: La Préhistoire de Blanc-Sablon*. Les Publications du Québec, Collection Dossiers du Patrimoine, Municipalité de Blanc-Sablon.

Plumet, Patrick
2002 Tuvaaluk/website http://www.unites.uqam.ca/tuvaaluk/cadre_prehistorique/menucadreprehist.html

1996 L'Esquimau: Essai de synthèse de la préhistoire de l'arctique eskimau. *Revue d'Archéologie Américaine* 10: 7-51.

1986 Questions et Réflexions Concernant la Pré-Histoire de l'Ungava. In *Palaeo-Eskimo Cultures in Newfoundland, Labrador and Ungava*, edited by J.A.Tuck and W.W. Fitzghuh, pp. 151-160. Memorial University of Newfoundland, Reports in Archaeology 1. St. John's.

Plumet Patrick and Serge Lebel
1997 Dorset Tip Fluting: A Second "American" Invention. *Arctic Anthropology* 34 (2): 132-162.

Rabottin, Jean-Louis
1999 Projet de mise en valeur d'un site archéologique à Saint-Pierre et Miquelon (1999-2003). Projet déposé à la Préfecture de la Collectivité Territoriale de Saint-Pierre et Miquelon, 15p. ms.

Rabu, Dominique and Jean-Jacques Chauvel, in collaboration with C. Alsac, M-P Dabard, T.P. Fletcher, C. Guerrot, G.L. Pilota, M. Tegyey and D. Thieblemeont
1993 *Excursion Géologique à Saint-Pierre et Miquelon. Livret-guide, 28 août- 2 septembre 1993*. Rapport BRGM n° 93R37721 – SGN/CSG. Orléans.

Ramsden, P.G. and J.A. Tuck
2001 A Comment on the Pre-Dorset/Dorset Transition in the Eastern Arctic. *Anthropological Papers of the University of Alaska, NS.* 1 (1): 7-11.

Rast, Timothy L
1999 Investigating Palaeo-Eskimo and Indian Settlement Patterns along a Submerging Coast at Burgeo, Newfoundland. Unpublished M.A. thesis. Department of Anthropology, Memorial University of Newfoundland. St. John's.

Renouf, M.A.P.
2006 Re-investigating a Middle Phase Dorset dwelling at Phillip's Garden, Port au Choix, Newfoundland, In *Dynamics of Northern Societies: Proceedings of the SILA/NABO Conference on Arctic and North Atlantic Archaeology, Copenhagen, May 10th-14th 2004*, edited by J. Arneborg and B. Grønnow, pp. 119-128. National Museum, Studies in Archaeology and History, Vol. 10. Copenhagen.

2005 Phillip's Garden West: A Newfoundland Groswater Variant, In *Contributions to the Study of the Dorset Palaeo-Eskimos*, edited by Patricia D. Sutherland, pp. 57-80. Mercury Series, Archaeology Paper 167. Canadian Museum of Civilization, Gatineau.

1994 Two transitional sites at Port au Choix. In *Threads of Arctic Prehistory: Papers in honour of William E. Taylor, Jr.*, edited by D. Morrison and J.P. Pilon, pp. 166-195. Mercury Series, Archaeological Survey of Canada, Paper 149. Canadian Museum of Civilization, Hull.

1987 Archaeological Excavations at the Port au Choix National Historic Park: Report of the 1986 Field Activities. Unpublished report on file at the Archaeology Division, Parks Canada, Atlantic Region. Halifax.

1986 Report of 1985 Excavations at the Point Riche and Phillip's Garden sites, Port au Choix National Historic Park. Unpublished report on file at the Archaeological Division, Parks Canada, Atlantic Region. Halifax.

Robbins, Douglas T.
1986 "Newfoundland Dorset" Culture. In *Palaeo-Eskimo Cultures in Newfoundland, Labrador and Ungava*, edited by J.A. Tuck and W.W. Fitzhugh, pp. 119-123. Memorial University of Newfoundland, Reports in Archaeology 1. St. John's.

1985 Stock Cove, Trinity Bay: the Dorset Eskimo Occupation of Newfoundland from a Southeastern Perspective. Unpublished M.A. thesis. Department of Anthropology, Memorial University of Newfoundland. St. John's.

Ryan, A. B.
1983 Geology of the west coast of Newfoundland. Newfoundland. *Journal of Geological Education* Vol. 7 (2).

Schlanger, Nathan
1991 Le fait technique total. La raison pratique et les raisons de la pratique dans l'oeuvre de Marcel Mauss. *Terrain* 16:114-130.

Schlederman, P.
1978 Prehistoric demographic trends in the Canadian High Arctic. *Canadian Journal of Archaeology* 2: 43-58.

Shanks, M. and C. Tilley
1987 *Re-Constructing Archaeology: Theory and Practice*. Routledge, London.

Shott, Michael J.
1995 How Much is a Scraper? Curation, Use Rates, and the Formation of Scraper assemblages. *Lithic Technology* 20: 53-72.

Simpson, David N.
1986 Prehistoric Archaeology of the Port au Port Peninsula, Western Newfoundland. Unpublished M.A. thesis. Department of Anthropology, Memorial University of Newfoundland. St. John's.

The Staff of Asarco Inc. and Abitibi Price MRD in Cooperation with the Department of Mines Energy and Energy, Information Division.
2001 *Volcanoes. Some Questions and Answers*. Halifax.

Stark, M.T.
1998 Technological choices and social boundaries in material culture patterning: an introduction. In *The Archaeology of Social Boundaries*, edited by M.T. Stark, pp. 1-11. Smithsonian Institution Press, Washington.

Sutherland, Patricia D.
2000a Strands of Culture Contact: Dorset-Norse Interactions in the Canadian Eastern Arctic. In *Identities and Cultural Contacts in the Arctic*, edited by M. Appelt, J. Berglund and H.C. Gulløv, pp. 159-169. The Danish National Museum & Danish Polar Centre, Copenhagen.

2000b The Norse and Native North Americans. In *Vikings. The North Atlantic Saga* edited by W.W. Fitzhugh, pp. 238-247. Smithsonian Institution Press, Washington.

1996 Continuity and Change in the Paleo-Eskimo Prehistory of Northern Ellesmere Island. In *The Paleo-Eskimo Cultures of Greenland. New Perspectives in Greenlandic Archaeology. Papers from a Symposium at the Institute of Archaeology and Ethnology, University of Copenhagen, May 21-24, 1992,* edited by B. Grønnow, pp. 271-294. Danish Polar Centre, Copenhagen.

Sutherland, Patricia D, and Robert McGhee
1997 Lost Visions, Forgotten Dreams. Life and Art of an Ancient Arctic People. Exhibit Guide – Canadian Museum of Civilization. Gatineau.

The Rock-Color Chart Committee
1995 *The Geological Society of America Rock-Color Chart*. The Geological Society of America. Boulder, Colorado.

Tuck, James A.
1983 Excavations at Shamblers Cove – 1982: A Stage 3 Impact Report. Unpublished report on file, Department of Tourism and Culture, Historic Resources Division, Government of Newfoundland and Labrador. St. John's.

1978 Excavations at Cow Head, Newfoundland an interim report. *Études/Inuit/Studies* 2 (1): 138-141.

1975 *Prehistory of Saglek Bay, Labrador: Archaic and Palaeo-Eskimo Occupations*. National Museums of Man, Mercury Series, Archaeology Survey of Canada Paper No. 32. Ottawa.

n.d. Prehistory of Atlantic Canada. Unpublished manuscript in author's possession.

Tuck, J.A. and William W. Fitzhugh
1986 Palaeo-Eskimo Traditions of Newfoundland and Labrador: A re-appraisal. In *Palaeo-Eskimo Cultures in Newfoundland, Labrador and Ungava*, edited by J.A. Tuck and W.W. Fitzhugh, pp. 161-167. Memorial University of Newfoundland, Reports in Archaeology 1. St. John's.

Williams, Harold W.
2003 Geologic Ancestors to the Atlantic. The Geology of Newfoundland. *Newfoundland Quarterly* 96 (3): 11-18.

2001 *Field Trip at Geological cross-section of the Appalachian Orogen*. Geological Association of Canada and Mineralogy Association of Canada, St. John's.

1995 Preamble (Dunnage Zone), In Chapter 3 of *Geology of the Appalachian-Caledonian Orogen in Canada and Greenland*, edited by H. Williams, pp. 139-142. Geological Survey of Canada, Geology of Canada No. 6.

Williams, H.W., E. Burden, L.Quinn, P. von Burden and. A. Bashforth
1996 *Geology and Paleontology of the Port au Port Peninsula, Western Newfoundland. A Field Guide*. Canadian Paleontology Conference Field Trip, Guidebook No.5. Geological Association of Canada - Paleontology Division. Department of Earth Sciences, Memorial University of Newfoundland. St. John's.

Williams, H., S.J. O'Brien, A.F. King, and M.M.Anderson
1995 Avalon Zone-Newfoundland. In Chapter 3 of *Geology of the Appalachian-Caledonian Orogen in Canada and Greenland*, edited by H. Williams, pp. 226-237. Geological Survey of Canada, Geology of Canada No. 6.

Wintemberg W. J.
1940 Eskimo Sites of the Dorset Culture in Newfoundland: Part II. *American Antiquity* 5 (4): 309-333.
1939 Eskimo Sites of the Dorset Culture in Newfoundland. Part I. *American Antiquity* 5 (2): 83-102.

Won, Mun-Zu and W.J. Iams
2002 Late Cambrian radiolarian faunas and biostratigraphy of the Cow Head Group, western Newfoundland. *Journal of Paleontology* 76 (1): 1-33.

www.ingramcontent.com/pod-product-compliance
Lightning Source LLC
Chambersburg PA
CBHW061546010526
44113CB00023B/2815